Legal Writing

W9-CNM-985

and
Research Manual

Legal Writing and Research Manual

John A. Yogis, Q.C.
B.A., LL.B., LL.M. (Dal.), LL.M. (Mich.)
Associate Dean of Law, Professor of Law, Dalhousie University

and

Innis M. Christie
B.A., LL.B., LL.M. (Dal.), LL.B. (Camb.), LL.M. (Yale)
Professor of Law, Dalhousie University

Fifth Edition

by

Michael J. Iosipescu
B.A., B.Sc., M.A., LL.B. (Dal.)
Lecturer in Law, Dalhousie University
Director of Research, Legal Research Council

and

Michael E. Deturbide
B.Sc., B.J., LL.B. (Dal.), LL.M. (Dal.)
Assistant Professor, Dalhousie Law School

 Butterworths
Toronto and Vancouver

Legal Writing and Research Manual, Fifth Edition
© Butterworths Canada Ltd. 2000
February 2000

The Butterworth Group of Companies

Canada:
75 Clegg Road, MARKHAM, Ontario L6G 1A1
and
1732-808 Nelson Street, Box 12148, VANCOUVER, B.C. V6Z 2H2

Australia:
Butterworths Pty Ltd., SYDNEY

Ireland:
Butterworth (Ireland) Ltd., DUBLIN

Malaysia:
Malayan Law Journal Sdn Bhd, KUALA LUMPUR

New Zealand:
Butterworths of New Zealand Ltd., WELLINGTON

Singapore:
Butterworths Asia, SINGAPORE

South Africa:
Butterworth Publishers (Pty.) Ltd., DURBAN

United Kingdom:
Butterworth & Co. (Publishers) Ltd., LONDON

United States:
LEXIS Publishing, CHARLOTTESVILLE, Virginia

Canadian Cataloguing in Publication Data
The National Library of Canada has catalogued this publication as follows:
Main entry under title:
Legal Writing and Research Manual
Yogis, John A., 1940-
Legal writing and research manual
5th ed.
Includes bibliographical references and index.
ISBN 0-433-40900-2 (bound)   ISBN 0-433-40902-9 (pbk.)

    1. Legal composition. 2. Legal research — Canada. 3. Citation of legal authorities — Canada. I. Christie, Innis, 1937- . II. Iosipescu, Michael J. III. Deturbide, Michael E. (Michael Eugene), 1957- . IV Title.

KE265.Y64 2000   808'.06634   C99-933059-4
KF250.Y64 2000

Printed and bound in Canada.

Preface to the Fifth Edition

The fifth edition of this manual preserves the basic goal of the first edition, which was to assist first-year law students in becoming familiar with the research tools available to lawyers. It also provides basic information on the use of these tools.

Some of the material in the fourth edition has been updated. The text is organized to simplify the students' entry into all major Canadian and English abridgments, encyclopedias and digest services. The chapter on "Suggestions for Legal Research and Writing" includes a step by step guide to basic legal research and a sample memorandum of law. The chapter on "Computerized Legal Research" has been revised to update programs such as LEXIS-NEXIS and to include references to the useful Internet sites.

We wish to express special appreciation to Sean Moreman for many hours of hard work on the fifth edition during the past semester. We also wish to thank the law librarian, Ann Morrison, for her assistance in updating the material.

Dalhousie Law School
Halifax, Nova Scotia   Michael E. Deturbide
January 2000   Michael J. Iosipescu

Table of Contents

CHAPTER 2
SECONDARY LEGAL MATERIALS

CHAPTER 3
SUGGESTIONS FOR LEGAL RESEARCH AND WRITING

Introduction

This manual is designed primarily for use by first-year law students as an aid in legal writing and research. The manual has six broad objectives:

(1) to introduce students to the systems of publication and organization of primary source materials. Primary materials are those materials which state the law and which are formulated by those constitutionally vested with authority to declare law. In Canada primary material is found in the form of:

(i)   constitutional documents and statutes;
(ii)   regulations passed under the authority of statutes;
(iii)   Orders-in-Council;
(iv)   reasons for judgment in decided cases; and
(v)   reasons for decisions of boards, tribunals and commissions;

(2) to familiarize students with the major sources of secondary legal materials that may be found in a law library. Secondary materials are preliminary research tools that assist in finding, evaluating, and understanding primary materials. Secondary materials include:

(i)   encyclopedias;
(ii)   abridgments;
(iii)   digests;
(iv)   statute citators;
(v)   case annotators and citators;
(vi)   words and phrases;
(vii)   dictionaries;
(viii) legal periodicals; and
(ix)   textbooks and treatises;

(3) to provide instruction on the research techniques used to locate statutes, regulations and cases;

(4) to provide instruction on the citation of primary legal materials and on the general rules of style in legal writing;

(5) to provide basic instruction on how to research a legal problem and prepare a legal memorandum; and

(6) to provide a basic awareness of computer-assisted legal research, including resources available to the legal researcher on the World Wide Web.

This manual is not a comprehensive reference work. It deals primarily with Canadian statutes, regulations, case reports, encyclopedias, and Internet sites. As well, it provides a detailed summary of the major sources of English legal materials to be found in major Canadian law libraries. Finally, it gives a brief overview of American legal materials.

Chapter 1 discusses statutes, regulations, and case reports for each province. In addition, it provides an extensive overview of federal statutes and regulations. The discussion of English materials focuses on Halsbury's Statutes of England.

Chapter 2 discusses the major Canadian and English encyclopedias with particular emphasis given to The Canadian Abridgment, Canadian Encyclopedic Digest, and Halsbury's Laws of England.

Chapter 3 outlines the basic steps of conventional library research and provides commentary on how to incorporate computer research. In addition, it contains guidelines for the preparation of a legal memorandum and includes a sample memorandum.

Chapter 4 is devoted to American legal materials. It itemizes and provides brief descriptions of some of the major sources of federal and state law. It also mentions the major American encyclopedias and digests.

Chapter 5 discusses the use of commmercial databases in legal research with particular reference to the main commercial databuases and the Internet.

CHAPTER 1
Primary Legal Materials

A. STATUTES

Primary materials are the records of rules laid down by those bodies vested with the authority to declare law. Generally, the most important primary materials are legislation and case reports. Legislation includes statutes and subordinate legislation. Subordinate legislation is made under powers conferred by a statute. It includes regulations, orders, rules, bylaws and ordinances. Case reports are the records of court decisions. This chapter discusses statutes, regulations, and case reports from Canada and the United Kingdom.

A statute, or "act", has been defined in English law as "a pronouncement by the Sovereign in Parliament, that is to say, made by the Queen by and with the advice and consent of both Houses of Parliament, or, in certain circumstances, the House of Commons alone, the effect of which is either to declare the law, or to change the law (normally for the future only, but sometimes with retrospective effect), or to do both".[1]

Statutes may be classified in various ways based on the scope of their operation. A public general act (or public statute) applies to the whole community (for example, the *Ontario Human Rights Code*); a local act is generally restricted in terms of area (for example, the *London-Middlesex Act, 1992* of Ontario); a private act may be restricted to specific individuals or groups (for example, the *Women in Crisis (Northumberland County) Act, 1992*). The distinction between public general acts and local acts is often difficult to determine. Many jurisdictions have abolished the distinction and classify statutes as public general or private acts. In the sessional or annual volumes of statutes, public general acts are found in the first section and private and local acts are found in the second section. Only public general acts are included in revised editions of statutes.

Because of their broader application, public general statutes are of primary interest to lawyers and will be the exclusive subject of the discussion that follows.

The main functions of public general statutes are:

(i) to codify an area of law which has become excessively convoluted through the accretion of case law (for example, the *Sale of Goods* legislation in the common law provinces and territories);

---

[1] *Halsbury* (4th), Vol. 44, at 484.

(ii)   to change or reform the case law (for example, the Ontario *Occupiers' Liability Act* removed a confusing common law distinction between an "invitee" and a "licensee"); and

(iii) to deal with areas previously untouched by case law (for example, the federal *Atomic Energy Control Act*).

The following discussion is designed to familiarize the student with the publication and organization of Canadian and United Kingdom statutes and to detail the basic steps to statute research.

The discussion is in three parts:

(a)   publication and organization;
(b)   research techniques; and
(c)   citation.

1. Canadian Statutes

(A) Publication and Organization

Preceding official publication, a federal public statute begins as a legislative proposal called a bill and is introduced during a legislative session. When a bill is introduced into a legislature, it is given a number. For example, Bill C-8 respecting the *Special Import Measures Act* was the eighth bill introduced in 1984 during the second session of the thirty-second Parliament. Before it can become law, a bill must pass through three readings in the House of Commons and the Senate. A bill is published in pamphlet form one or more times during its passage through the legislature. If approved, after the third reading, federal bills are sent to the Governor-General to receive Royal Assent. At this stage a bill officially becomes law. Upon receiving Royal Assent the new statutes are given consecutive chapter numbers and published again in pamphlet form (for instance, the *Special Import Measures Act* became chapter 25 of the 1984 *Statutes of Canada*). New acts are also published in *The Canada Gazette, Part III*. At the close of the calendar year, all the acts are bound in an annual volume, referred to as the *Statutes of Canada*.[2] The acts appear in the order that they received Royal Assent.

The *Statutes of Canada* annual bound volumes include amendments to previously existing acts, new acts and subsequent amendments to new acts up to the end of the most recent calendar year (allowing some lag time for publication).

---

[2]   Federal statutes are accumulated annually and one copy of those acts, in English and French, given to the Registrar-General pursuant to the *Publication of Statutes Act*, R.S.C. 1985, c. S-21, s. 6.

The annual volume also includes a "Table of Contents", a "Table of Public Statutes", a table of the "Proclamations of Canada", and an "Index" detailing the contents of each act.

The procedure for provincial bills is similar, taking into account the absence of an upper house. Royal Assent is accorded by the provincial Lieutenant-Governor. Ontario, Québec, Northwest Territories and Manitoba follow the federal practice and publish their statutes in annual volumes. This means that statutes are collected and bound at the end of each year. The acts are assigned a series of consecutive chapter numbers within each calendar year and the publication in bound form may be available within a few months of the end of the year. Alberta, British Columbia, New Brunswick, Newfoundland, Nova Scotia, Prince Edward Island, Saskatchewan and the Yukon publish their statutes in sessional volumes. A session of a legislature may be only a few months long or may span more than one year. The acts are given a series of consecutive chapter numbers for the session and are published in bound form at the end of the session.

Sessional or annual volumes include an invaluable cumulative "Table of Public Statutes"[3] which lists in alphabetical order, by short title, all public general acts from the current sessional or annual volume and all previous sessional or annual volumes as far back as the last revision of statutes for the jurisdiction. The table includes the revised statutes, subsequent amendments, new acts, amendments to those acts, and a few acts that are still in force which may not have been included in a revision.

Every 10 to 20 years[4] both federal and provincial governments establish commissions to revise and consolidate their respective public general acts in order to eliminate errors, consolidate amendments, and, in particular, to reorganize and renumber statutes, combine or eliminate sections or subsections, and add, delete, or replace certain words. When a revision is completed, the revised statutes are proclaimed in force and the former versions are repealed.[5]

---

[3] Manitoba's *Table of Public Statutes* lists (i) all statutes in the C.C.S.M.; (ii) public acts not in the C.C.S.M.; (iii) municipal acts not in the C.C.S.M.; (iv) private acts; and (v) acts and parts of acts coming into force on proclamation.

  Saskatchewan publishes two bound volumes: *Table of Public Statutes* and *Table of Regulations*. The Law Society of Saskatchewan Libraries has published an *Index to the Statutes of Saskatchewan, Second Edition*, which is updated regularly.

  The "Table of Public Statutes" in the *Statutes of Canada* is found at the back of the annual volumes and from time to time is also published separately in a softcover edition.

[4] The last federal revision was in 1985. The last provincial or territorial revisions are as follows: Alberta in 1980; British Columbia, 1996: New Brunswick, 1973; Newfoundland, 1990; Northwest Territories, 1988; Nova Scotia, 1989: Ontario, 1990; Prince Edward Island, 1988; Québec, 1977; Saskatchewan, 1978; Yukon Territory, 1986. In 1987, Manitoba published what are referred to as *Re-enacted Statutes*.

[5] Most provinces have looseleaf versions of the latest revised statutes. These publications are called "continuing consolidations" because they incorporate new acts and amendments since the last revision. Their value is in keeping the statute law current under one cover. In addition, the publication of looseleaf versions lessens the need for periodic revisions. Ontario and Newfoundland do not have looseleaf statutes. All but Manitoba's and Québec's are unofficial; nonetheless,

Two points should be noted concerning revised statutes. First, no new material is added to the law by a revision. Secondly, a few acts remain unconsolidated and unrepealed. An illustration of this is *An Act to provide for the recognition of the Beaver (Castor Canadensis) as a symbol of the sovereignty of Canada.*

The most recent revision of the federal statutes is the *Revised Statutes of Canada, 1985.* This set consists of 17 volumes, which includes eight volumes of federal statute law, five supplements, two indices, a table of concordance and a volume of appendices. The eight volumes of the set consolidate federal statute law to December 31, 1984. The supplements contain new acts and amendments to the *Revised Statutes of Canada* made between December 31, 1984 and November 30, 1991. The supplements also contain acts not included in the main revision, such as the *Divorce Act* and the *Income Tax Act.* The appendices include a schedule of acts repealed, constitutional documents, and the *Bill of Rights, 1960.*

Statutes are published in both English and French versions in the *Revised Statutes of Canada.* The acts are arranged alphabetically by the short title[6] and each act is given an alphanumeric designation. For example, the *Copyright Act* in the *Revised Statutes of Canada, 1985*, is chapter C-42. In the example, the alpha designation refers to the first letter of the first word of the act and the numeric designation is the number of the act in its alphabetical order within that letter. The *Revised Statutes of Canada* is also published in a looseleaf format and is kept up to date with regular releases.

The revised statutes of most provinces are also arranged alphabetically by the short title of the act,[7] but not all have adopted an alphanumeric system of numbering chapters. The *Revised Statutes of Nova Scotia* and the *Revised Statutes of British Columbia*, for example, still use a simple numeric system.

The alphanumeric systems adopted by some provinces have unique features designed to complement the publication of their revised statutes in a looseleaf format. The looseleaf edition of the Manitoba statutes is entitled the *Continuing Consolidation of the Statutes of Manitoba* and contains re-enacted (and revised) acts. Chapters are designated to allow acts passed since the completion of the re-enactment to be easily incorporated into the binder. For example, *The Ecological Reserves Act*, *The Education Administration Act*, and *The Elderly and Infirm Persons' Housing Act*, all re-enacted statutes, appear as chapters E5, E10, and E20, respectively. *The Economic Innovation and Technology Council Act* which has been passed since the re-enactment appears as chapter E7. The looseleaf service is current to the date noted by the publisher. Acts passed by the legislature after that date are not included in the service. For these, the student

---

in several provinces, it is becoming increasingly common to include a reference to the consolidation in a citation.

[6] When they are enacted all statutes have a long title found at the head of the text and most also have a short title located in the first or last section. When a statute appears in a revision the long title is usually omitted and the short title is placed at the head of the text.

[7] The *Revised Statutes of Newfoundland* have a long title and usually a shorter title.

should consult the appropriate red-bound annual volume or the separate chapters of acts available from the Queen's Printer.

The bound edition of the *Revised Statutes of Prince Edward Island* uses the same basic alphanumeric system as the *Revised Statutes of Canada*. However, the system has been modified by incorporating a decimal notation which permits infinite expansion for use in the looseleaf edition. For example, the *Lending Agency Act*, passed after the 1988 *Revised Statutes of Prince Edward Island*, was numbered chapter L-8.1 following the *Legislative Assembly Retirement Allowances Act* which is chapter L-8. A similar system is used for the *Revised Statutes of New Brunswick*, the *Revised Statutes of Saskatchewan*, the *Revised Statutes of Québec* and the *Revised Statutes of Alberta*. In Prince Edward Island, however, the decimal notation appears only in the "Table of Public Statutes", and not in the body of the statute volume itself (as in Saskatchewan, for instance).

(B) RESEARCH TECHNIQUES

(1) Finding a Statute

As mentioned earlier, federal statutes are published in bound form in the *Revised Statutes of Canada* or in the annual volumes of the *Statutes of Canada*. To locate a statute a student need only refer to the "Table of Public Statutes" in the latest annual volume of the *Statutes of Canada* or to the "Table of Public Statutes" issued with the *Canada Gazette, Part III*. It lists[8] all acts in force as of December 31st of that year.

The student may also refer to the "Table of Public Statutes" when only the subject-matter is known, since most titles of acts suggest the subject-matter with which the act is concerned.

It is not always necessary to consult the table. If the short title and date are known, the student may simply refer to the "Table of Contents" for that annual volume. Also, if the name of the act and its alphanumeric designation for the *Revised Statutes of Canada* is known, refer directly to the volume that includes that chapter. (The chapter numbers of the statutes contained in each volume are printed on the spine.)

The procedure for finding provincial statutes is similar to that for finding federal statutes. To locate a particular provincial statute the student should refer to the "Table of Public Statutes" in the latest annual or sessional volume for the selected jurisdiction. The "Table of Public Statutes" may also be of assistance in determining whether there has been any legislation on a selected topic. Alternatively, the student may refer to a separately bound subject index, if one is available for the selected jurisdiction.[9]

---

[8]   The acts in the table are listed alphabetically by the short title. Thus, if only the long title is known, guess at the short title before reading the table.

[9]   Maritime Law Book Co., for example, has prepared an index for New Brunswick.

(2) Checking for Amendments

To find all the amendments to a federal statute, refer to the text of amendments, if any, under the title of the statute in the "Table of Public Statutes" in the latest annual or volumes of the *Statutes of Canada*. It lists all the amendments enacted as of December 31st of that year. The amendments will usually be found in statutes bearing the name of the revised statute; however, in some instances the amendments will be included in an umbrella statute, commonly referred to as an "omnibus act". For example, amendments to the *Access to Information Act* and the *Broadcasting Act*, in 1987, were included in the *Miscellaneous Statute Law Amendment Act, 1987*, which is found in chapter 1 of the *Revised Statutes of Canada, 1985* (4th Supplement).

Some of the amendments to the *Transfer of Offenders Act* which appear in the "Table of Public Statutes" in the 1998 *Statutes of Canada* are reproduced in Table 1 below.

On the left of the table, the section numbers (in bold-face type) refer to the sections of the *Transfer of Offenders Act* which have been amended. The dates refer to the bound volumes of statutes (or the supplement to the revision) in which the amending statutes are found. The chapter and section numbers (in light-face type) refer to the amending acts.

TABLE 1

Transfer of Offenders Act — R.S., 1985, c. T-15
(Transfèrement des délinquants, Loi sur le)

s. 2, 1992, c. 20, s. 216(1)(*f*); 1993, c. 34, s. 121
s. 6, R.S., c. 31 (1st Supp.), s. 104
s. 8, 1992, c. 20, s. 208; 1995, c. 42, s. 83
s. 10, 1992, c. 20, s. 209; 1995, c. 42, ss. 71(*d*)(F) and 72(*d*)(F)
s. 11, 1992, c. 20, s. 210; 1995, c. 42, s. 84
s. 11.1, added, 1995, c. 42, s. 84
s. 12, 1992, c. 20, s. 211; 1995, c. 42, s. 84
s. 16, R.S., c. 27 (1st Supp.), s. 203; 1995, c. 22, s. 17 (Sch. III, items 6 to 9)
s. 17, 1993, c. 34, s. 122
s. 23, c. 34, s. 123
s. 24, R.S., c. 31 (1st Supp.), s. 105
s. 25, repealed, 1993, c. 34, s. 124
Sch., SOR/86-49, SOR/86-297; SOR/87-583; SOR/89-156; SOR/91-91; SOR/95-293; SOR/97-83; SOR/98-441
General, 1992, c. 20, s.216(2)
General, 1995, c. 22, s.26
CIF, R.S. c. 27 (1st Supp.), s.203 proclaimed in force 04.12.85 *see* SI/85-211

CIF, R.S., c. 31 (1st Supp.), ss.104 and 105 proclaimed in force 15.10.85 *see* SI/85-188
CIF, 1992, c. 20, ss. 208 to 211 and 216 in force 01.11.92 *see* SI/92-197
CIF, 1993, c. 34, ss. 121 to 124 in force on assent 23.06.93
CIF, 1995, c. 22, s. 17 (Sch. III, items 6 to 9) and s. 26 in force 03.09.96 *see* SI/96-79
CIF, 1995, c. 42, ss. 71(F), 72(F), 83 and 84 in force 24.01.96 *see* SI/96-10

The student may also find amendments to a federal statute in the *Canada Statute Citator*. The *Citator* lists the names of the acts of Canada with a reference to their location in the *Revised Statutes of Canada* or in a bound volume of statutes. The *Citator* includes the text of all amendments (except for amendments to the *Criminal Code* and the *Income Tax Act*) to the acts, arranging them according to the section numbers of the original act.

The procedure for finding amendments to provincial statutes is similar to that used for finding amendments to a federal statute. The student should refer to the "Table of Public Statutes" in the latest bound volume of statutes for all jurisdictions, except for Saskatchewan where the statute volumes include a separate part for "Public Acts" and "Amending and Repealing and Temporary Public Acts".[10] The tables list the amendments (new sections and repealed sections are also included) in force as of December 31st of the year of the volume. The tables are not, however, uniformly prepared. For example, the "Table of Public Statutes" in the *Statutes of Ontario*, by and large, does not list the specific sections of statutes which have been amended.

A statute citator is an efficient tool for locating amendments to provincial acts. Currently there are publications known as "Statute Citators" for British Columbia, Nova Scotia and Ontario. A publication similar to a citator, entitled "Statutes Judicially Considered" often includes amendments. Such a publication is available for Alberta, British Columbia, Manitoba and Saskatchewan. There are also publications known as "Decisions Citators" for British Columbia, Alberta, Saskatchewan and Manitoba which include digests and reported cases which have considered statutes. Again, the various citators and statutes judicially considered publications are not uniformly prepared. For example, the *Ontario Statute Citator* provides the full text of amendments to acts; whereas the *British Columbia Statute Citator* merely lists the amendments.

(3) Canadian Statutes on the Internet

The Internet has quickly established itself as an important legal research tool. The federal government and most provincial governments have developed useful World Wide Web sites that contain a wealth of information on government

---

[10] There is a companion volume entitled "Saskatchewan Tables" or *Table of Public Statutes* and *Table of Regulations*.

statutes, bills, regulations, policies and reports. Most of these sites provide the information for free (see below for exceptions).

The text of statutes on government-sponsored Web pages is updated regularly, so the statutes are usually consolidated and up-to-date. However, it is important that the researcher determine when the last update to the site occurred. Most government Web sites indicate the date of last updating, usually at the beginning or end of the document.

Disclaimers on most sites indicate that all information available on the Web site, including statutes, is provided for convenience of reference only, and has no official sanction.

The *Consolidated Statutes of Canada* may be accessed online: Department of Justice Canada <http://www.canada.justice.gc.ca>.

After choosing to view the site in either official language, the home page of the Department of Justice appears. Click on Laws of Canada to view the *Consolidated Statutes of Canada*, and constitutional documents.

Although most federal statutes are available through the Department of Justice site, a notable exception is the *Income Tax Act* which, because of frequent annual amendments, has been left to commercial publishers to consolidate.

Connect to the following Web sites to view the consolidated statutes in each respective jurisdiction:

British Columbia	online: British Columbia Queen's Printer <http://www.qp.gov.bc.ca/bcstats/>,
Yukon	online: Access to Justice Network <http://legis.acjnet.org/ACJNET/Yukon/index_en.html>,
Northwest Territories	online: Access to Justice Network <http://legis.acjnet.org/ACJNet/TNO/index_en.html>,
Alberta	online: Alberta Queen's Printer <http://www.gov.ab.ca/qp/>,
Saskatchewan	online: Queen's Printer for Saskatchewan <http://www.qp.justice.gov.sk.ca>, (Note: There is a fee for electronic access)
Manitoba	online: Manitoba Government <http://www.gov.mb.ca/chc/statpub/free/index.html>,
Ontario	online: The Legislative Assembly of Ontario <http://www.gov.on.ca/MBS/english/publications/statregs/index.html>,
Québec	online: Québec Ministry of Justice and Les Publications du Québec <http://doc.gouv.qc.ca/servlets/Dbml/indes2.html>, (click on "Lois et Règlements")
New Brunswick	online: New Brunswick Department of Justice <http://www.gov.nb.ca/justice/asrlste.htm>,
Nova Scotia	online: Government of Nova Scotia <http://www.gov.ns.ca/legi/legc/>.

(4) *Checking for New Acts or Recent Amendments for the Current Year*

New acts, amendments, or repealed acts passed after the publication of the latest annual volume of the *Statutes of Canada* may be found in *The Canada Gazette, Part III*, or, failing that, in the collection of third reading of bills which is kept in most libraries.

The student may also refer to the most recent "Cumulative Table" in *The Canada Gazette, Part III*, or to the "Table of Contents" for individual volumes of *The Canada Gazette, Part III*, not yet included in the "Cumulative Table". As a final check, the student may refer to the *Canada Statute Citator* which lists acts not yet included in the last published "Table of Public Statutes".

Proposed changes to federal statutes which are still in the form of a bill may be discovered by means of secondary tools, including the following:

(i) "Progress of Bills Through Parliament", found in the *Newsletter of the Ottawa Letter*;
(ii) "Canada Statute Citator Monthly Bulletin Service";
(iii) "Progress of Bills", found in *Canadian Current Law - Legislation*;
(iv) *Status of Bills and Motions Reported*, published under authority of the Speaker of the House of Commons;
(v) votes and proceedings of the House of Commons and Senate; and
(vi) QUICKLAW's Canada Status of Bills database (CSB).

New acts, amendments, or repealed acts which are not included in the "Table of Public Statutes" in the bound volume of provincial statutes often may be found in the looseleaf edition of the revised statutes for selected jurisdictions.[11] Alternatively, the student may contact the librarian of the provincial legislature or the provincial government bookstore for the selected jurisdiction. The latter may have selected acts reprinted in pamphlet form.

Proposed changes to provincial statutes which are still in the form of a bill may be discovered by means of secondary tools, including the following:

(i) "Ontario Statute Citator Weekly Bulletin Service", found in the *Ontario Statute Citator* (or as a companion volume);
(ii) "Legislative Record", found in *Provincial Pulse*; and
(iii) *Ontario Legislative Digest Service*.

In addition to these sources, a number of tables and indices relating to the status of bills are published by the Legislative Counsel of most provinces and by law libraries.

---

[11] Always check acts in a consolidation against the original legislation, if possible, in those jurisdictions for which the consolidation is not authoritative. The consolidations of Alberta and Saskatchewan, for example, are not authoritative. The student should refer to the title page to determine the status of the consolidation for the selected jurisdiction.

Perhaps the quickest way to determine the status of bills before the legislatures is to consult the particular jurisdiction's Web page. These pages usually provide up to date information on new bills, including changes that have been made between readings, and a history of recently proclaimed laws. It is vital to check the date of the last updating of the Web page, especially during a period when the legislature or parliament is sitting.

The following sites may be consulted to determine the status of bills before the legislature of each jurisdiction:

Federal	online: Parliamentary Internet <http://www.parl.gc.ca/>,
British Columbia	online: The Legislative Assembly of British Columbia <http://www.legis.gov.bc.ca/bills.htm>,
Alberta	online: The Legislative Assembly of Alberta <http://www.assembly.ab.ca>,
Saskatchewan	online: The Legislative Assembly of Saskatchewan <http://www.legassembly.sk.ca/bills/progbill.htm>,
Manitoba	online: Manitoba Government <http://www.gov.mb.ca/chc/statpub/free/index.html>,
Newfoundland	online: Newfoundland House of Assembly <http:/www.gov.nf.ca/house/>,
Ontario	online: The Legislative Assembly of Ontario <http://www.ontla.on.ca/Documents/documentsindex.htm>,
Québec	online: Assemblée nationale du Québec <http://www.assnat.qc.ca/fra/publications/index.html>,
New Brunswick	online: The Legislative Assembly of New Brunswick <http://www.gov.nb.ca/legis/busi/busi.htm>,
Prince Edward Island	online: Government of Prince Edward Island <http://www.gov.pe.ca/leg/bills/index.php3>,
Nova Scotia	online: Government of Nova Scotia <http://www.gov.ns.ca/legi/legc/>.

(5) Determining the Date of Coming into Force

Following the third reading in the appropriate legislative body, a bill receives Royal Assent and becomes law; however, the date of Royal Assent, usually noted below the title of an act in a statute book, is not usually the same date as the date of coming into force (the effective date).

There are three ways that a federal law may be brought into force:

(i)   The act may provide for its own coming into force. Reference should be made to the last section of the statute;

(ii)   The act may state that it will come into force on a date to be set by proclamation. If so,

(a)   refer to the "Table of Public Statutes" or to the table of "Proclamations of Canada" in the latest annual volume of the *Statutes of Canada*, or

- (b) refer to the table of proclamations in *The Canada Gazette, Part III*, or
- (c) refer to the table of proclamations in the quarterly index of *The Canada Gazette, Part I*, or
- (d) refer to the heading "Proclamations" in the index to individual volumes of *The Canada Gazette, Part I*; or
- (iii) The act may be silent as to the date of coming into force. Reference should be made to the *Interpretation Act*, R.S.C. 1985, c. I-21, s. 6(2).

NOTE: Other secondary sources for finding proclamation dates include the "Statutes Amended, Repealed, or Proclaimed in Force" section of *Canadian Current Law - Legislation*, the *Canada Statute Citator* and the *Ottawa Letter*.

Provincial acts, like federal acts, may be brought into force in three ways:

- (i) The act may provide for its own coming into force. Refer to the last section of the statute; or
- (ii) The act may state that it will come into force on a date to be set by proclamation. If so, check one or more of the following sources for the selected province:
  - (a) a table of proclamations or the "Table of Public Statutes" in the latest bound volume of statutes;
  - (b) "Acts Proclaimed" (Saskatchewan); "Acts in Force" (British Columbia); "Proclamation" (Ontario, Québec, Alberta, Manitoba); "Proclamations" (New Brunswick, Nova Scotia, Prince Edward Island, Northwest Territories); "A Proclamation" (Newfoundland); "Statutory Instruments" (Yukon) in the appropriate provincial or territorial Gazette;
  - (c) the "Statutes Amended, Repealed, or Proclaimed in Force" section in *Canadian Current Law - Legislation*;
  - (d) a statute citator (for example, *Ontario Statute Citator*); or
- (iii) The act may be silent as to the date of coming into force.

In the latter case, the dates of coming into force are governed by the following general provisions for each province:

Alta. -	*Interpretation Act*, R.S.A. 1980, c. I-7, s. 4(1).
B.C. -	*Interpretation Act*, R.S.B.C. 1996, c. 238, s. 3(2).
Man. -	*The Interpretation Act*, R.S.M. 1987, c. I80, s. 5(4) (C.C.S.M. I80).
N.B. -	*Interpretation Act*, R.S.N.B. 1973, c. I-13, s. 3(2).
Nfld. -	*The Statutes Act*, R.S.N. 1990, c. S-26, s. 4.
N.W.T. -	*Interpretation Act*, R.S.N.W.T. 1988, c. I-8, s. 4(1).
N.S. -	*Interpretation Act*, R.S.N.S. 1989, c. 235, s. 3.
Ont. -	*Statutes Act*, R.S.O. 1990, c. S.21, s. 5(1).

P.E.I. -   *Interpretation Act*, R.S.P.E.I. 1988, c. I-8, s. 3(1).
Qué. -   *Interpretation Act*, R.S.Q. 1977, c. I-16, s. 5, as am. by S.Q. 1982,
            c. 62.
Sask. -   *Interpretation Act*, S.S. 1995, c. I-11.2, s. 4(2).
Yukon -   *Interpretation Act*, R.S.Y.T. 1986, c. 93, s. 3.

(C) CITATION

One of the more difficult tasks for the first-year law student is to master the proper citation of statutes which have been published in the official statute volumes. The introduction, in recent years, of looseleaf editions of statutes has added to the difficulty. The outline below will assist the student in mastering the basic "rules" of citation. Appendix I lists the recommended method of citation for federal acts and for provincial acts.

Rule 1: Title

Refer to the short title, if there is one. The correct form of the short title is that which appears in the provision for the short title in the bound volume of statutes or in the revised statutes. Note in particular that if the year or the word "the" appear in the title, they are reproduced in a citation. The titles of statutes in all Canadian jurisdictions should be italicized.

Rule 2: Statutory Reference and Jurisdiction

(i)   Refer to a statute as "S." and to a revised or re-enacted statute as "R.S.".
(ii)   Combine "S." or "R.S." with the following abbreviations for Canada and for each province and territory: C., B.C., A., S., M., O., Q., N.B., P.E.I., N., N.S., Y. and N.W.T.

Rule 3: Year or Session

(i)   Include the year in any citation of a statute found in a revision or an annual volume.

Examples:

R.S.C. 1985, c. A-2.
S.O. 1985, c. 20.

(ii)   Include the year or years in any citation of a statute found in a sessional volume.

Examples:

S.N.S. 1984, c. 1.
S.C. 1980-81-82-83, c. 5.

(iii)   Include a reference to the number of the session where there is more than one session in a year, each of which are numbered separately.

Example:

S.O. 1971 (2nd Sess.), c. 2.

(iv)   Supplements to the *Revised Statutes of Canada* contain statutes that were passed after the cut-off date and before the release date for the set. Such statutes should be cited to the supplement and it is necessary to include the number of the supplement, unless it is the first one.

Example:

R.S.C. 1985, c. 8 (2nd Supp.), s. 2.

Rule 4: Chapter and Schedule

(i)   When citing a chapter use the designation "c.", and "cc." for more than one chapter, notwithstanding any other abbreviation which might be used in the statute volume in the jurisdiction.[12] Refer to Schedule as "Sch.", and Schedules as "Schs.".

Rule 5: Section, Subsection and Paragraph

(i)   Refer to a section with the designation "s.". Refer to more than one section as "ss.".[13] Otherwise, include the number of the subsection in brackets, *e.g.*, s. 91(1). Refer to paragraph as "para.", and paragraphs as "paras.".

Rule 6: Citation of New Acts

Acts which have not been included in a revision or re-enactment are cited to the appropriate bound volume published after the revision or re-enactment.

---

[12]   Prior to 1977, statutes in Newfoundland sessional volumes were referred to by number and not chapter and the abbreviation "No." was used in the citation of a statute.

[13]   Provisions of the *Québec Code* are referred to as articles rather than sections; therefore, use the abbreviations "art." and "arts.".

Example:

Gaming Services Act, 1992, S.O. 1992, c. 24.

Rule 7: Citation of Amending and Repealing Acts

(i)   Refer to an amendment as "as am. by", to a repealed act as "as rep. by", and if repealed and substituted as "re-en.".

(ii)   Refer to amending acts by, first, citing the revised statute, if there is one, and, second, citing the bound volumes of statutes.

Examples:

Horse Racing Commission Act, R.S.N.S. 1989, c. 204, as am. by S.N.S. 1991, c. 11.
Regional Transit Authority Act, R.S.N.S. 1989, c. 389, as am. by S.N.S. 1990, c. 19, ss. 83-84.

NOTE: In citing amendments, the title of the amending act is always omitted unless it has a different title than the original act. If the difference is found only in the words "An Act to amend", it is not necessary to repeat the title. The jurisdiction may also be omitted.

(iii)   Include a reference to the amended and amending sections if the point under consideration involves only a particular section or subsection of a statute.

Example:

An amendment to section 20(1) of the *Alberta Oil Sands Technology and Research Authority Act* is cited R.S.A. 1980, c. O-6, s. 20(1), as am. by S.A. 1984, c. 30, s. 3.

(iv)   Include the amending section if the amendment is included in a general purpose act (commonly referred to as an "omnibus act").

Example:

A 1984 amendment to the *Oil and Gas Conservation Act* located in the *Miscellaneous Statutes Amendment Act, 1984* is cited: *Oil and Gas Conservation Act*, R.S.A. 1980, c. 0-5, as am. by S.A. 1984, c. 55, s. 35.

(v)   Refer to a new or additional section with the designation "added" or "add".

Example:

Criminal Records Act, R.S.C. 1985, c. C-47, s. 2.2(1) added, S.C. 1992, c. 22, s. 2(1).

Rule 8: Punctuation

Include periods after every abbreviation, commas after the title, a chapter or section designation, if required (see example above), and year, as well as before modifications, *e.g.*, "as am. by".

Rule 9: Pinpoint Reference of Acts

A pinpoint reference to a specific section of an act follows the chapter designation.

Example:

Waste Management Act, 1992, S.O. 1992, c. 1, s. 2.

Rule 10: Looseleaf Statute Services

There are looseleaf consolidations for Canada and most provinces,[14] but these various jurisdictions have not adopted a standard form of designation for the consolidations, as is the case for revised or bound volumes of the statutes. The practice generally appears to be to refer not to the name of the consolidation but only to chapter references of the consolidation in a citation, if it is different than the revision or the bound volume.

Canada

When referring to acts in the bound edition of the *Revised Statutes of Canada, 1985*, cite the revision. When referring to subsequent acts, cite to the *Statutes of Canada*. Do not cite to the looseleaf.

Alberta

The consolidation does not have official status. Thus, cite to the revision and subsequent bound volumes.

Examples:

Land Titles Act, R.S.A. 1980, c. L-5.

---

[14] Except for Ontario and Newfoundland. None of the Territories have a looseleaf edition.

Legal Professions Act, S.A. 1990, c. L-9.1.

NOTE: The same chapter designations are used in the consolidation and in the bound volumes.

British Columbia

Statutes are cited to the revision. Acts which were passed after the last revision are cited to the bound volume of statutes.

Examples:

Fish Protection Act, S.B.C. 1997, c. 21.

Manitoba

The consolidation of the statutes of Manitoba is now generally referred to as C.C.S.M. (*i.e.*, *Continuing Consolidation of the Statutes of Manitoba*) and the designation has been adopted by several Canadian texts on legal citation.

Examples:

The Emergency Measures Act, S.M. 1987-88, c. 11, C.C.S.M., c. E80.
The Business Practices Act, S.M. 1990-91, c. 6, C.C.S.M., c. B120.

Re-enacted Statutes of Manitoba in bilingual format are contained in the consolidation and appear with the same chapter numbers as are found in the bound re-enactment volumes.

Example:

The Employment Standards Act, R.S.M. 1987, c. E110, C.C.S.M., c. E110.

New Brunswick

Statutes contained in the *Revised Statutes of New Brunswick, 1973*, and which were incorporated in the looseleaf service, use the same alphanumeric numbering system. Cite to the revision.

Example:

Companies Act, R.S.N.B. 1973, c. C-13.

Acts which are included in the supplement to the revision and new acts passed after the revision are assigned an alphanumeric designation (with a decimal notation). It is used in the bound volumes and in the consolidation. Thus, the citation below applies to both.

Example:

Quarriable Substances Act, S.N.B. 1991, c. Q-1.1.

Amending acts are numbered in the traditional alphanumeric manner in the sessional volume and incorporated into the appropriate act in the consolidation. A reference to an amendment to the revised statute appears as follows:

Plant Diseases Act, R.S.N.B. 1973, c. P-9, as am. by S.N.B. 1979, c. 55; 1986, c. 8, s. 98; 1990, c. 61, s. 108.

Similarly, amendments to a new act will be cited as follows:

Advanced Life Support Services Act, S.N.B. 1976, c. A-3.01, as am. by S.N.B. 1985, c. 4, s. 1; 1986, c. 8, s. 1; 1990, c. 61, s. 3; 1992, c. 52, s. 1; 1994, c. 78, s.1.

Nova Scotia

A new revision and a new consolidation were published in 1989. Both have the same chapter designations and are cited in the traditional manner to the bound revision and sessional volume.

Examples:

Architects Act, R.S.N.S. 1989, c. 21.
Public Sector Compensation Restraint Act, S.N.S. 1991, c. 5.
Insurance Brokers' Association of Nova Scotia Act, S.N.S. 1949, c. 105, as am. by S.N.S. 1990, c. 43; 1992, c. 73.

Prince Edward Island

The revised statutes of 1988 were published in bound and looseleaf formats. Acts passed after the *Revised Statutes of Prince Edward Island, 1988*, are given a different chapter number in the continuing consolidation than in the bound volume. The looseleaf reference is indicated in brackets at the end of the citation to the bound volume of the *Statutes of Prince Edward Island*.

Example:

Credit Union Act, S.P.E.I. 1990, c. 14 (c. C-29.1).

Québec

Québec statutes may be cited to either the bound revision or to the looseleaf revision. The citation, *Charter of Human Rights and Freedoms*, R.S.Q. 1977, c. C-12, is a reference to the bound 1977 revision. Statutes passed after the revision are cited to the looseleaf service or to the *Statutes of Québec*.

Examples:

An Act Respecting Trust Companies and Savings Companies, R.S.Q., c. S-29.01.
An Act Respecting the Composition of the Office of the National Assembly, S.Q. 1990, c. 2.

Saskatchewan

The *Revised Statutes of Saskatchewan, 1978*, are published in bound and looseleaf formats. The looseleaf consolidation is not officially sanctioned for use in a court of law. Cite to the bound volume of statutes.

Examples:

The Police Act, 1990, S.S. 1990-91, c. P-15.01.
The Crown Employment Contracts Act, S.S. 1991, c. C-50.11.
The Absconding Debtors Act, R.S.S. 1978, c. A-2.

NOTE: An alphanumeric system with decimal notation has been adopted for acts assented to after the revision for ease of use with a looseleaf format, presumably at some later date.

2. United Kingdom Statutes

(A) PUBLICATION AND ORGANIZATION

Two basic distinctions should be drawn between English and Canadian statutes. First, English statute law does not undergo the periodic and systematic consolidations that Canadian statute law enjoys. Nevertheless, there is a continuing process of updating which involves consolidation of individual statutes and their amendments into new acts and the repeal of spent and undesired statutes. The second distinction is that while only one or two series of statute volumes serves each Canadian jurisdiction, there are a number of series containing United Kingdom statutes:

(1)   Modern Sources of United Kingdom Statutes

(i)   Public General Acts and Measures (1932 to date)

The most comprehensive official source of statutes of the United Kingdom is a series of red bound volumes called the *Public General Acts and Measures*. The series began in 1832 and, until 1939 the volumes of the statutes contained all the acts passed in a particular session of the British Parliament. After that date, the volumes contained all the acts passed in a calendar year. At the beginning of each volume are alphabetical and chronological tables of short titles, a subject index, a table showing their effect on existing legislation, and a table showing the derivations of consolidating acts.

(ii) Statutes in Force (1972 to date)

This is an official looseleaf edition of the public general acts of the United Kingdom. It contains all the acts currently in force in the United Kingdom and is kept up to date by periodic releases in booklet form.

There are a number of important finding aids for the set including:

(a)   a comprehensive general index;
(b)   an index to each subject group;
(c)   an alphabetical list of acts with cross-references to subject headings;
(d)   a chronological list of acts with cross-references to subject headings; and
(e)   an annual cumulative supplement.

(iii) Halsbury's Statutes of England, Third Edition

This is the most comprehensive and best indexed unofficial source of statutes of the United Kingdom and one that will generally be consulted before the official sources. It reprints the text of statutes as amended and provides annotations in the form of explanatory notes, effects on other legislation, statutory instruments, and judicial consideration. It is arranged by subject title. The third edition was replaced by a fourth edition, but it is kept on some law library shelves for historical purposes.

The following publications are included in the set:

(a) Main Third Edition Volumes 1 to 39. These provide a comprehensive record of acts passed by the British Parliament and were published between 1968 and

1972. The cut-off date for materials contained in individual volumes is noted after the title page.

(b) Continuation Volumes 40 to 54(2). These contain the statutes passed after the publication of the main volumes. Each volume includes a "Table of Statutes" and an "Index". These volumes were published annually between 1971 and 1984. The cut-off date for materials in individual volumes is noted after the title page.

(c) Consolidated Tables and Index for Volumes 1-50. This is a single-volume index for the main set and part of the continuation volumes. It covers all legislation in force on January 1, 1981. It contains an "Alphabetical List of Statutes", a "Chronological List of Statutes", a "General Index" and a "Words and Phrases" index.

(d) Cumulative Supplement. This work records the amendments, additions, and other changes to the material in the main and continuation volumes. It includes alphabetical and chronological lists of statutes and a table of cases. These supplement the lists contained in the *Consolidated Tables and Index* for volumes 1-50.

(iv) Halsbury's Statutes of England and Wales, Fourth Edition

This set, like its predecessor, *Halsbury's Statutes of England, Third Edition*, is intended to provide a complete record of all acts of the English Parliament grouped according to subject-matter.

The following publications are included in the set:

(a) Main Fourth Edition Volumes 1 to 50. These replace the 39 main and continuation volumes of the third edition. The complete set contains all acts under 146 subject titles. The cut-off date for materials in individual volumes is noted following the title page.

(b) Reissue Volumes. These are intended to replace main volumes which have undergone numerous changes. They include all relevant acts, and exclude any repealed statutory provisions. They have been published regularly since 1987.

(c) Cumulative Supplement. This work records the amendments, additions, and other changes to the main, reissue and *Current Statutes Service* volumes. It is updated and published annually.

(d) Noter-Up Service. This is a looseleaf service binder. It records amendments, additions and other changes made during the current year to the material in the main volumes and the *Current Statutes Service*. The "Noter-Up" also contains

material relating to "Unannotated Acts" and updates the annual volumes of *Halsbury's Is it in Force?*. Each issue of the "Noter-Up" supersedes the last, and three issues are published each year. The "Noter-Up" is used in conjunction with the current *Cumulative Supplement*.

(e) Current Statutes Service. This is a multi-volume looseleaf publication which contains the text of all acts which post-date the main and reissue volumes. The *Current Statutes Service* is classified by subject-matter and divided by guide cards bearing the number of the parent volume to which the new material relates. It includes an "Alphabetical List of Statutes" and a "Chronological List of Statutes", along with a subject index, all of which are supplementary to the annual *Table of Statutes and General Index* volume. It is updated six times a year. When a bound volume is reissued, the material that is contained in the *Current Statute Service* binder for that title is incorporated into the reissue volume.

(f) Table of Statutes and General Index. This service contains the annual index to the fourth edition of *Halsbury's Statutes of England*. It lists the acts which are contained in the main and reissue volumes, as well as in the service binders. Each volume also includes chronological and alphabetical lists of statutes, as well as volume and service indexes. It was first published in 1989 and has been updated since then.

(g) Is it in Force? This work lists the commencement dates and other information for every act of general application in England and Wales and General Synod Measures passed since January 1, 1963. The text is arranged according to calendar year beginning with the most recent year. The work is updated and published annually. It lists (a) the dates on which the acts received Royal Assent; (b) the date or dates which have been appointed for the provision of the acts to come into force; and (c) provisions which are not in force. The cut-off date for material contained in the volume is noted in the Preface. Commencement dates and other changes for the current year are listed following the guide "Is it in Force?" in the *Noter-Up Service* binder.

(v) Current Law Statutes Annotated (1948 to date)

This is a series of blue bound volumes of the statutes of the United Kingdom Parliament. The acts are arranged chronologically and the more important acts are annotated. Each annual publication (consisting of one or more volumes) contains a "Statute Citator" and includes statutes affected by statutory instrument, judicially considered, and repealed and amended. A looseleaf service provides any new acts not yet published in a bound volume.

A companion volume, *Current Law Statute Citator* (1947-1971) includes the following information:

(a)   a list of all U.K. acts since 1947;
(b)   a section-by-section list of citations to amendments and repeals made to
       U.K. acts since 1947; and
(c)   a section-by-section record of cases decided on particular statutory pro-
       visions since 1947.

A further update may be found in both the *Current Law Legislation Citator*
(1972-1988) and the *Current Law Legislation Citators* (1989 - date). This last
publication is produced annually, but is kept up to date with monthly paperback
issues. The Citators both contain sections entitled "Statute Citator" and "Statutory Instrument Citator".

(vi) The Law Reports, Statutes (1866 to date)

This set is published by the Incorporated Council of Law Reporting as part of
The Law Reports. It contains a verbatim reprint of the official statutes. These are
initially issued in booklet form and later replaced by an annual volume or volumes.

(2) Older Sources of United Kingdom Statutes

(i) The Statutes Revised, Third Edition (1235 to 1948)

This is the "official" series for statutes 1714 to 1948, containing a compilation of
acts from 1235 to 1948, which were in force at the end of 1948. Statutes are
printed in chronological order in 32 volumes. Although each volume has an
index, there is no general index to the set.

(ii) Statutes of the Realm (1235 to 1713)

This is the "official" series for statutes enacted before 1714. Statutes are listed in
chronological order. There is a chronological table of statutes and a subject
index to each volume and to the set as a whole.

(iii) Statutes at Large

This refers to a collection of various editions of the statutes published between
the thirteenth and eighteenth centuries. The edition of Tomlins & Raithby, containing acts from the *Magna Carta* to 1869, is generally considered to be the
most accurate.

(B) RESEARCH TECHNIQUES

(1) Finding United Kingdom Statutes

(i) Public General Acts and Measures

If both the title and date are known, consult the alphabetical list of statutes in the official *Public General Acts and Measures* for that year.

(ii) Halsbury's Statutes

If the name of the act is known (and if the act is likely to appear in a particular title), consult the spines of the volumes or the list of titles (at the front of each volume) to find the appropriate act. For example, volume 8 contains the title "Companies", where the *Companies Act, 1985*, appears.

Alternatively, refer to the alphabetical or chronological lists of acts in the selected volume for what appears to be the appropriate title. For example, the "Table of Statutes" at the front of the "Companies" title in volume 8 (1999 Reissue) shows that the *Companies Act, 1985*, begins on page 88.

If the name of the act is not known, but you have a general idea of the particular area of law, *i.e.*, the title, consult the spines of individual volumes, or the list of titles published at the front of each volume or at the front of the *Table of Statutes and General Index*. The *Table of Statutes and General Index* is also a useful source of information where the name of the particular act relating to a certain area is known and one wishes to check for additional legislation on that subject. Simply by looking up the relevant subject area in the *General Index* any other acts dealing with that subject will be identified. For example, to find the *Restrictive Trade Practices Act, 1976*, use the "Alphabetical List of Statutes" at the front of the *Table of Statutes and General Index*.

To update a search or to find a very recent act, refer to the "Alphabetical List of Statutes" at the front of the first binder of the *Current Statutes Service*.

(2) Checking for Amendments

The amended text of statutes is reprinted in *Halsbury's Statutes*. For more recent amendments, consult:

(i)   the latest annual *Cumulative Supplement*. This *Supplement* directs the user to the main volumes, reissue volumes and the *Current Statutes Service*, updating the act, section and schedule found in those sources; and

(ii) the *Noter-Up Service*. The "Noter-Up" directs the user to the main volumes, reissue volumes and to the *Current Statutes Service*. The "Noter-Up" is a preview of what will appear in the next *Cumulative*

Supplement. It is the final check on the state of a given act and should always be used in conjunction with the *Cumulative Supplement.*

(3) Determining the Date of Coming into Force

Unless another date is specified, a statute of the United Kingdom comes into force on the date of Royal Assent: *Acts of Parliament (Commencement) Act, 1793* (U.K.), 33 Geo. III, c. 13. The date of Royal Assent will be found under the long title. If the date of commencement is to be fixed by proclamation, consult "Is it in Force?" of *Halsbury's Statutes, Fourth Edition*, or the "Dates of Commencement" in the monthly issues or year books of *Current Law.*

(4) U.K. Statutory Materials on the Internet

Since 1996, all new public acts in the U.K. have been published on the Internet, online: Acts of the UK Parliament <http://www.hmso.gov.uk/acts.htm>.

(C) CITATION

United Kingdom statutes are cited in the same way as Canadian statutes with the following exceptions:

(1) Date: The regnal year must be used for the date when you cite a statute passed before 1963. The calendar year may be used when you cite a statute passed during or after 1963.

(2) Jurisdiction: Although it would not appear in an English work, an indication of the jurisdiction should be included when you are writing for Canadian lawyers. The abbreviation in parenthesis, either "(Imp.)" or "(U.K.)", should be inserted after the date.

Examples:

Punishment of Incest Act, 1908 (Imp.), 8 Edw. VII, c. 45.
Militia Act, 1882 (Imp.), 45 & 46 Vict., c. 49.
Guardianship Act, 1973 (U.K.), 1973, c. 29.
Road Traffic (Driving Instruction) Act, 1967 (U.K.), 1967, c. 79.

NOTE: Many statutes of the United Kingdom include a date in the short title. In such cases, the date must be included again in its proper place.

B. SUBORDINATE LEGISLATION

Subordinate legislation has been defined as "legislation enacted by a person, body or tribunal, subordinate to a sovereign legislative body".[15]

Subordinate legislation includes regulations, orders, rules, bylaws, and municipal ordinances. The most important of these, for purposes of general research, are regulations and orders. The term "regulation" is generally taken to comprise subordinate legislation of general and substantive effect. The term "order" is generally understood as comprising subordinate legislation issued for a particular situation. These definitions are loose and often difficult to apply to a particular instrument. In any case, most jurisdictions provide functional definitions of these terms in statutes which govern subordinate legislation. Owing to the limited scope of this book, the following outline confines itself to those pieces of subordinate legislation which are defined as "regulations" in Canadian jurisdictions and as "statutory instruments" in the United Kingdom.

In all jurisdictions in Canada, there is a statute of general effect which systematizes the central filing and publication of regulations. For example, the *Regulations Act* of Ontario (R.S.O. 1990, c. R.21, s. 5) provides that "[e]very regulation shall be published in *The Ontario Gazette* within one month of its filing". Subsection 2(1) provides, in part, that "[e]very regulation shall be filed in duplicate with the Registrar together with a certificate in duplicate of its making signed by the authority making it or a responsible officer thereof..."

These statutes also provide important information relating to the following:

(i)   definition of "regulation" or "statutory instrument";
(ii)   commencement date of regulations;
(iii) regulations exempt from publication; and
(iv)   indexing, revision, and consolidation of regulations.

The following outline offers a method for researching regulations from the federal and provincial jurisdictions of Canada. For each jurisdiction, there is, first, a summary of the publication procedure and, second, a suggested method of researching regulations. This method involves the following four steps:

(1)   finding a regulation;
(2)   updating the regulation;
(3)   determining the date of coming into force; and
(4)   citation.

---

[15] G.L. Gall, *The Canadian Legal System*, 3rd ed. (Toronto: Carswell Legal Publications, 1990), at 37. For example, s. 39 of the *Public Libraries Act*, c. P.44 of the 1990 *Revised Statutes of Ontario*, states, in part, that "the Lieutenant Governor in Council may make regulations".

1. Regulations in Canada

(A) FEDERAL REGULATIONS

The *Statutory Instruments Act*, R.S.C. 1985, c. S-22, governs the publication of federal regulations. Section 5 of the Act provides that "every regulation-making authority shall, within seven days after making a regulation, transmit copies...to the Clerk of the Privy Council for registration". Section 11 of the Act requires all regulations to be published in *The Canada Gazette* within 23 days of registration, unless exempted.

The main body of federal regulations is published in a 19-volume set, the *Consolidated Regulations of Canada, 1978*, which brings together regulations in force on December 31, 1977. The consolidation has a "Table of Contents" listing all the regulations (except those exempt from publication) made under each federal statute. The consolidation has a supplement referred to as *The Canada Gazette, Part II, Special Issue*. The *Special Issue* contains amending regulations made between December 31, 1977, and December 31, 1978. The "Schedule", volume 19, is a list of regulations which have been revoked.

(1) Finding Federal Regulations

The indispensable tool for finding federal regulations is the *Consolidated Index of Statutory Instruments*.

NOTE: This is not a subject index to the regulations. As such, the student must know the name of the regulation or statute under which the regulation was made.

This cumulative index is published quarterly in conjunction with *The Canada Gazette, Part II*. It consists of three tables.

Table I lists, alphabetically, *inter alia*, by title, regulations showing the statutes under which regulations were made and, below each statute, lists the regulations and amendments to regulations which the statute has authorized.

Table II lists, *inter alia*, in alphabetical order and by short title, the statutes under which regulations were made and, below each statute, lists the regulations and amendments to regulations that the statute has authorized.

Table III lists those statutes whose regulations are exempt from publication.

Hence, the first step in finding a federal regulation is to consult the third table in the *Consolidated Index of Statutory Instruments* in order to determine whether the regulation was exempt from publication. The second step, if the title of the regulation is known, is to consult the first table in the *Consolidated Index* in order to discover the short title of the statute under which the regulation was made. The third step, once the short title of the enabling statute is known, is to consult the second table of the *Consolidated Index* under the short title of the enabling statute. It contains a list of regulations with references to their location in the *Consolidated Regulations of Canada, 1978. The Canada Gazette, Part II*, or the Consolidation of 1955.

(2) Updating the Regulations of Canada

A search is brought up to date by consulting the bi-weekly issues of *The Canada Gazette, Part II*, published since the last *Consolidated Index of Statutory Instruments*. Each issue includes an index of regulations contained in that issue.

(3) Coming Into Force

If a federal regulation does not itself specify the date, it comes into force on the day it was registered which is indicated at the top of the text. If the regulation is exempt from registration, it comes into force on the day it was made (*Statutory Instruments Act*, R.S.C. 1985, c. S-22, s. 9(1)).

(4) Citation

Regulations published in *The Canada Gazette, Part II*, are cited as follows:

Access to Information Regulations, SOR/83-507.

"SOR" abbreviates "Statutory Order and Regulations"; "83" indicates the year; "507" indicates the number of the order or regulation.
Regulations published in the 1978 Consolidation are cited as shown below:

Arctic Waters Pollution Prevention Regulation, C.R.C., c. 354 (1978).

"C.R.C." abbreviates *Consolidated Regulations of Canada*.[16]
Amendments to the consolidation are cited, first, to the consolidation and, second, to a regulation number appearing in *The Canada Gazette, Part II*, as shown below:

Children of Deceased Veterans Education Assistance Regulations, C.R.C., c. 399 as am. by SOR/91-310, ss. 2-3; SOR/86-807, s.1.

Amendments to regulations passed after the consolidation are cited:

Steering Appliances and Equipment Regulations, SOR/83-810, as am. by 86-1027.

---

[16] Note that it is not necessary to include either the volume or the page number of the consolidation. The inclusion of the year is optional.

NOTE: Alternative sources for finding federal regulations include: (a) QUICKLAW's federal regulations database (SOR); (b) Carswell's *Canada Regulations Index*; (c) LEXIS-NEXIS; and (d) The "Regulations" table in *Canadian Current Law - Legislation Annual* and the supplement to the *Legislation Annual (Canadian Abridgment (2nd))*. There is a detailed description of *Canadian Current Law - Legislation* on page 103.

(5) Federal Regulations on the Internet

The organization and reporting of regulations can sometimes leave even the most determined researcher exasperated. Fortunately, the advent of the World Wide Web has provided the impetus for governments to provide ongoing consolidation and updating of regulations via government Web sites. As with online statutes, the regulations on government Web sites are not official.

The federal Department of Justice Homepage provides a quick link to the text of regulations made pursuant to federal statutes, online: Department of Justice Canada <http://canada.justice.gc.ca/index_en.html>.

(B) ALBERTA REGULATIONS

Regulations are published in *The Alberta Gazette, Part II*, issued every two weeks. A cumulative index is published every month in conjunction with *The Alberta Gazette, Part II*.

The Alberta regulations are consolidated annually in a bound volume which contains a cumulative index of regulations arranged in alphabetical order by the short title of the enabling statute.

(1) Finding Alberta Regulations

The index in each bound volume of Alberta regulations lists all regulations filed under the *Regulations Act* that are still in force as of December 31st of the given year. Thus, to find Alberta regulations (as well as amendments thereto), consult the index in the most recent annual volume of the regulations. Alternatively, refer to the "Table of Regulations" at the back of *Statutes of Alberta Judicially Considered*.

(2) Updating Alberta Regulations

To find regulations and amendments published after the latest annual volume, refer to a "Cumulative Index" issued in conjunction with *The Alberta Gazette, Part II*. Then refer to individual issues of *The Alberta Gazette, Part II*, which were published after the latest "Cumulative Index". As a final check, consult *Canadian Current Law - Legislation*. There is a detailed description of *Canadian Current Law - Legislation* on page 105.

NOTE: In the early part of the year you may find the "Cumulative Index" for the last calendar year, as well as for the current year.

(3) Coming Into Force

An Alberta regulation comes into force on the day it is filed, unless a later date is provided. The filing date appears under the title (*Regulations Act*, R.S.A. 1980, c. R-13, s. 2(2)).

(4) Citation

Alberta regulations are cited to a regulation number printed in *The Alberta Gazette*. For example, the *Fair Actual Value Regulation*, which was filed in 1985, is cited:

Alta. Reg. 397/85.

(5) Alberta Regulations on the Internet

The text of regulations made pursuant to Alberta statutes may be found online: Alberta Queen's Printer <http://www.gov.ab.ca/qp/>.

(C) BRITISH COLUMBIA REGULATIONS

Regulations are published in *The British Columbia Gazette, Part II*, which is issued every two weeks. The regulations are consolidated in a multi-volume looseleaf set. The regulations are listed under the enabling statutes in the "Table of Contents". New regulations and amendments to regulations are incorporated in the consolidation up to the date noted at the bottom of the pages containing the text of the regulations. Any amendments subsequent to that date may be found in *The British Columbia Gazette, Part II*.

(1) Finding British Columbia Regulations

To find a British Columbia regulation (or an amendment to a regulation), consult the "Index of Current B.C. Regulations" in volume 1 of the consolidation or in the paperback bi-annual publication of the Ministry of the Attorney General. The notation at the bottom left corner of each page indicates the currency of the index.

(2) Updating British Columbia Regulations

To find new regulations or amendments to regulations which may have been published after the cut-off date for the consolidation, refer to the "Index to Published Regulations", found at the back of the latest bound annual volume of the collected parts of *The British Columbia Gazette, Part II.* Since 1985, these bound volumes have been titled "British Columbia Regulations". If this is not as current as the paperback index or the index in the consolidation, consult the indices to the individual paper parts of *The British Columbia Gazette, Part II,* after the cut-off date noted in the "Index to Current B.C. Regulations". As a final check refer to *Canadian Current Law - Legislation.* There is a detailed description of *Canadian Current Law - Legislation* on page 105.

(3) Coming Into Force

A British Columbia regulation comes into force on the day it is deposited with the Registrar, unless a day is specifically prescribed, or a later date is presented in the regulations or an earlier date is authorized by the enabling statute (*Regulations Act,* R.S.B.C. 1996, c. 402, s. 4(1)).

(4) Citation

British Columbia regulations are cited to a regulation number printed in *The British Columbia Gazette Part II.* For example, the *Adoption Reunion Regulation,* which was deposited with the Registrar of Regulations in 1991, is cited:

B.C. Reg. 257/91.

(5) British Columbia Regulations on the Internet

At the time of writing, only *Bulletins of British Columbia* regulations were available online: British Columbia Queen's Printer <http://www.qp.gov.bc.ca/stat_reg/regs/bulletin/>.

(D) MANITOBA REGULATIONS

Regulations are published in *The Manitoba Gazette, Part II,* which is issued every week. Regulations are collected in annual volumes, which also contain an "Index to Regulations Registered under the Regulations Act in Force as of December 31st, [year]" (yellow pages). This is a cumulative index of all regulations to the end of the given year. It is arranged according to enabling statute. A quarterly index of regulations is published in *The Manitoba Gazette, Part II.* Generally, no regulations are published in the *Continuing Consolidation of the Statutes of Manitoba* (C.C.S.M.). An index of regulations is provided in the "Information Tables". The index is current to the date specified at the bottom of each page of the index.

(1) Finding Manitoba Regulations

To find Manitoba regulations, consult the "Index of Regulations Registered under the *Regulations Act* in Force as of December 31st, [year of volume]" (yellow pages) published in the latest bound annual volume of *The Manitoba Gazette, Part II*, or as a separate insert in an issue of *The Manitoba Gazette, Part II*, for the current year. This index indicates any amendments.

(2) Updating Manitoba Regulations

To check for new regulations and recent amendments for the current year, consult the "Table of Contents" in *The Manitoba Gazette, Part II*. Alternatively, refer to *Canadian Current Law - Legislation*. There is a detailed description of *Canadian Current Law - Legislation* on page 105.

(3) Coming Into Force

Unless a later day is provided, Manitoba regulations come into force on the day of filing with the Registrar. This date is indicated under the title of the regulation (*The Regulations Act*, S.M. 1988-89, c. 7, C.C.S.M. R60, s. 3).

(4) Citation

Regulations are cited with reference to a regulation number in *The Manitoba Gazette, Part II*. For example, *The Private Vocational Schools Regulation*, which was filed in 1988, is cited:

Man. Reg. 182/88.

In 1987 and 1988, most of Manitoba's regulations were re-enacted in French and English. When citing a regulation that was re-enacted, an "R" is added to the number. For example, *The Tobacco Tax Regulation* is cited as follows:

Man. Reg. 77/88 R.

Amendments to *The Tobacco Tax Regulation* are cited:

Man. Reg. 77/88 R, as am. by 345/88; 476/88; 156/89; 236/90; 99/91; 211/93; 20/95; 133/95.

NOTE: Each of the amended regulations is published in English and in French.

(E) NEW BRUNSWICK REGULATIONS

New Brunswick regulations are published in *The Royal Gazette* under the heading "Statutory Orders and Regulations, Part II". The regulations are collected in annual volumes. Each volume contains a "Cumulative Index of New Brunswick Regulations" and a "Table of New Brunswick Regulations Subject Matter".[17] There is also a multi-volume consolidated looseleaf edition for these regulations.

The consolidation was effective as of November 1, 1984. New regulations and amendments are incorporated into the looseleaf set on a regular basis. The cut-off date for the most recent releases for the consolidation is indicated at the beginning of volume 1. Regulations are filed under the name of the enabling statute. The consolidation includes a "Table of Contents" which lists in order of appearance all regulations contained in the consolidation, a "Cumulative Index of New Brunswick Regulations" which lists all regulations recorded as filed with the Registrar of Regulations from 1963 to the date of consolidation and an index of "Not Consolidated Not Repealed Regulations".

(1) Finding New Brunswick Regulations

To find New Brunswick regulations, refer to the "Cumulative Index" in the last volume of the consolidated looseleaf edition of the *Regulations of New Brunswick*. It contains a list of the regulations in force as of the date of publication, with amendments.[18]

(2) Updating New Brunswick Regulations

To find the most recent regulations or amendments to regulations, check the paperbound "Index" of *The Royal Gazette* published after the cut-off date noted in the "Cumulative Index" to the consolidation, if available. As well, refer to the heading "Statutory Orders and Regulations" in individual issues of *The Royal Gazette* after the cut-off dates noted in the indices and to *Canadian Current Law - Legislation*. There is a detailed description of *Canadian Current Law - Legislation* on page 105.

(3) Coming Into Force

Unless a later date is specified, New Brunswick regulations come into force on the date of filing. The date of filing is indicated beneath the title of the regulation (*Regulations Act*, S.N.B. 1991, c. R-7.1, s. 3).

---

[17] If more than one volume is published for the year, the first volume includes the "Subject Matter" index and, the second volume, the "Cumulative Index".

[18] If the volume is not available, refer to the "Cumulative Index" in the latest annual volume of the *Regulations of New Brunswick*; although this will not usually be as current as the index in the consolidation.

(4) Citation

New Brunswick regulations are cited to a regulation number printed in *The Royal Gazette*. For example, the *Public Utilities Board Regulation - Insurance Act*, which was filed in New Brunswick in 1986, is cited:

N.B. Reg. 86-78.[19]

(5) New Brunswick Regulations on the Internet

The text of regulations made pursuant to New Brunswick statutes may be found online: The Government of New Brunswick <http://www.gov.nb.ca/justice/asrlste.htm>.

(F) NEWFOUNDLAND REGULATIONS

The Newfoundland regulations are published in *The Newfoundland Gazette, Part II*, issued every week. The Office of the Legislative Counsel publishes an *Index of Subordinate Legislation* for *The Newfoundland Gazette*. The *Index* is arranged alphabetically with respect to the acts that provide for the making of the subordinate legislation. The *Index* is updated and printed on a regular basis. The title page indicates the cut-off date for entries to the *Index*.

(1) Finding Newfoundland Regulations

To find a Newfoundland regulation or an amendment, refer to the *Index of Subordinate Legislation*. The regulations appear under the name of the enabling statute. There are separate entries for the number of the regulation, amendments to the regulation and its location in *The Newfoundland Gazette*.

(2) Updating Newfoundland Regulations

To find regulations published after the cut-off date for the *Index of Subordinate Legislation* (noted on the second page of the *Index*), refer to the "Continuing Index of Subordinate Legislation" in the issues of *The Newfoundland Gazette, Part II*, published after the cut-off date. Also check *Canadian Current Law - Legislation*. There is a detailed description of *Canadian Current Law - Legislation* on page 105.

---

[19] In citing New Brunswick regulations, the year appears first and the number of the regulation appears second.

(3) Coming Into Force

Unless another day is provided, subordinate legislation comes into force on the day it is published (*Statutes and Subordinate Legislation Act*, R.S.N. 1990, c. S-27, s. 10(2) as am. by S.N. 1996, c. R-10.1, s. 69(1)).

(4) Citation

Newfoundland regulations are cited to a regulation number printed in *The Newfoundland Gazette, Part II*. For example, the *Archives Public Records Management Regulations, 1991*, which were assented to in 1991, are cited:

Nfld. Reg. 93/91.

(G) NORTHWEST TERRITORIES REGULATIONS

Northwest Territories regulations are published in the *Northwest Territories Gazette, Part II*, under the heading "Regulations". These are collected in annual binders, and each binder contains a cumulative index of regulations to the cut-off date, with amendments. Table A and Table B of the index list repealed and spent regulations, respectively, and Table C (pink and yellow-page inserts) lists regulations currently in force, under their enabling statutes. A complete revision of the regulations was published in five volumes in 1990.

(1) Finding Northwest Territories Regulations

To find Northwest Territories regulations, refer to Table C (pink-page sections) following the tab "Part 2" in a recent *Northwest Territories Gazette* binder. It contains a list of the regulations in force as of the date of publication, with amendments.

(2) Updating Northwest Territories Regulations

To find new regulations or amendments subsequent to the cut-off date for Table C, refer to the heading "Regulations" in individual issues of the *Northwest Territories Gazette, Part II*. Also check *Canadian Current Law - Legislation*. There is a detailed description of *Canadian Current Law - Legislation* on page 105.

(3) Coming Into Force

Unless a different date is specified, Northwest Territories regulations come into force on the day of registration. This date is indicated in the *Northwest Territories Gazette* (*Statutory Instruments Act*, R.S.N.W.T. 1988, c. S-13, s. 8).

(4) Citation

Regulations published in the revision are cited to the *Revised Regulations of the Northwest Territories, 1990*. For example, the *Fort Good Hope Snowmobile Regulations*, are cited:

R.R.N.W.T. 1990, c. A-3.

Amendments to the revision are cited, first, to the revision and, second, to a regulation number printed in the *Northwest Territories Gazette, Part II*. For example, the *Petroleum Products Tax Regulations*, which were amended by regulation number 081 in 1992, are cited:

R.R.N.W.T. 1990, c. P-3, as am. by N.W.T. Reg. R-081-92.

New regulations passed since the revision are cited by reference to a regulation number in the *Northwest Territories Gazette, Part II*. For example, the *Snare Lake Liquor Prohibition Regulations*, which were filed in 1991, are cited:

N.W.T. Reg. R-097-91.[20]

(5) Northwest Territories Regulations on the Internet

The text of regulations made pursuant to statutes of the Northwest Territories may be found online: Access to Justice Web site <http://legis.acjnet.org/ACJNet/TNO/index_en.html>.

(H) NOVA SCOTIA REGULATIONS

Nova Scotia regulations have been published in the *Royal Gazette, Part II*, since 1977. There is no current official consolidation or revision of the regulations of Nova Scotia. A bi-weekly and an annual index are published in conjunction with the *Royal Gazette, Part II*.[21]

NOTE: A five-volume set, *Regulations of Nova Scotia*, was issued for the years 1973 to 1977. Prior to this, selected regulations were published in the sessional volumes of the *Statutes of Nova Scotia* (1943 to 1973) under the heading "Rules and Regulations".

---

[20] The prescribed method of determining regulation numbers is derived from the *Revised Regulations*, R.R.N.W.T. 1980, Reg. 239, s. 4(6).

[21] The Registrar of Regulations publishes an unofficial *Sectional Index to Nova Scotia Regulations*. This looseleaf index lists all post-1977 regulations currently in force, up to the cut-off date at the front of the binder. Part A of the *Index* has the name of each regulation listed under its enabling statute, and cross-indexes each statute to a more detailed index in Part B. Part B also lists regulations by their respective statutes, lists amendments by section, and provides a history of repealed regulations. Part C is a consolidated list of proclamations.

(1) Finding Nova Scotia Regulations

To find Nova Scotia regulations, refer to the annual indices commencing with 1977.[22]

NOTE: For 1973 to 1977, refer to *Regulations of Nova Scotia*. Finding regulations prior to 1973 requires perseverance. Assistance may be obtained by referring to the "Index to the Regulations" for 1942 to 1970, contained in the 1970-71 volume of the *Statutes of Nova Scotia*, or to a single-volume consolidation of selected regulations published in 1942.

(2) Updating Nova Scotia Regulations

To check for new regulations and amendments since the last annual index, refer to the bi-weekly index which is published in conjunction with the *Royal Gazette, Part II*. Also check *Canadian Current Law – Legislation*. There is a detailed description of *Canadian Current Law – Legislation* on page 105.

(3) Coming Into Force

Unless a later date is provided, a regulation comes into force on the day it is filed with the Registrar of Regulations (*Regulations Act*, R.S.N.S. 1989, c. 393, s. 3(6) (s. 3(6) not yet proclaimed)).

(4) Citation

Current Nova Scotia regulations are cited to a regulation number printed in the *Royal Gazette, Part II*. For example, the *Health Services Tax Vendor Trust Account Regulations* which were filed in 1993 are cited:

N.S. Reg. 65/93.

(5) Nova Scotia Regulations on the Internet

The text of regulations made pursuant to Nova Scotia statutes may be found online: The Government of Nova Scotia <http://www.gov.ns.ca/just/regulations/>.

(l) ONTARIO REGULATIONS

Regulations are published in *The Ontario Gazette*, which is issued every week. They are consolidated in annual volumes with a cumulative "Table of Regulations". A complete revision of the regulations was published in 1990. This

---

[22] Alternatively, simply refer to the listing of the regulation under its enabling statute in Part B of the *Sectional Index*.

nine-volume set brings together all regulations in force on December 31, 1990. A three-volume supplement to the revision contains regulations after the cut-off date of December 31, 1990 and before November 16, 1992, the day the revision was proclaimed in force.

(1) Finding Ontario Regulations

To find Ontario regulations, refer to the "Table of Regulations" in the latest bound annual volume of the *Statutes of Ontario* or the *Ontario Regulations*. This shows, *inter alia*, the regulations contained in the revision and subsequent regulations and amendments to regulations to December 31st of the last calendar year of publication. The table has three columns: the first gives the number of the regulation, if it is located in the revision; the second gives the number of the regulation, if it was made after December 31, 1990; and the third shows amendments to the regulations. Alternatively, refer to Carswell's *Ontario Regulations Service* (check the annual consolidated index and the monthly cumulative index) and QUICKLAW's Regulations of Ontario (RO) database.

(2) Updating Ontario Regulations

To check for new regulations and amendments to regulations after the cut-off date noted above, refer to the most recent "Table of Regulations" which is issued with a weekly edition of *The Ontario Gazette*. As well, consult the semi-annual index of *The Ontario Gazette* (if available) and the index on the overleaf of the back cover of each subsequent issue of the *Gazette* (not included in the "Table of Regulations" or the semi-annual index) under the heading "Publications under the Regulations Act". Refer as well to *Canadian Current Law - Legislation*. There is a detailed description of *Canadian Current Law - Legislation* on page 105.

(3) Coming Into Force

Unless otherwise stated, an Ontario regulation comes into effect on the day it is filed. The filing date is indicated immediately beneath the title of the regulation (*Regulations Act*, R.S.O. 1990, c. R.21, s. 3).

(4) Citation

Regulations published in the revision are cited to the *Revised Regulations of Ontario*. For example, the *Anatomy Act Regulation*, which is the 21st regulation in the revision, is cited:

R.R.O. 1990, Reg. 21 as am. by O. Reg. 772/94.

Amendments to the revision are cited, first, to the revision and, second, to a regulation number printed in *The Ontario Gazette*. For example, the *Bailiffs Act*

Regulation, which appeared as number 53 in the revision and was amended by regulation number 689 in 1991, is cited:

R.R.O. 1990, Reg. 53, as am. by O. Reg. 689/91; 513/97.

New regulations passed since the revision are cited by reference to a regulation number in *The Ontario Gazette*. For example. the *Specified Employee Ownership Corporations Regulation*, made under the *Labour Sponsored Venture Capital Corporations Act, 1992*, is cited:

O. Reg. 591/92.

(5) Ontario Regulations on the Internet

The text of regulations made pursuant to Ontario statutes may be found online: The Government of Ontario <http://www.gov.on.ca/MBS/english/publications/statregs/index.html>.

(J) PRINCE EDWARD ISLAND REGULATIONS

Regulations are published in the *Royal Gazette, Part II*, and issued every week. The regulations are consolidated in looseleaf binders, *The Revised Regulations of Prince Edward Island*.

New regulations and amendments to regulations found in the revision are incorporated on a continuing basis. The cut-off date for the revision is noted on the pages of the regulations. The revision contains a "Table of Contents" which lists the regulations under the name of the enabling statute. It also includes a "Table of Regulations" (blue pages) which provides a history of regulating provisions, including their derivations and modifications.

(1) Finding Prince Edward Island Regulations

To find a Prince Edward Island regulation, refer to the "Table of Contents" in the revision under the name of the enabling statute. To check for amendments, consult the "Table of Regulations".

(2) Updating Prince Edward Island Regulations

To find new regulations and amendments to regulations, refer to the "Continuing Index to the Regulations of Prince Edward Island" and to the "Regulations Index" in all issues of the *Royal Gazette, Part II*,[23] after the cut-off date for the

---

[23] This will usually entail a search through the individual issues of the *Royal Gazette, Part II*, for the current year.

latest "Table of Regulations". Refer as well to *Canadian Current Law - Legislation*. There is a detailed description of *Canadian Current Law - Legislation* on page 105.

(3) Coming Into Force

Every regulation not expressed to come into force on a particular day comes into force on the day the regulation is published in the *Royal Gazette* (*Interpretation Act*, R.S.P.E.I. 1988, c. I-8, s. 3(4)).

(4) Citation

Prince Edward Island regulations published in the revision are cited to the *Revised Regulations of Prince Edward Island*. The "EC number" of revised regulations is found in the *"Table of Regulations"* at the back of the binder (blue pages). For example, the *Animal Protection Regulations*, are cited:

R.R.P.E.I. EC 71/90.

Regulations not yet included in the revision are cited to a regulation number printed in the *Royal Gazette, Part II*. For example, the *Education Negotiating Agency Regulations Amendment*, which were issued in 1999, are cited:

EC 286/99.

(K) QUÉBEC REGULATIONS

Regulations are published in the *Québec Official Gazette, Part II*, which is issued every week. The regulations are consolidated in a 12-volume set, the *Revised Regulations of Québec, 1981*. A companion work, the *Tableau des modifications et index sommaire*[24] permits access to the revision and indicates amendments to regulations. This volume is updated and replaced once or twice annually. An earlier work, the *Index cumulatif des textes reglementaires de 1867 au 1er juillet 1981* covers regulations and amendments before the revision.

(1) Finding Québec Regulations

To find Québec regulations, consult the "Tableau des modifications" in the *Tableau des modifications et index sommaire*. The cut-off date for the table is indicated on the title page.

---

[24] Prior to 1985, this work was referred to as the *Index cumulatif des actes reglementaires*.

(2) Updating Québec Regulations

To check for new regulations and amendments to regulations after the cut-off date in the *Tableau des modifications et index sommaire*, refer to the latest paper part "Index Statutory Instruments" issued as part of the *Québec Official Gazette, Part II*. Alternatively, it may be easier to check under the heading "Regulations", in the "Table of Contents" in the back pages of the "Index". Also check *Canadian Current Law - Legislation*. There is a detailed description of *Canadian Current Law - Legislation* on page 105.

(3) Coming Into Force

Unless another date is specified, a regulation comes into force 15 days after the date of publication in the *Québec Official Gazette* (*Regulations Act*, S.Q. 1986, c. 22, s. 17).

(4) Citation

Regulations published in the revision are cited to the *Revised Regulations of Québec*. For example, the *Regulation Respecting the Quality of the Work Environment* is cited:

R.R.Q. 1981, c. S-2.1, r. 15.

Amendments to the revision are cited, first, to the revision and, second, to a regulation number printed in the *Québec Official Gazette*. For example, an amendment to the *Regulation Respecting the Application of the Legal Aid Act* is cited:

R.R.Q. 1981, c. A-14, r. 1, as am. by O.C. 941-83, 11 May 1983, G.O.Q. 1983.II.1971.

A textual reference will appear in the following form:

The *Regulation Respecting the Sale of Livestock by Auction*, R.R.Q. 1981, c. P-42, r. 4, made under the *Animal Health Protection Act*, R.S.Q. c. P-42, s. 45, is amended by O.C. 1262-86, 20 August 1986, G.O.Q. 1986.II.3749; 1135-87, 22 July 1987, G.O.Q. 1987.II.5297; 1766-90, 19 December 1990, G.O.Q. 1990.II.1776; 337-93, 17 March 1993, G.O.Q. 1993.II.1954.

New regulations passed after the revision are cited by referring to a regulation number in the *Québec Official Gazette*. For example, the *Grain Regulation* is cited:

O.C. 1982-83, 21 September 1983, G.O.Q. 1983.II.3447.

NOTE: In the examples, the citations include a reference to the *Québec Official Gazette*.

(5) Québec Regulations on the Internet

Québec regulations may be searched and downloaded online: <http://www.doc.gouv.qc.ca/servlets/Dbml/index2.html> (click "Lois et Règlements").

(L) SASKATCHEWAN REGULATIONS

There are two official sources of Saskatchewan regulations: *The Saskatchewan Gazette, Part II*, and *The Saskatchewan Gazette, Part III*. *Part II* contains revised regulations and amendments to revised regulations. The regulations printed in *Part III* are new regulations and amendments to existing regulations which have not been revised.[25]

Saskatchewan regulations have been consolidated in a multi-volume looseleaf set entitled *The Regulations of Saskatchewan*. This looseleaf publication consists of consolidations of *The Revised Regulations of Saskatchewan* and the amendments to those regulations printed in *The Saskatchewan Gazette, Part II*. The cut-off date for the consolidation is indicated on the first page. The looseleaf publication is supplemented semi-annually. Saskatchewan regulations printed in *Part III* are not included in the consolidation.

(1) Finding Saskatchewan Regulations

To find Saskatchewan regulations and amendments to the regulations, refer to the "Table of Regulations" printed in the *Tables to the Statutes of Saskatchewan and Saskatchewan Regulations*. As well, refer to the "Table of Repealed Revised Regulations" in the same publication.

(2) Updating Saskatchewan Regulations

To find regulations and amendments which are not included in the "Table of Regulations" and the "Table of Repealed Revised Regulations", refer to *Canadian Current Law - Legislation* (a detailed description of *Canadian Current Law - Legislation* can be found on page 105) or to the *Saskatchewan Decisions Citator*. There is also an "Index of Revised Regulations" and an "Index of Unrevised Regulations" published in the current paper part of *The Saskatchewan Gazette*.

---

[25] The regulations printed in *Part II* are a component of the *Revised Regulations of Saskatchewan* which are being compiled over a period of years.

(3) Coming Into Force

A Saskatchewan regulation comes into force on the day it is published, if no other date is specified, or on the day it is filed, if it has been exempted from publication and no other date is specified (*The Regulations Act*, S.S. 1995, R.16.2, s. 5).

(4) Citation

The *Revised Regulations of Saskatchewan* are cited to their short titles, which appear in section 1 of the regulations, together with their location in *The Revised Regulations of Saskatchewan*. For example, *The Agri-Food Regulations*, passed in 1990 under the authority of *The Agri-Food Act*, are cited:

R.R.S. 1990, c. A-15.2, Reg. 1.

An amendment to a revised regulation is given a Saskatchewan regulation number in *The Saskatchewan Gazette*. For example, the amendment to *The Municipal Police Equipment Regulations, 1991*, made under the authority of *The Police Act*, are cited:

R.R.S., c. P-15.01, Reg. 3, as am. by Sask. Reg. 66/93.

Regulations which have not been revised are given a Saskatchewan regulation number. For example, *The Power Corporation Transportation Regulations*, which were issued in 1986, are cited:

Sask. Reg. 84/86.

The Day Care Amendment Regulations, 1986, amending *The Day Care Regulations* of 1975 (which have not been revised to date), are cited:

Sask. Reg. 213/75, as am. by 63/86.

(5) Saskatchewan Regulations on the Internet

The government of Saskatchewan requires registration and a fee for electronic access to its publications, including regulations online: Queen's Printer for Saskatchewan <http://www.qp.justice.gov.sk.ca>.

(M) YUKON REGULATIONS

Regulations of the Yukon Territory are published in a continuing looseleaf consolidation; they do not always appear in *The Yukon Gazette*, as only the titles of the regulations are required to be published there. The first volume of the consolidation contains a cumulative "Index of Regulations in Force", listing all regulations under their respective enabling statutes and amendments.

(1) Finding Yukon Regulations

To find Yukon regulations, refer to the "Index of Regulations in Force" in the first binder of the consolidation, under the regulation's enabling statute. Besides indicating the regulation number, the index also cross-indexes each statute with a corresponding tab number in the consolidation; each tab marks the location of all regulations enacted pursuant to that statute. Unpublished regulations can be obtained from the Yukon government.

(2) Updating Yukon Regulations

To find the titles of new regulations, or amendments subsequent to the latest update of the consolidation, refer to the heading "Regulations" in *The Yukon Gazette, Part II*, or to *Canadian Current Law - Legislation*. There is a detailed description of *Canadian Current Law - Legislation* on page 105.

(3) Coming Into Force

Unless a later date is specified, Yukon regulations come into force on the date of filing. This date is printed above the regulation's title in *The Yukon Gazette* (*Regulations Act*, R.S.Y.T. 1986, c. 151, s. 2(2)).

(4) Citation

Yukon regulations are cited to the numbers of the Orders-in-Council registering them and the years of registration. For example, the *Meat Inspection and Abbatoir Regulations*, which were registered by the 104th Order-in-Council of 1988, are cited:

Yukon O.I.C. 1988/104.

Amendments are cited in a similar manner. For example, the 1983 *Bear Creek Development Area Regulation*, which was amended in 1989, is cited:

Yukon O.I.C. 1983/132, as am. by 1989/136.

(5) Yukon Regulations on the Internet

The text of regulations made pursuant to statutes of the Yukon may be found online: Access to Justice Network <http://legis.acjnet.org/ACJNET/Yukon/index_en.html>.

2. Subordinate Legislation of the United Kingdom

As mentioned earlier, in the United Kingdom rules and regulations are referred to as "Statutory Instruments" and, as in Canada, all statutory instruments enacted under the authority of a statute must be published within a prescribed period. There are three main sources for the statutory instruments of the United Kingdom.

(A) MAIN SOURCES

(1) *Statutory Rules, Orders, and Statutory Instruments (Revised to December 31, 1948)*

This is the official source of statutory instruments for the United Kingdom. It is a 25-volume set which revises and consolidates all the statutory instruments in force in the United Kingdom as of December 31, 1948. The set is arranged by subject-matter and the last volume of the set includes indices and tables.

(2) *Statutory Instruments*

This is the successor to *Statutory Rules, Orders and Statutory Instruments*. Individual volumes are issued every four months. This set also includes indices and tables. A new format was introduced in 1987; refer to the "Preface" (found in Part I, Section I) for a detailed description of the contents.

(3) *Halsbury's Statutory Instruments*

This multi-volume set covers every statutory instrument of general application in force in England and Wales. The set is arranged by subject-matter. It reprints the text of selected statutory instruments and provides summaries and notations for the others. The set is kept up to date with "reissue" volumes (the title page notes the effective date of reissue) and a set of looseleaf service binders. The cut-off date for materials included in each section of the binders is noted on the tab page or the following page.

There are some secondary tools or finding aids which permit access to the statutory instruments of the United Kingdom. They include:

(i) *Index to Government Orders*

This is a multi-volume set which indexes, by subject-matter and enabling legislation, all subordinate legislation in force as of the 31st day of December of the last calendar year of publication. In the preliminary (green) pages, there are two tables: (1) the "Table of Abbreviations" and (2) the "Table of Statutes". The "Table of Statutes" lists the acts and measures and their sections that confer powers to make subordinate legislation, as well as the subject headings under which those powers or other relevant statutory provisions are indexed.

The body of the *Index* (white pages) records the powers and their exercise. Under the main subject headings (which appear in alphabetical order), there are brief summaries of all the powers to make subordinate legislation which have been conferred by public general acts. Particulars are given of the enactment conferring the power and of the effect of any subsequent enactment which has extended or modified it. Particulars of the authorities (*e.g.*, Ministers) responsible for subordinate legislation, of the relevant parliamentary control, and of the commencement of acts by order can be found under a parliamentary subheading of many headings.

Under each power, there is a list of the general statutory instruments made in exercise of that power and in force on the 31st day of December of the given year.

(ii) Table of Government Orders

This is a table of legislative instruments with notations commencing as early as 1671. For each instrument listed, the reader will find:

(1)   the year in which the instrument was made;

(2)   the serial number of the instrument in that year or, if it was not numbered, the date upon which it was made;

(3)   the title of the instrument, or subject-matter if it has no title, printed in bold type if the instrument or any part of it is in force, and in italics if it is wholly revoked, spent or otherwise without effect;

(4)   if the instrument was made before 1961, a volume and page reference in brackets, showing where its text may be found;

(5)   if the instrument is wholly or partly in force (and so in bold type), short particulars of any amendment or modification effected after 1948; and

(6)   if the instrument is no longer in force (and so in italics), short particulars of the revoking provision or the reason why it has ceased to have effect (*e.g.*, "spent", "superseded", "expired").

(iii) Halsbury's Statutory Instruments Consolidated Index

This single-volume softcover publication contains the "Consolidated Index to Halsbury's Statutory Instruments" and a complete "Alphabetical List of Statutory Instruments" contained in the work. The *Consolidated Index* covers all the main volumes to the work current on the date mentioned in the "Publisher's Note" and the annual *Supplement*. The "Alphabetical List of Statutory Instruments" comprises all the instruments included in the main volumes and in the service to *Halsbury's Statutory Instruments* which were in force on the date given in the "Publisher's Note". The "Publisher's Note" at the start of the volume states the cut-off date for the *Index*. For more recent instruments, see the "Chronological List of Instruments" in Service Binder No. 1.

A full list of the volumes to which the *Consolidated Index* refers is set out on the overleaf to the "Publisher's Note". Main volumes that are reissued after the publication of the volume are covered by their own indices, which supersede the relevant entries in the *Consolidated Index*.

Entries in the *Consolidated Index* refer to the volume and page number at which the relevant information appears in the main volume, and also, where appropriate, give details of the actual statutory instrument involved. A typical reference to a bound volume (this reference appears under "Appeals: foreign marriages, refusal to solemnise") is: **12**, 13 (1970/1539), art. 3(2). The figure printed in bold type is the volume number and it is followed by the page number and, in brackets, the citation of the relevant instrument, in this case SI 1970/1539.

The "Alphabetical List of Statutory Instruments" indicates the title (or titles) under which each instrument is dealt with in the work. The list is designed for use where the user does not know the year and serial number of an instrument. Where the year and serial number are known, reference should be made to the "Chronological List of Instruments" in Service Binder No. 1. That list is updated every month.

There are a number of sources which may be consulted for recent statutory instruments and amendments. These include the *Lists of Statutory Instruments*, *Daily List of Government Publications*, *Current Law*, and the service binders for *Halsbury's Statutory Instruments*.

(B) FINDING UNITED KINGDOM SUBORDINATE LEGISLATION

If only the subject-matter is known, consult:

(i)   the *Consolidated Index* for *Halsbury's Statutory Instruments*; or

NOTE: Always check the "List of Volumes" at the beginning of the *Consolidated Index*. This lists the main volumes covered by the service and notes the cut-off date for the law contained in each volume.

(ii)   the updating "Monthly Survey Index" in Service Binder No. 1 for *Halsbury's Statutory Instruments*.

If you know that the statutory instrument was published before 1949 and the number of the instrument is also known, consult:

(i)   the "Numerical Table of Statutory Instruments, Part I" in volume XXV of *Statutory Rules, Orders and Statutory Instruments* (Revised to December 31, 1948).

If you have a reference to a statutory instrument for the period after 1948, consult:

(i) *Statutory Instruments* for the given year; or
(ii) the "Chronological List of Instruments" located in the service binder for *Halsbury's Statutory Instruments*. The list directs the user to the location of the instrument in a main volume or a service binder.

(C) CHECKING FOR AMENDMENTS

Consult the *Table of Government Orders.*[26] It is published annually and its currency is maintained by a *Noter-Up Service*. Alternatively, refer to the appropriate main volume of *Halsbury's Statutory Instruments* and update the information with the service binders.

(D) DETERMINING THE DATE OF COMING INTO FORCE

First, locate the desired regulation in the *Consolidated Index* for *Halsbury's Statutory Instruments*. It will direct you to a main volume or to a service binder. Next, locate the desired statutory instrument and refer to "Commencement". If necessary, consult the "Monthly Survey Summaries" in Service Binder No. 1.

Once you have determined the number of the statutory instrument and its commencement date, confirm the accuracy of the latter in the official *Statutory Instruments*.

(E) CITATION

For "Statutory Rules and Orders" issued prior to 1949, the following form of citation is recommended:

Water Abstraction Regulations, 1947, SR & O 1947/2342,

NOTE: In the example, "SR & O" refers to "Statutory Rules and Orders" and is the form commonly used for subordinate legislation prior to 1949.

For statutory instruments issued after 1948, the following form of citation is recommended:

Statutory Sick Pay (Medical Evidence) Regulations, 1985, SI 1985/1604.

---

[26] See Section B, 2(A) (3)(*ii*), *supra*.

C. CASE REPORTS

Since the middle of the last century, approximately 200 distinct report series have been published in Canada and the United Kingdom. A few, like the *Chancery Reports*, have been published continuously since that time. Many more flourished for a few years and then ceased publication; nonetheless, they are retained on library shelves because they usually contain judgments which do not appear elsewhere. Throughout this period, as well, most case reports have covered a particular jurisdiction or court. Recently, there has been a rapid growth in case reports exclusively concerned with special areas of the law. The following discussion of case reports is in five parts:

(1)   publication;
(2)   format;
(3)   Canadian case reports;
(4)   English case reports; and
(5)   general rules of citation.

1. Publication

The publication of law reports in Canada is carried out largely by private publishing houses.[27] The publishers gather the relevant written judgments[28] from the various courts soon after they have been delivered and publish them in small groups in paperbound form[29] under a particular name.[30] These unbound parts may be issued weekly, bi-weekly, monthly, or eight to ten times a year. The cases are arranged more or less chronologically. The paperbound parts are later discarded when replaced by bound volumes.

The bound volumes of English and Canadian reports are generally arranged into series or sets, each covering a specific period. One example is the *All England Law Reports* set which consists, at present, of over 150 volumes spanning the period 1936 to 1999. Another example is the *Dominion Law Reports*. At present, this set consists of approximately 527 volumes covering the period 1912 to 1999.[31] A final example is the *Western Weekly Digest*, a short-lived publication which consists of two volumes covering the period 1975 to 1976.

---

[27]   The *Supreme Court of Canada Reports* and *Federal Court Reports* are two notable exceptions. Both are published by the Queen's Printer.

[28]   Not all cases heard in Canada are reported; although, most decisions of superior courts are reported and some report series make a point of reporting lower court judgments which raise interesting points of law.

[29]   The release of advance paperbound parts before the publication of bound volumes is a relatively recent practice.

[30]   A few examples are *Carswell's Practice Cases, Canadian Cases on the Law of Insurance, Ontario Law Reports* and *Canada Tax Cases*.

[31]   For the purposes of citation, this set is categorized into four series. For further discussion of the citation of the *Dominion Law Reports*, see *infra* at Section C, 3(A)(1).

2. Format

Case reports in English and Canadian report series follow the same basic format. The following information will generally be included:

(i)   the full name of the judgment;
(ii)   the date the decision was rendered;
(iii) the court (in multi-jurisdictional reports);
(iv) the judge or judges;
(v)   the counsel;
(vi) catchwords (a summary of key facts and legal principles);
(vii) headnote (a summary of facts and the judgment);
(viii) notes (provide cross-reference to other major works);
(ix) annotation (for selected cases in some reports);
(x)   a list of cases, statutes, rules and authorities cited;
(xi) the summarized arguments of counsel (in some reports);
(xii) the text of the decision or decisions; and
(xiii) order.

3. Canadian Case Reports

For the purposes of description, Canadian case reports may be classified as follows:

(a)   national reports;
(b)   regional reports;
(c)   provincial reports; and
(d)   subject reports.

The case reports described below are the most important of the modern Canadian case reports.

NOTE: Case reports may also be classified as official, semi-official, and unofficial. Official reports are those published under the authority of the court whose decisions are reported. Unofficial reports are those published without authority by private organizations. Semi-official reports fall midway between the two: they are privately published but have been accorded a measure of authority through custom or sponsorship. The distinction may be important for two reasons. First, where there is a discrepancy among reports, the official report is preferred to the unofficial. Second, when citing collateral reports, the official report should be cited before the semi-official and the semi-official report should be cited before the unofficial. See Appendix VII for a classification of reports in accordance with the above-noted designations.

(A) NATIONAL REPORTS

(1) Dominion Law Reports, 1912 to date (cited D.L.R.)

Since 1912, the unofficial *Dominion Law Reports* have provided the most extensive coverage of Canadian cases. The set includes a wide selection of decisions on all branches of the law from all jurisdictions of Canada. At present, it is published in weekly paperbound parts which are later consolidated in bound volumes. For the purposes of citation, there have been five sets:

(i)   1912 to 1922. The volumes are numbered consecutively throughout this period.

Example:

Re Walker (1919), 49 D.L.R. 415 (Ont. C.A.).

(ii)   1923 to 1955. The volumes are numbered consecutively throughout each year.

Example:

Guay v. *Sun Publishing Co.,* [1953] 4 D.L.R. 577 (S.C.C.).

(iii)   1956 to 1968. The volumes are numbered consecutively throughout this period. This series is distinguished from its predecessors by inserting (2d) after "D.L.R.".

Example:

Smuck v. *Seburn* (1968), 65 D.L.R. (2d) 692 (Ont. H.C.J.).

(iv)   1969 to 1984. The volumes are numbered consecutively throughout this period. This series is distinguished from its predecessors by inserting (3d) after "D.L.R.".

Example:

Furber v. *Furber* (1972), 31 D.L.R. (3d) 642 (B.C.S.C.).

(v)   1984 to date. The volumes are numbered consecutively throughout this period. This series is distinguished from its predecessors by inserting (4th) after "D.L.R.".

Examples:

Demeter v. *British Pacific Life Insurance Co.* (1984), 13 D.L.R. (4th) 318 (Ont. C.A.). *Bell Canada* v. *Unitel Communications Inc.* (1992), 99 D.L.R. (4th) 533 (F.C.A.).

There are four important companion publications to the *Dominion Law Reports*:

(i)   *Dominion Law Reports (Second Series) Consolidated Table of Cases*;
(ii) *Dominion Law Reports Annotation Service (Second and Third Series)* and *Consolidated Table of Cases (Third Series)*;
(iii) *Dominion Law Reports (Third Series) Index*, Volumes 1 to 150; and
(iv) *Dominion Law Reports (Fourth Series) Index Annotations* and *Table of Cases* (beginning with Volume 1, 1988).

NOTE: The annotation service acts as a citator for cases reported in the *Dominion Law Reports*. The purpose of the citator is to show whether a reported case has been appealed or judicially considered elsewhere in the set.

These indices are organized according to a unique classification scheme devised by the reports' publisher, Canada Law Book. This scheme lists key headings and subheadings on every topic and appears at the front of every index volume. Thus, when researching the *Dominion Law Reports*, the student should first examine this scheme for the key headings pertaining to the subject under investigation. Once these are known, the student then need only look under these same headings in the index. This will refer the student to pertinent cases. Furthermore, each listing includes a "catchline", which is a short précis of the specific questions decided in each case, in addition to the volume and page number where it can be found.

(2) Supreme Court Reports, 1876 to date (cited S.C.R.)

This set has been the official report series of the Supreme Court of Canada since that court was established in 1875. It contains virtually all the decisions of the Supreme Court of Canada. It is printed in both French and English. For the purpose of citation, it is useful to distinguish three separate publishing periods:

(i)   1876 to 1922. The volumes are numbered consecutively throughout this period and called *Reports of the Supreme Court of Canada* but are referred to as the *Supreme Court Reports*.

Example:

Dominion Fire Insurance Co. v. *Nakata* (1915), 52 S.C.R. 294.

(ii)   1923 to 1975. The volumes are indicated by the year of publication and are called *Canada Law Reports, Supreme Court* but are referred to as the *Supreme Court Reports.*

Example:

Quebec Asbestos Corp. v. *Couture*, [1929] S.C.R. 166.

(iii)   1975 to date. The volumes are numbered consecutively through each year and are called *Canada, Supreme Court Reports* but are referred to as *Supreme Court Reports.*

Examples:

Halifax (City) v. *S. Cunard & Co.*, [1975] 1 S.C.R. 458. *R.* v. *Ewert*, [1992] 3 S.C.R. 161.

NOTE: Judgments of the current year are published in paperbound parts (red jacket).

(3) Federal Court Reports,[32] 1971 to date (cited F.C.)

This series has been the official report of the Federal Court of Canada since that court was established in 1971. The *Federal Court Reports* are printed in both French and English and contain virtually all decisions since the Court's inception. A selection of judgments is reported and all judgments not reported are digested.

Examples:

Bland v. *National Capital Commission*, [1993] 1 F.C. 541 (C.A.). *Smyth* v. *Minister of National Revenue*, [1968] 2 Ex. C.R. 189.

---

[32]   The predecessor of the Federal Court was the Exchequer Court which was established in 1875. From its inception to 1922, decisions of this court were contained in the *Reports of the Exchequer Court of Canada.* From 1922 to 1969 they were contained in the *Canada Law Reports, Exchequer Court.* There are also two volumes for 1970: one called *Canada, Exchequer Court Reports* and the other *Canada Law Reports, Exchequer Court.* Throughout this period they have been usually referred to as the *Exchequer Court Reports.*

(4) Federal Trial Reports, 1986 to date (cited F.T.R.)

This is a series of law reports covering judgments of the Trial Division of the Federal Court of Canada. It is an unofficial publication of the Maritime Law Book Company and is part of the National Reporter System.

Example:

> *Minister of National Revenue* v. *National Bank of Canada* (1993), 63 F.T.R. 9.

It is serviced with a digest which includes 15 different consolidated indices. The main finding aid is the "Topical Index", found in each volume, which incorporates a key number classification system. A student may find a key number (all points of law in the reports have a key number) by referring to the looseleaf *Master Key Word Index*. This index provides cross-references to the "Topical Index" and replaces the "Key Word Index" in the volumes and digests. Use the *Master Key Word Index* to find a key number. For example, if you are looking for cases on "entrapment", the following entry is in the *Master Key Word Index*:

Entrapment - Criminal Law 205

The title and key number of "Criminal Law" can be used to search in all reports of the Maritime Law Book Company either manually or by computer.

NOTE: The "Index to Cases Reported, Appeal Notes and Unreported Cases" is a useful companion looseleaf service to the main set.

(5) National Reporter, 1974 to date (cited N.R.)

This is part of the National Reporter System. It contains all of the judgments of the Supreme Court of Canada and all of the judgments of the Federal Court of Appeal. The unofficial *National Reporter* also includes the disposition of all motions for recent leave to appeal to the Supreme Court of Canada. The decisions appear first in paperbound parts and later in bound volumes. Several volumes are issued annually and digests are published for every ten volumes in the set. The digest volumes include brief summaries of reported cases and a consolidation of the various indices which appear in individual volumes.

Each volume of the *National Reporter* includes the following indices:

(i)   "Index to Cases and Motions Reported";
(ii)   "Index to Case Comments";
(iii) "Index to Unedited/Unreported Cases";
(iv)   "Index to Cases Noticed";
(v)   "Index to Statutes Noticed";

(vi)   "Index to Authors and Works Noticed"
(vii) "Index to Words and Phrases"; and
(viii) "Topical Index with Topic Numbers".

The most valuable indices for researching a legal issue are the "Topical Index" and the *Master Key Word Index* published in a looseleaf format as a companion volume to all reports in the set. A familiarity with the latter allows the user to find a topic and number which may be used in the "Topical Index" to quickly search all of the digest volumes of the report series, as well as individual volumes which have not been included in a digest, to find cases on a selected point.

NOTE: The same key-word and topical index system is used in all other case reports which form part of the National Reporter System: *Alberta Reports, Atlantic Provinces Reports, British Columbia Appeal Cases, Federal Trial Reports, Manitoba Reports (2d), New Brunswick Reports (2d), Newfoundland and Prince Edward Island Reports, Nova Scotia Reports (2d), Ontario Appeal Cases, Saskatchewan Reports* and *Western Appeal Cases*. The same system applies to *British Columbia Trial Cases, New Brunswick Reports (2d) Supp.* and *Ontario Trial Cases*, which are all available electronically.

As a result, the same topic (or subtopic) number may be used to conduct research in all of these reports. For example, given the topic key and number "Contracts - 1205", the user may scan the topical indices in the digest and individual volumes of the *National Reporter* to find cases dealing with "what constitutes an offer?". Then, the user may scan the topical indices in the digest and individual volumes of any one or more of the other case reports mentioned using the same topic and key number to find other cases dealing with "what constitutes an offer?".

All headnotes from these publications are in a computer database called the National Reporter System or "NRS" operated by QUICKLAW. All 151 titles and over 25,000 key numbers which cover individual points of law are listed in a separate database called M.L.B. Key Number Database also operated by QUICKLAW. A search of these databases by using a word such as "confession" will indicate a key number, which can then be used to search the computer databases, or to search the digest and individual volumes of one or more report series in the set.

(B) REGIONAL REPORTS

(1) Western Weekly Reports, 1911 to date (cited W.W.R.)

This unofficial set contains a wide variety of cases from the four western provinces and the three territories.[33] It is published in weekly paperbound parts which are regularly replaced by bound volumes. For the purposes of citation, there have been five series to date:

(i)   1911 to 1916. The volumes are numbered consecutively throughout this period.

Example:

Heron v. *Lalonde* (1915), 9 W.W.R. 440 (B.C.C.A.).

(ii)   1917 to 1950. The volumes are numbered consecutively through each year.

Example:

Royal Bank of Canada v. *Dodge*, [1942] 1 W.W.R. 270 (Alta. S.C.).

(iii)   1951 to 1954. The volumes are numbered consecutively throughout this period. The letters "N.S." are included in the citation of volumes 1 to 13 since this is a new series.

Example:

Prudential Trust Co. v. *Cugnet* (1954), 11 W.W.R. (N.S.) 634 (Sask. Q.B.).

(iv)   1955 to 1970. The volumes are numbered consecutively throughout this period, continuing from the preceding period. The letters "N.S." are dropped.

Example:

R. v. *Ostrove* (1967), 60 W.W.R. 267 (Man. Q.B.).

(v)   1971 to date. The volumes are numbered consecutively through each year.

---

[33]   The set also includes judgments of the Supreme Court of Canada and the Federal Court of Canada on appeal from the western provinces and the three territories.

Examples:

Minister of Finance v. *Piker*, [1973] 1 W.W.R. 169 (B.C.C.A.). *Rodriguez* v. *British Columbia (A.G.)*, [1993] 3 W.W.R 553 (B.C.C.A.).

There are several indices for the following periods: 1951-1970 covering vols. 1 to 75; [1971] vol. 1 to [1980] vol. 6; [1981] vol. 1 to [1985] vol. 6; [1986] vol. 1 to [1988] vol. 6; and [1989] vol. 1 to [1991] vol. 6; [1992] vol. 1 to [1994] vol. 10; [1995] vol. 1 to [1996] vol. 10; [1997] vol. 1 to [1998] vol. 10. As well, there is a paperbound *Cumulative Index* for decisions made after the last bound consolidation. This will be later incorporated into a new hardbound consolidated index.

(2) Atlantic Provinces Reports,[34] 1975 to date (cited A.P.R.)

This unofficial set was first published in 1975. It reprints the decisions appearing in the current *New Brunswick Reports*, *Nova Scotia Reports* and *Newfoundland and Prince Edward Island Reports*. Advance paperbound parts are not published for this set. The parallel series (and the appropriate volume of that series) is provided in each volume of the A.P.R. series.

Examples:

Re Lundrigans Ltd. (Bankrupt) (1993), 336 A.P.R. 113 (Nfld. S.C., T.D.).
Campobello Fisheries v. *Jackson Bros. Ltd.* (1992), 337 A.P.R. 91 (N.B.Q.B., T.D.).
Coalition of Citizens for a Charter v. *Metropolitan Authority* (1993), 338 A.P.R. 1 (N.S.S.C.).

NOTE: The *Lundrigans* case can be found in volume 107 of the Nfld. & P.E.I.R. series, as indicated in volume 336 of the A.P.R. series, at page 113 (the same page number as in A.P.R.). The *Campobello* case can be found in volume 132 of the N.B.R. (2d) series, as indicated in volume 337 of the A.P.R. series, at page 91. The *Coalition* case can be found in volume 122 of the N.S.R. (2d) series, at page 1.

(3) Western Appeal Cases, 1992 to date (cited W.A.C.)

This unofficial set was first published in 1992 by Maritime Law Book Company. It includes judgments of the Courts of Appeal of Alberta, British Columbia,

---

[34] Prior to 1975, coverage of the decisions from the Atlantic provinces was provided by the *Dominion Law Reports* and the *Maritime Provinces Reports* (cited M.P.R.). The latter was published from 1930 to 1968 in 53 volumes.

Manitoba and Saskatchewan. Advance paperbound parts are not published for this set. The parallel series is given in each individual volume in the *Western Appeal Cases*.

Example:

Christie v. *Insurance Corp. of British Columbia* (1993), 47 W.A.C. 262 (B.C.C.A.) (and 28 B.C.A.C. 262).

NOTE: The above example can be found in volume 28 of the *British Columbia Appeal Cases* (B.C.A.C.), at page 262, as indicated in volume 47 of the W.A.C. series, at page 262.

(C) PROVINCIAL REPORTS

(1) British Columbia

(i) British Columbia Law Reports[35] (cited B.C.L.R.)

This unofficial set includes selected cases from the British Columbia Court of Appeal, other British Columbia courts, as well as decisions of the Supreme Court of Canada emanating from British Columbia. It includes, like its sister publications beginning with the *Federal Trial Reports*, discussed at page 53, separate indices and companion digest volumes. For the purposes of citation, there have been three series to date:

First Series, 1976 to 1986. The volumes are numbered consecutively throughout this period. An example citation is:

Shea v. *Shea* (1983), 47 B.C.L.R. 59 (S.C.).

Second Series, 1986 to 1995 volume 100. The volumes are numbered consecutively throughout this period. Two example citations are:

British Columbia Government Employee's Union v. *Labour Relations Board of British Columbia* (1986), 2 B.C.L.R. (2d) 66 (C.A.).
Evans v. *Campbell* (1993), 77 B.C.L.R. (2d) 211 (C.A.).

Third Series, 1995 to date. The volumes are numbered consecutively throughout this period. An example of citation is:

---

[35] There are a number of earlier case reports which covered selected British Columbia cases, including the *Western Law Reporter*, 1905 to 1916 (cited W.L.R.), and the *British Columbia Reports*, 1867 to 1947 (cited B.C.R.).

Paz v. *Hardouin* (1995), 10 B.C.L.R. (3d) 232 (C.A.).

NOTE: The British Columbia Court of Appeal cases are available in a separate Maritime Law Book Company publication, the *British Columbia Appeal Cases.*

(2) Alberta

(i) Alberta Reports,[36] 1977 to date (cited A.R.)

This unofficial set was formerly (until 1986) issued under the authority of the Law Society of Alberta and contains all of the judgments of the Alberta Court of Appeal and selected trial judgments from other courts. It includes, like its sister publications beginning with the *Federal Trial Reports*, discussed at page 53, separate indices and companion digest volumes. The main volumes are numbered consecutively throughout the set. Two example citations are:

Bank of British Columbia v. *Lupul* (1985), 65 A.R. 75 (Q.B.).
R. v. *Leaming* (P.L.) (1992), 134 A.R. 146 (Prov. Ct.).

(ii) Alberta Law Reports

This unofficial set contains all of the judgments of the Alberta Court of Appeal and selected trial court judgments including the Court of Queen's Bench, the Surrogate Court and the Provincial Court, as well as judgments of the Supreme Court of Canada emanating from Alberta.

Second Series, 1976 to 1992 (cited Alta. L.R. (2d)). The volumes are numbered consecutively throughout this period. An example citation is:

Western Mack Truck (Edmonton) Ltd. v. *Heikel* (1976), 1 Alta. L.R. (2d) 184 (Dist. Ct.).

Third Series, 1992 to date (cited Alta. L.R. (3d)). This series is also numbered consecutively throughout this period. An example citation is:

R. v. *Badger* (1993), 8 Alta. L.R. (3d) 354 (C.A.).

---

[36] There are a number of earlier case reports which covered selected Alberta cases, including the *Western Law Reporter*, 1905 to 1916 (cited W.L.R.), and *Alberta Law Reports*, 1908 to 1932 (cited Alta. L.R.).

(3) Saskatchewan

(i) Saskatchewan Reports,[37] 1979 to date (cited Sask. R.)

This unofficial set includes all of the judgments of the Saskatchewan Court of Appeal and most trial court judgments and selected decisions of the Provincial Courts. It includes, like its sister publications beginning with the *Federal Trial Reports*, discussed at page 53, separate indices and companion digest volumes. Two example citations are:

> *Levesque* v. *Bramalea Ltd.* (1983), 26 Sask. R. 9 (Q.B.).
> *Pearce* v. *Hubic Estate* (1992), 104 Sask. R. 182 (Q.B.).

(4) Manitoba

(i) Manitoba Reports (Second Series),[38] 1979 to date (cited Man. R. (2d))

This unofficial set includes all of the judgments of the Manitoba Court of Appeal and most trial court judgments from the Court of Queen's Bench, selected decisions of the Provincial Court and judgments of the Supreme Court of Canada emanating from Manitoba. It includes, like its sister publications beginning with *Federal Trial Reports*, discussed at page 53, separate indices and companion digest volumes. Two example citations are:

> *R.* v. *Godfrey* (1984), 26 Man. R. (2d) 61 (C.A.).
> *Moge* v. *Moge* (1992), 81 Man. R. (2d) 161 (S.C.C.).

---

[37] There a number of earlier case reports which covered selected Saskatchewan cases, including the *Western Law Reporter*, 1905 to 1916 (cited W.L.R.), and the *Saskatchewan Law Reports*, 1907 to 1931 (cited Sask. L.R.).

[38] There are a number of earlier case reports which covered selected Manitoba cases, including the *Western Law Reporter*, 1905 to 1916 (cited W.L.R.), the *Manitoba Law Reports*, 1884 to 1890 (cited Man. L.R.), vols. 1 to 6, and the *Manitoba Reports*, 1890 to 1967 (cited Man. R.), vols. 7 to 67.

(5) Ontario

(i) Ontario Reports (Second Series),[39] 1974 to 1991 (cited O.R. (2d))

This semi-official set was published under the authority of the Law Society of Upper Canada. It contains cases from the Court of Appeal, the Court of Justice (General Division and Provincial Division), Small Claims Court, as well as summaries of decisions from the Supreme Court of Canada. Companion volumes entitled "Consolidated Index" provide a consolidated alphabetical table of cases and a consolidated subject index to cases found in the individual volumes of the set. An example citation is:

Re Butt (1986), 53 O.R. (2d) 297 (Surr. Ct.).

(ii) Ontario Reports (Third Series), 1991 to date (cited O.R. (3d))

This semi-official set is also published under the authority of the Law Society of Upper Canada. It contains cases from the Court of Appeal of the Ontario Court of Justice (General Division and Provincial Division), as well as summaries of decisions from the Supreme Court of Canada. A companion volume entitled *Consolidated Index* provides a consolidated alphabetical table of cases and a consolidated subject index to cases found in the individual volumes of the set. Two example citations are:

Paramount Pictures Corp. v. *Howley* (1991), 5 O.R. (3d) 573 (Gen. Div.).
First City Capital Ltd. v. *Hall* (1993), 11 O.R. (3d) 792 (C.A.).

(iii) Ontario Appeal Cases,[40] 1984 to date (cited O.A.C.)

This unofficial set reports all cases from the Ontario Court of Appeal and the Ontario Divisional Court. It includes, like its sister publications beginning with *Federal Trial Reports*, discussed at page 53, separate indices and companion digest volumes. Two example citations are:

Aliferis v. *Parfeniuk* (1985), 9 O.A.C. 215 (C.A.).
Black Action Defence Committee v. *Huxter* (1992), 59 O.A.C. 327 (Div. Ct.).

---

[39] There have been a number of earlier Ontario case reports including the *Ontario Reports*, 1931 to 1973 (cited [year] O.R.), the *Ontario Appeal Reports*. 1876 to 1900 (cited O.A.R.), the *Ontario Law Reports*, 1901 to 1930 (cited O.L.R.), the *Ontario Reports*, 1882 to 1900 (cited O.R.), the *Ontario Weekly Notes*, 1909 to 1932 (cited O.W.N.), and the *Ontario Weekly Notes*, 1933 to 1962 (cited [year] O.W.N.).

[40] An earlier set with a similar name, *Ontario Appeal Reports* (cited O.A.R.) was published between 1876 and 1900.

(6) Québec

(i) *Recueils de jurisprudence du Québec*, 1986 to date (cited [year] R.J.Q.)

This official set contains judgments of the Cour d'Appel, Cour supérieure, Cour provinciale, Cour des sessions de la paix, and Tribunal de la jeunesse.[41] A "Cumulative Index" is published annually.[42] Two example citations are:

Meyers v. *Royal Bank of Canada*, [1986] R.J.Q. 15 (C.S.).
R. v. *Doré*, [1992] R.J.Q. 2955 (C.Q.).

(7) New Brunswick

(i) *New Brunswick Reports (Second Series)*,[43] 1969 to date (cited N.B.R. (2d))

This semi-official set, issued under the authority of the Law Society of New Brunswick, includes all of the judgments of the New Brunswick Court of Appeal, most judgments of the Court of Queen's Bench, including selected cases of the Family Division and some decisions of the Provincial Court. It includes, like its sister publications beginning with *Federal Trial Reports*, discussed at page 53, separate indices and companion digest volumes. Two example citations are:

Belyea v. *Belyea* (1992), 130 N.B.R. (2d) 297 (Q.B.).
Léger v. *Léger* (1993), 132 N.B.R. (2d) 238 (Q.B., Fam. Div.).

---

41 Before 1986, the *Recueils de jurisprudence du Québec* was published in five parts: *Cour d'Appel* (cited [year] C.A.); *Cour supérieure* (cited [year] C.S.); *Cour provinciale* (cited [year[C.P.), *Cour des sessions de la paix* (cited [year] C.S.P.); and *Tribunal de la jeunesse* (cited [year] T.J.). Prior to 1975, only the first two series were published. The predecessor series, 1892 to 1967, was referred to as *Rapports Judiciares de Québec*. Maritime Law Book Co. commenced a new series in 1987, the *Québec Appeal Cases* (cited Q.A.C.). The set was discontinued in 1995.

42 The *Cumulative Index* is located at the end of the last volume of each year.

43 There are a number of earlier case reports which covered selected New Brunswick cases, including *Maritime Provinces Reports*, 1930 to 1968, *Eastern Law Reporter*, 1906 to 1914 (cited E.L.R.), and *New Brunswick Reports*, 1825 to 1929 (cited N.B.R.).

(8) Nova Scotia

(i) Nova Scotia Reports (Second Series),[44] 1969 to date (cited N.S.R. (2d))

This semi-official set is issued under the authority of the Nova Scotia Barristers' Society and includes all of the judgments of the Nova Scotia Court of Appeal and selected judgments from the Nova Scotia Supreme Court, County Courts, Family Courts, and Provincial Courts. It includes, like its sister publications beginning with *Federal Trial Reports*, discussed at page 53, separate indices and companion digest volumes. Two example citations are:

Ward's Estate v. *Ward* (1985), 68 N.S.R. (2d) 178 (S.C., A.D.).

NOTE: Since January 1, 1993, there has been a consolidation of Nova Scotia courts. Thus, a decision of the Court of Appeal would be now cited as *Schaller* v. *Schaller* (1993), 120 N.S.R. (2d) 82 (C.A.). Formerly, the highest court was referred to as the Supreme Court, Appeal Division, and was cited as (S.C., A.D.).

R. v. *Doucette* (1993), 121 N.S.R. (2d) 163 (Prov. Ct.).

A five-volume companion set, *Nova Scotia Reports, 1965-69* (cited N.S.R.), brings together decisions rendered between 1965 and 1969. There is a single-volume digest[45] which summarizes the cases contained in *Nova Scotia Reports* (1965-69) and the first ten volumes of the *Nova Scotia Reports (2d)*.

(9) Newfoundland and Prince Edward Island

(i) Newfoundland and Prince Edward Island Reports,[46] 1970 to date (cited Nfld. & P.E.I.R.)

This semi-official set, issued under the authority of the Law Society of Newfoundland and the Law Society of Prince Edward Island, includes all of the judgments of the Newfoundland and Prince Edward Island Courts of Appeal, and selected judgments from the Supreme Court of Newfoundland, Trial

---

[44] There have been a number of earlier case reports dealing with selected Nova Scotia cases, including *Maritime Provinces Reports*, 1930 to 1968, *Eastern Law Reporter*, 1906 to 1914, and *Nova Scotia Reports*, 1834 to 1929 (cited N.S.R.).

[45] Referred to as *Digest and Indexes* for volumes 1 to 10 and for *Nova Scotia Reports, 1965-69*, volumes 1 to 5.

[46] There are a number of earlier case reports which covered selected Prince Edward Island cases, including *Eastern Law Reporter*, 1906 to 1914, and *Maritime Provinces Reports*, 1930 to 1968. The latter included Newfoundland cases beginning in 1949.

Division, Newfoundland Family Court, Newfoundland Provincial Court, Prince Edward Island Supreme Court, Trial Division, and the Provincial Court of Prince Edward Island. It includes, like its sister publications beginning with *Federal Trial Reports*, discussed on page 53, separate indices and companion digest volumes. Three example citations are:

> *R. v. King* (1985), 54 Nfld. & P.E.I.R. 286 (Nfld. Dist. Ct.).
> *R.S. v. I.S.* (1992), 102 Nfld. & P.E.I.R. 246 (Nfld. Prov. Ct.).
> *Llewellyn v. MacSwain* (1993), 106 Nfld. & P.E.I.R. 101 (P.E.I.S.C., TD.).

(10) Northwest Territories

(i) Northwest Territories Reports, 1983 to date (cited [year] N.W.T.R.)

This semi-official set is issued under the authority of the Law Society of the Northwest Territories and contains judgments of the Northwest Territories Court of Appeal, and selected trial court judgments, including the Territorial Court and the Youth Court. It also reports judgments on appeal from the Northwest Territories to the Supreme Court of Canada. The volumes are identified by year. Two example citations are:

> *R. v. J.S.O.*, [1985] N.W.T.R. 255 (Terr. Ct.).
> *R. v. Spencer*, [1992] N.W.T.R. 124 (S.C.).

(11) Yukon Territory

(i) Yukon Reports, 1987 to 1989 (cited Y.R.)

This semi-official set was issued under the authority of the Law Society of the Yukon and contained judgments of the Yukon Court of Appeal and selected trial judgments, including the Yukon Territorial Court and Yukon Supreme Court. It also reported judgments on appeal from the Yukon Territory to the Supreme Court of Canada. The volumes were numbered consecutively. An example citation is:

> *M.B.W. Surveys Ltd. v. Bank of Nova Scotia* (1986), 1 Y.R. 157 (S.C.).

(D) SUBJECT REPORTS

There are nationwide report series in specialized fields. They usually include both decisions of special boards or tribunals, as well as conventional courts which are omitted by other case reports. Some, like the *Labour Arbitration Cases*, contain only the decisions of special tribunals.

Most of the subject case reports contain extensive indices, digests, annotations,[47] and other features designed to assist the user to find cases as well as related legislation and articles more quickly. Many of the cases reported in these series appear as well in national, regional, or provincial case reports.

Appendix III contains the publication periods and the recommended citations for the major subject reports.

4. Canadian Judicial Decisions on the Internet

Judicial decisions from several courts in Canada are now quickly available through the Internet without the need to subscribe to computerized databases. Some of these sites even have search engines which allow for searching by case name or legal topic. One can also subscribe to receive newly released decisions via e-mail from some courts.

These Web sites cannot replace basic library research or searching via commercial databases (see Chapter 5). Only a few superior courts in Canada provide decisions via Web sites, and those sites with a search engine do not search the databases of any of the others. Therefore, one would have to consult each court's Web page to find all relevant cases on a particular topic from each court.

Nevertheless, the following sites provide up to date releases from their respective courts, and are welcome additions for the legal researcher:

(1) Supreme Court of Canada

Offers a searchable database, weekly bulletins, timely releases of Supreme Court of Canada decisions, a free subscription service, and access to the Supreme Court Reports online: The Supreme Court of Canada <http://www.droit.umontreal.ca/doc/csc-scc/en/index.html>

(2) Federal Court of Canada

Provides access to Federal Court decisions, the Federal Court Rules, a free subscription service, searchable databases online: Federal Court of Canada <http://www.fja.gc.ca/en/cf>.

(3) The Superior Courts of British Columbia

Provides access to decisions of the British Columbia Supreme Court and Court of Appeal, a legal "compendium" that describes the laws and judiciary in British Columbia, and searchable databases online: British Columbia Superior Courts <http://www.courts.gov.bc.ca>.

---

[47] There is often extensive commentary on selected cases which is very useful in helping the reader understand the case in the context of earlier law and in terms of perceived trends.

(4) Alberta Courts

Contains decisions not only of Alberta's Superior Courts (Court of Queen's Bench and Court of Appeal), but also includes decisions of the Alberta Provincial Court, which includes Family Court; also provides a searchable database online: Alberta Courts <http://www.albertacourts.ab.ca>.

(5) Ontario Courts

Provides decisions from the Ontario Court of Appeal, notices and rules from the Superior Court of Justice and Ontario Court of Justice; no search engine online: Ontario Courts: <http://www.ontariocourts.on.ca>.

5. English Case Reports

(A) EARLY ENGLISH REPORTS

(1) Nominate Reports

In 1535, law reports began to appear in England in the form which we now know. This is the period of the "Nominate Reports", which lasted from 1535 to 1865. The "Nominate Reports" is not a specific report series, but rather it is a broad term describing a multitude of commercial reports prepared by private reporters. Hundreds of these case reports were published with varying degrees of completeness and accuracy.

(2) English Reports (cited E.R.)

The *English Reports* series was prepared around the turn of the century by a group of leading jurists in order to make the great mass of "Nominate Reports" more accessible. It constitutes a collection of most of the more reliable reports published between 1378 and 1866. The set consists of 176 volumes of cases arranged by court and a two-volume *Index of Cases*. Each case is reprinted verbatim with the original footnotes. In parenthesis beneath the name of the case, the editors have provided citations to collateral reports (preceded by "S.C." for "same case"), to the history of the case, and to subsequent judicial consideration. The original pagination is indicated in bold type within the text. Some editorial comment is provided.

To find a case in the *English Reports*, given only the citation to the original "Nominate Reporter", consult the *Chart to the English Reports* (the Chart is framed and hung beside the set in most law libraries), or consult a separate publication entitled "Chart of Reports". The Chart contains an alphabetical list of the names of all the reporters whose work has been reprinted in the *English Reports*. The Chart will indicate in what volume of the *English Reports* the desired case can be found. For example, if you are given the citation (1835), 1 Y. & C.

Ex. 247, first refer to an index of law reports, journals and abbreviations (such as is found in *Osborn's Concise Law Dictionary*, 8th ed.) to determine what Y. & C. Ex. means. Once you know that Y. & C. Ex. refers to *Younge & Collyer's Reports*, consult the Chart. (Students will often know from looking at the Chart that Y. & C. Ex. is a reference to *Younge & Collyer's Reports, Exchequer in Equity*.) The Chart shows that volumes 1-4 of *Younge & Collyer's Reports, Exchequer in Equity*, are reprinted in volume 160 of the *English Reports*. Next, scan the top of the pages in volume 160 for the abbreviation 1 Y. & C. Ex. and the original page number 247 (or the number closest to it). You will find a reference to *Bennett* v. *Attkins* at page 101 of this volume of the *English Reports*.

If you know the name of the case, find the case name in the "Index of Cases to the English Reports" and note the references to the original "Nominate Reporter", the volume in bold type and page number in the *English Reports*, where the cases can be found. It shows, for example, that *Bale* v. *Cleland*, originally reported in 4 F. & F. 117, is located in volume 176 (appears in bold type) at page 494 in the *English Reports*.

The *English Reports* are generally cited in preference to many other collections because they contain verbatim reprints of the original reports. When citing a case from the *English Reports*, the student should include a citation to the original report so that the reader may assess the reliability of the report. A citation to the *English Reports* should follow for the reader's convenience. Where the *Index of Cases* discloses several reports of the same case, alternate citations should be included.

Example:

Wigmore's Case (1707), Holt 459, 90 E.R. 1152 and 2 Salk. 438, 91 E.R. 380 (K.B.).

(3) Revised Reports (cited R.R.)

The *Revised Reports* were prepared shortly after the *English Reports* and contain a practical selection of case reports from "Nominate Reports" during the period 1785 to 1865. The set consists of 149 volumes of case reports, a one-volume "Table of Cases" and a two-volume "Index Digest". At the beginning of volume 149 there is a "Table of Comparative Reference" which shows the correspondence between the volumes of the original reports and the volumes of the *Revised Reports*. To a great extent, the coverage of the *Revised Reports* duplicates that of the *English Reports*, and, therefore, it is preferable to cite the version in the *English Reports*.

Example:

Royal British Bank v. *Turquand* (1855), 5 El. & B1. 248, 103 R.R. 461 (Q.B.).

(4) *All England Law Reports Reprint* (cited All E.R. Rep.)

The *All England Law Reports Reprint* is a recent collection of nominate and commercial reports from the period 1558 to 1935. The set consists of 36 volumes of cases arranged in chronological order and a one-volume *Index* which includes a "Table of Cases". In addition to the judgments, which remain virtually unaltered from the original, each case report includes citation to all parallel reports of the same case and a comprehensive list of cases where the original case has been judicially considered. There is a supplementary series, entitled the *All England Law Reports Reprint Extension Volumes*, covering the period 1861 to 1935. The *Extension Series*, consisting of 17 volumes of cases, a one-volume *Index* and a pamphlet which is a "Table of Cases", is arranged in the same manner as the original series.

Examples:

Rylands v. *Fletcher*, [1866] All E.R. Rep. 1 (H.L.).
Butler v. *Rice*, [1908-10] All E.R. Rep. Ext. 51 (Ch.).

NOTE: Very few (if any) Canadian law schools keep copies of the *Extension Series* in their libraries.

(B) MODERN ENGLISH REPORTS

Modern English law reporting began in the mid-nineteenth century with the appearance of several commercial series of case reports. Among those series which have been discontinued, the most important were the *Law Journal Reports* (1822-1949), the *Weekly Reporter* (1853-1906), the *Law Times* (1860-1947), and the *Times Law Reports* (1884-1952).

The most important current reports of a general nature are the semi-official *Law Reports*, the unofficial *Weekly Law Reports* and *All England Law Reports*. There are, of course, many specialized reports currently published in the United Kingdom.

(1) *Law Journal Reports* (1822-1949) Volumes 1-118

This set consists of approximately 300 volumes containing selected equity and common law court decisions. The set has two parts, an old series and a new series. The arrangement of the set is as follows:

Old Series

1822-1831 Volumes 1-9: Each volume contains judgments of the courts of equity and common law courts. The volumes are identified by the names of the individual courts. The reports of individual cases are grouped according to the court which gave the decision and they are given separate pages within the volume. A citation to a case in this part of the set includes the abbreviation for the name of the court and the abbreviation O.S. for "Old Series".

Example:

Graves v. *Dolphin* (1826), 5 L.J.O.S. Ch. 45.

New Series

1832-1835 Volumes 1-4: Each volume contains judgments of the courts of equity and common law courts. The volumes are identified by the names of individual courts. The reports of individual cases are grouped according to the court which gave the decision and paged separately within the volume.

A citation to a case in this part includes the abbreviation for the name of the court but does not include a reference to a "New Series".

Example:

Abbott v. *Pomfret* (1835), 4 L.J.C.P. 139.

1836-1875 Volumes 5-44: In this period, two volumes having the same number were published each year. Generally, one is identified as "Equity & Bankruptcy", the other as "Common Law". The reports of the individual cases, in each volume, are grouped according to the court which gave the decision and paged separately within a volume. A citation to a case includes a reference to the abbreviation for the name of the court but not to the abbreviations for "Equity & Bankruptcy" and "Common Law".

Examples:

Equity: *Eyre* v. *Mason* (1838), 7 L.J. Ch. 220.
Common Law: *Briscoe* v. *Lomax* (1838), 7 L.J.Q.B. 148.

1876-1946 Volumes 45-115: In this period, two or three similarly numbered volumes were published in each year. The reference to "Common Law" and "Equity & Bankruptcy" on the spines of individual volumes is dropped but the cases are still broadly distinguished as "Equity & Bankruptcy" and "Common Law". The volumes are identified by the name of the individual courts. The individual cases are grouped according to the court which gave the decision and paged separately within a volume. A citation to a case includes the abbreviation for the name of the court.

Examples:

Equity: *Hilliard* v. *Fulford* (1876), 46 L.J. Ch. 43.
Common Law: *Nichols* v. *Marsland* (1876), 46 L.J.Q.B. 174.

1947-1949 Volumes 116-118: During this period a single volume which reported the decisions of all courts was published each year and the practice of paging separately the reports of cases in different courts was discontinued. A citation to a case includes the abbreviation for the name of the court.

Example:

Cow v. *Casey* (1948), 118 L.J.C.A. 565.

(2) The Law Reports

This set is published by the Incorporated Council of Law Reporting for England and Wales and includes cases of interest from the several divisions of the High Court of Justice. The individual series which constitute *The Law Reports* are named after the division of the High Court of Justice whose decisions they report. Originally there were 11 sets. Owing to the changes in the English system of courts, particularly as a result of the *Judicature Act, 1875*, the component sets have undergone several changes in name and in coverage. From the 11 original series, four current series have evolved.

1.   *Appeal Cases*, 1891 to date (cited [year] A.C.)

Examples:

Castle Insurance Co. v. *Hong Kong Islands Shipping Co.*, [1984] A.C. 226 (P.C.).
Swingcastle Ltd. v. *Gibson*, [1991] 2 A.C. 223 (H.L.).[48]

2.   *Chancery Division*, 1891 to date (cited [year] Ch.)[49]

Example:

Mills v. *Silver*, [1991] Ch. 271 (C.A.).

---

[48] Certain years have published more than one volume.
[49] These reports along with the *Family Reports* are combined in monthly paperback issues.

3.   *Queen's (King's) Bench Division*, 1891 to date (cited [year] Q.B. or K.B.)

Examples:

Meek v. *Powell*, [1952] 1 K.B. 164 (K.B.D.).
Corbett v. *Barking Health Authority*, [1991] 2 Q.B. 408 (C.A.).

4.   *Family Division*, 1972 to date (cited [year] Fam.)

Examples:

Marsden v. *Marsden*, [1972] Fam. 280 (C.A.).
Wookey v. *Wookey*, [1991] Fam. 121 (C.A.).

NOTE: Prior to 1972, *Family Division* was known as *Probate* (short for Probate, Divorce and Admiralty).

Each of these series is published in monthly parts and regularly consolidated in bound volumes.

The shelving of *The Law Reports* in a law library often leads to confusion for the beginning student. Each current set is shelved with its predecessor sets, many of which have different names. For example, the *Appeal Cases* reports were preceded historically by the *Privy Council Appeals* (1865-75), a seven-volume set of the *English & Irish Appeals* (1866-75), a two-volume set of the *Scotch & Divorce Appeals* (1866-75), and a 15-volume set of *Appeal Cases* (1875-90). Thus, these are shelved before the *Appeal Cases* reports. The same arrangement is applied to the *Chancery Division* reports, *Queen's Bench Division* reports, and *Family Division* reports.

This means that in the overall arrangement of *The Law Reports* very recent volumes of one set (for example, 1994) may be shelved next to the earliest volumes of a second set (for example, 1865). Table II shows the four current sets of *The Law Reports* and each of their predecessor sets.[50]

TABLE II

Privy Council Appeals	Eng. & Irish Appeals	Sco. & Div. Appeals	Appeal Cases	Appeal Cases
(1865-75)	(1866-75)	(1866-75)	(1875-90)	(1891-date)
Vols. 1-6	Vols. 1-7	Vols. 1-2	Vols. 1-15	

---

[50]   See also Appendix II which details the complete arrangement of *The Law Reports*.

Chancery Appeals (1865-75) Vols. 1-10	Equity Cases (1865-75) Vols. 1-20	Chancery Division (1875-90) Vols. 1-45	Chancery Division (1891-date)
Crown Cases Reserved (1865-75) Vols. 1-2	Queen 's Bench Cases (1865-75) Vols. 1-10		
Common Pleas Cases (1865-75) Vols. 1-10	Common Pleas Division (1875-80) Vols. 1-5	Queen's Bench Division (1875-90) Vols. 1-25	Queen's (or King's) Bench Division (1891-date)
Exchequer Cases (1865-75) Vols. 1-10	Exchequer Division (1875-80) Vols. 1-5		
Admiralty & Ecclesiastical Cases (1865-75) Vols. 1-4	Probate Division[1] (1876-90) Vols. 1-15	Probate Division[2] (1891-1971) by year	
Probate & Divorce Cases (1865-75) Vols. 1-3		Since 1972 Family Division[3]	

[1] Probate, Divorce, Admiralty, Ecclesiastical & Privy Council.
[2] Probate, Divorce, Admiralty, Court of Appeal. Ecclesiastical & Privy Council.
[3] Family, Court of Appeal, Ecclesiastical.

Citation of *The Law Reports*

In the following explanation, note that the name of the court is included only when the court is not evident from the main citation.

(i)   From 1865 to 1875. In each set the volumes are numbered consecutively. Thus, the 20 volumes of the "Equity Cases" published between 1865 and 1875 are numbered 1 to 20. It is the volume number, not the year, which is important in locating the correct volume.

Example:

Murray v. *Bush* (1873), L.R. 6 H.L. 37.

In the example citation, the letters "L.R." are placed before the volume number, 6, in order to distinguish *The Law Reports* from other publications. The date is placed in round brackets to show that it is not essential to finding the volume.

(ii)   From 1875 to 1890. As a result of the *Judicature Act, 1875*, the courts became divisions of the High Court of Justice. "D" was therefore included in the citation. "L.R." was dropped and the consecutive numbering of volumes started afresh.

Example:

Wylson v. *Dunn* (1887), 34 Ch.D. 569.

(iii)   From 1891 to date. The letter "D" was dropped. Volumes were numbered consecutively throughout the year. Thus, the year appears in brackets as an integral part of the citation.

Examples:

Petrofina (U.K.) Ltd. v. *Magnaload Ltd.*, [1984] Q.B. 127 (Q.B.D.).
Henderson v. *Arthur*, [1907] 1 K.B. 10 (C.A.).
Moon v. *Atherton*, [1972] 2 Q.B. 435 (C.A.).
W.H. Smith Do-It-All Ltd. v. *Peterborough City Council*, [1991] 1 Q.B. 304 (C.A.).

NOTE: The single exception to this rule is the citation of *Restrictive Practices Cases*,[51] where it was found convenient to cite in the original manner.

Example:

Re Yarn Spinners' Agreement (1959), L.R. 1 R.P. 118.

NOTE: Because of their semi-official status, always cite *The Law Reports* in preference to other series. If a number of reports are cited, refer first to *The Law Reports*.

(3) Industrial Cases Reports, 1975 to date (cited [year] I.C.R.)

This report series commenced in 1975 and includes decisions of the Employment Appeal Tribunal, the National Industrial Relations Court, High Court of Justice, Court of Appeal, and House of Lords concerning industrial relations.

---

[51]   Discussed in (3) below.

The predecessors of this series were the *Industrial Court Reports* (1972-74) and the *Reports of Restrictive Practices Cases* (1957-1972).

Examples:

Oxford Printing Co. v. *Letraset Ltd.* (1970), L.R. 7 R.P. 94 (Ch.D.).
Challinor v. *Taylor*, [1972] I.C.R. 129 (N.I.R.C.).
Meade v. *Haringey*, [1979] I.C.R. 494 (C.A.).
Bromwich v. *National Ear, Nose and Throat Hospital*, [1980] I.C.R. 450 (Q.B.D.).
Chisholm v. *Kirklees Borough Council*, [1993] I.C.R. 826 (Ch.D.).

(4) Weekly Law Reports

The semi-official *Weekly Law Reports* (1953 to date) includes every decision from all divisions likely to appear in any general series of reports. Appearing weekly, it constitutes an advance sheet for *The Law Reports* themselves. It also contains decisions which will not appear in *The Law Reports*.[52] Its predecessors were the *Weekly Notes* (1866 to 1952) and the *Times Law Reports* (1884 to 1952).

Examples:

R. v. *Hodgson*, [1973] 2 W.L.R. 570 (C.A.).
Tudor Grange Holdings Ltd. v. *Citibank N.A.*, [1991] 3 W.L.R. 750 (Ch.D.).

(5) All England Law Reports

The *All England Law Reports* is an unofficial series of weekly reports which began in 1936. It covers, *inter alia*, leading cases in all fields of law decided by the House of Lords, the Privy Council, the Court of Appeal, and all divisions of the High Court. The *All England Law Reports* are served by the following finding aids:

(i) *Tables and Index*, [year] (also referred to as the *Current Index*). This publication covers all cases reported in the *All England Law Reports* after the cut-off date for the consolidation to the date of issue. It includes a "Subject Index" and a table of "Cases Reported and Considered". The *Current Index* is a continuation of the *Consolidated Tables and Index* (described below).

(ii) *Consolidated Tables and Index*, [1936-1998]. This is a multi-volume set which covers all the cases reported in the *All England Law Reports*

---

[52] At the end of each year, the *Weekly Law Reports* are usually published in three bound volumes.

from 1936 to 1998. It includes a "Subject Index", a table of "Cases Reported and Considered", a table of "Statutes Considered" and a table of "Words and Phrases Considered".

The "Table of Cases Reported and Considered" includes a complete list of the names of all the cases reported in the *All England Law Reports* from 1936 forward. It provides, by way of annotations to the appropriate entries, the names and references of subsequent cases reported in the series in which the cases listed in the table have been judicially considered, *i.e.*, applied, distinguished, or overruled.

The purpose of the "Subject Index" is to enable the reader to obtain the names and references of cases on a particular topic. The arrangement of the index follows the conventional pattern of legal indices, being based on an alphabetical sequence of main headings each of which is subdivided into further subheadings, also arranged in alphabetical sequence, covering topics which fall within the generality of the main heading. For every entry, other than cross-reference entries, the process of subdivision has been taken two stages further. Each entry has been classified under a main index heading and three further subheadings in descending order of generality.

(iii) *Canadian Annotations to the Consolidated Tables and Index.* This looseleaf service lists all cases in the *All England Law Reports* which have been considered in a Canadian reporting series since 1936. It is updated several times yearly.

NOTE: The student searching for a particular case name, a case which may have been judicially considered, or cases on a particular topic should refer to the *Consolidated Index* and the *Current Index*. Such a search will cover all the published volumes and looseleaf parts other than a small number, not exceeding eight, of the most recently published paper parts. These paper parts have a "Digest of Cases", a cumulative case table and a "Noter-Up" (for cases and statutes) published in the inside back jacket.

(6) U.K. House of Lords Decisions on the Internet

Decisions of the House of Lords since 1996 are available online: United Kingdom Parliament <http://www.parliament.the-stationery-office.co.uk/pa/>.

6. General Rules of Citation

Because of the multiplicity of case reports and the variety in publication there is no single method of legal citation. The following "rules" cover most of the important points.

Rule 1: The Form of Citation

A complete case citation consists of:

(i)   the style of cause (or name of the parties) in italics;

NOTE: The name of an individual is not given in full; use the surname only. If there are multiple individuals give the surname of the first adversary party on each side. Do not use the words "and others" or "et al.". A criminal case is usually cited as *R.* v. *Jones*.

(ii) "v." separating the names of the opposing parties, not italicized.[53] When writing in English never use "c." instead of "v.", even if citing a case reported in French;

(iii) the year of the decision;[54]

(iv) the volume number (if any);

(v)   the abbreviated title of the case report;

(vi) the series;

(vii) the page at which the report begins;

(viii) the specific page reference where the relevant text material appears (if any); and

(ix) the abbreviated name of the jurisdiction and court (unless it is obvious from the name of the report series).

Examples:

Bank of Montreal v. *Faclaris* (1984), 13 D.L.R. (4th) 245 at 247 (Ont. H.C.J.).

Bradbury v. *Mundell* (1993), 13 O.R. (3d) 269 (Gen. Div.).

Sidoroff v. *Joe* (1992), 76 B.C.L.R. (2d) 82 at 84 (C.A.).

In these examples, the plaintiff's surname has been placed first in the report of the trial and the defendant's surname appears second.[55]

---

[53] The practice varies. Some publishers italicize the "v.". It is bad form when speaking to say "versus"; always say "A against B" or "A and B".

[54] Usually a volume of case reports includes several cases from the prior year. If so, the recommended practice is to cite the year of the decision in round brackets even if another year is indicated on the spine of the volume. If the year is necessary to find the volume, include the year which appears on the spine in square brackets. Note that some publishers indicate the appropriate citation for the volume on the title page.

[55] The practice on appeal is not uniform. In some reports the appellant's name (the one who appeals to the higher court) appears first on appeal while in other reports the plaintiff's name remains first regardless of which side appeals. The Canadian Law Information Council has developed a standard for identification of cases by name. Under the new standard a case keeps the same name as used in the original proceeding through all appeal levels.

In the first example, the decision was reported in 1984 in the 13th volume of the *Dominion Law Reports (Fourth Series)*. The report begins on page 245, the quoted passage is on page 247, and the decision was handed down by the Ontario High Court of Justice.

In the second example, the decision was reported in 1993 in the 13th volume of the *Ontario Reports (Third Series)*. The report began on page 269 and the decision was handed down by the General Division of the Ontario Court of Justice.

In the third example, the decision was reported in 1992 in the 76th volume of the *British Columbia Law Reports (Second Series)*. The report begins on page 82, the quoted passage is on page 84, and the decision was handed down by the British Columbia Court of Appeal.

Capitalize the first letter of a party name and the first letter of all words other than prepositions, connectives and the like. (Omit given names and initials of individuals, except when they appear in the name of a company.) If the style of cause appears in the body of a memorandum or other text material, it is not repeated in the footnote citation.

Rule 2: Style of Cause

(i)   The use of "*sub nom.*"

Where a case is reported under different names it may be necessary for clarity to indicate this to the reader by use of the explanatory phrase "*sub nom.*". "*Sub nom.*" is placed in brackets with the name.

Example:

> *Walton* v. *Hebb*, [1985] 1 W.W.R. 122, (*sub nom. Re Walton and Attorney General of Canada*) 13 D.L.R. (4th) 379 (N.W.T.S.C.).

The case of *Dalton and MacDonald* which appears in the *Western Weekly Reports* as In *Re Dalton and MacDonald Estate*, and in the *British Columbia Law Reports* as In *Re Testator's Family Maintenance Act and the Estate of Donald Alexander MacDonald* may be cited as follows:

> *Dalton* v. *MacDonald Estate*, [1938] 1 W.W.R. 758, (*sub nom. Re Testator's Family Maintenance Act and MacDonald Estate*) 52 B.C.L.R. 473 (C.A.).

Consider also the following example:

> *Reference Re Legislative Authority of Parliament of Canada*, [1980] 1 S.C.R. 54, (*sub nom. Reference Re Legislative Authority of Parliament to Alter or*

Replace Senate) 102 D.L.R. (3d) 1, (*sub nom. Re British North America Act and Federal Senate*) 30 N.R. 271.

"*Sub nom.*" is also used to show a difference in the parties' names at a lower court level, as shown below:

Giffels Associates Ltd. v. *Eastern Construction Co.* (1978), 84 D.L.R. (3d) 344 (S.C.C.); aff'g (1976), 68 D.L.R. (3d) 385 (Ont. C.A.); aff'g in part (*sub nom. Dominion Chain Co.* v. *Eastern Construction Co.*) (1974), 46 D.L.R. (3d) 28 (Ont. H.C.J.).

Where a case which has been heard at more than one level of court, has been reported in parallel series, and has appeared under different names, the complete citation may be written as follows:

Horsley v. *MacLaren*, [1972] S.C.R. 441, 22 D.L.R. (3d) 545; aff'g (1970), 2 O.R. 487, 11 D.L.R. (3d) 277 (C.A.); rev'g (*sub nom. Matthews* v. *MacLaren*; *Horsley* v. *MacLaren*) (1969), 2 O.R. 137, 4 D.L.R. (3d) 557 (H.C.).

(ii)   Corporate Status

The style of cause should be reproduced with some modifications from a law reporter; the initials of a corporate name, if given, are included, but the reference to "Ltd." or "Inc." is omitted if the corporate status of the business is clear from the name of the party. As well, with a few exceptions, a reference to a definite article, such as "the" which precedes a party name is also omitted.

Example:

Toys "R" Us (Canada) v. *Manjel Inc.* (1993), 51 C.P.R. (3d) 27 (F.C.T.D.).

NOTE: The word "Inc." is necessary in the defendant's name since there is no other term to indicate that the party is a business. The plaintiff is clearly a business, so it is not necessary to add "Inc." or "Ltd.".

(iii)   References to the Crown

With some exceptions, the Crown is referred to as "R." instead of "Regina", "The Queen", "La Reine", "Rex", "The King", or "Le Roi". This practice was standardized beginning in 1986.

Examples:

Deom v. *R.* (1981), 64 C.C.C. (2d) 222 (B.C.S.C.).
R. v. *Inkster* (1988), 69 Sask. R. 1 (Q.B.).

NOTE: The former case appears as *Re Deom et al. and The Queen* in the report series. If the style of cause in the citation adopts a reference to "v.", the "Re" is dropped; if not, the reference to "Re" is included, as in the following example:

Re Rosenbaum and Law Society of Manitoba (1983), 8 C.C.C. (3d) 255 (C.A.).

(iv)   The Use of the Phrase "Reference Re"

The phrase "Reference Re" is used to introduce the title of a constitutional matter which has been considered under the reference jurisdiction of a court.

Examples:

Reference Re Roman Catholic Separate High Schools Funding (1987), 22 O.A.C. 321 (S.C.C.).
Reference Re Language Rights Under Section 23 of the Manitoba Act, 1870, and Section 133 of the Constitution Act, 1867, [1985] 1 S.C.R. 721.

Rule 3: Use of Square or Round Brackets

Each volume of a case report must be identified to facilitate retrieval. To achieve this, publishers employ two methods:

(i)   Consecutive numbering

Each new volume is issued a number in a consecutive sequence and a date is indicated. The date in round brackets is the date of the decision rather than the date on the spine of the volume in a report series. It is followed by a comma. For an explanation of the citation of years and examples see (ii) below.

Examples:

Re Laidlaw Foundation (1984), 13 D.L.R. (4th) 491 (Ont. H.C.J., Div. Ct.).
Ottawa Mortgage Investment Corp. v. *Edwards* (1991), 5 O.R. (3d) 465 (Gen. Div.).

If there is more than one reference to the decision, then the other reporters are identified only by volume number (round bracket dates are dropped).

Example:

Cormier v. *Butler* (1992), 129 N.B.R. (2d) 81, 325 A.P.R. 81 (Q.B., T.D.).

(ii) Year

Each new volume is identified by the year it was issued. The year will appear in either round or square brackets, depending on the citation method used for the particular report series.

Examples:

Re McVey, [1992] 3 S.C.R. 475.

In the example *Re McVey*, the volume is identified by the reference to 1992 of the *Supreme Court Reports*. Without the date it would be impossible to learn from the citation in which of the many volumes, numbered 3, of the *Supreme Court Reports* the case is reported. The date is placed in square brackets and is preceded by a comma.[56]

NOTE: Some volumes are identified by a volume number in addition to the year the volume was issued.

Example:

Keddie v. *Currie*, [1992] 1 W.W.R. 340 (B.C.C.A.).

NOTE: When citing American materials the date of the report appears after the page number, in the same set of brackets as the name of the court.

Rule 4: Dropping Round Brackets

When indicated in a previous citation, a date in round brackets need not be repeated; however, never dispense with square brackets.

Examples:

Taylor v. *Co-operative Fire & Casualty Co.* (1984), 35 Alta. L.R. (2d) 77, 10 C.C.L.I. 284, 57 A.R. 328 (Q.B.).

---

[56] If there are too many cases to be reported in one volume, the report is divided into two or more volumes for the year. Thus, in 1985, the *Western Weekly Reports* were published in six volumes, each volume number following the square-bracketed date; thus, [1985] 3 W.W.R. 385.

Lizotte v. *Traders General Ins. Co. [B.C.]*, [1985] 1 W.W.R. 595, 10 C.C.L.I. 222, [1985] I.L.R. 1-1874 (B.C.S.C.).

Marwin v. *Canada (Minister of Employment & Immigration)* (1989), 93 N.S.R. (2d) 120, 242 A.P.R. 120, 38 Admin. L.R. 298, 9 Imm. L.R. (2d) 122 (S.C., T.D.).

Rule 5: Punctuation in the Citation

A comma always precedes the date when square brackets are used, and follows the date when round brackets are used.

Examples:

McLellan v. *Parent*, [1992] N.W.T.R. 226 (S.C.).
Canadian Indemnity Co. v. *Canadian Johns-Manville Co.* (1990), 50 C.C.L.I. 95 (S.C.C.).

Rule 6: Punctuation between Citations

When more than one parallel citation is given for a case they may be separated with a comma. When giving the history of a case, a comma is used between parallel citations within each court level and a semi-colon is used to separate citations for different court levels.

Examples:

Gershman Produce Co. v. *Motor Transport Bd.* (1984), 14 D.L.R. (4th) 722, [1985] 2 W.W.R. 63, 32 Man. R. (2d) 308, 10 Admin. L.R. 253, 31 M.V.R. 67 (Q.B.).
First City Development Corp. v. *Nogler* (1991), 102 N.S.R. (2d) 444, 279 A.P.R. 444 (S.C., T.D.).
Gateway Construction Co. v. *Provincial Drywall Supply*, [1988] 3 W.W.R. 547, 51 Man. R. (2d) 275, 50 D.L.R. (4th) 154 (C.A.); aff'g (1987), 51 Man. R. (2d) 277, 28 C.L.R. 302 (Q.B.).

Rule 7: Series or Editions

Many reporters have been published in more than one series. If so, it is necessary to indicate the series in the citation. This information ("N.S." for "New Series", or 2d, 3d, 4th, etc.) is given in round brackets after the abbreviation for the report series.

Example:

Comairco Equipment v. *Breault* (1985), 52 O.R. (2d) 695 (Dist. Ct.).

NOTE: The "(2d)" tells the reader that the case is found in the Second Series of the *Ontario Reports*.

Rule 8: Indication of the Court

Generally, the abbreviated name of the court is added in brackets after the jurisdiction and both follow the page reference to the reported case. If the name of the court is obvious from the name of the report series, the court may be excluded.

Examples:

Blakely v. *513953 Ontario Ltd.* (1985), 31 M.V.R. 10 (Ont. S.C. [H.C.J.]).
Banbury v. *Tahir* (1993), 13 O.R. (3d) 609 (Gen. Div.).
Coderre (R.) v. *M.N.R.*, [1992] 1 C.T.C. 2596 (T.C.C.).
Joy Oil Co. v. *R.*, [1951] S.C.R. 624, [1951] 3 D.L.R. 582.

Rule 9: Indication of the Jurisdiction

Generally, the abbreviation of the court jurisdiction is given in parenthesis following the page reference to the case reported. The jurisdiction need not be indicated when it is evident from either the name of the series or the name of the court where the case was decided.

For example, when citing from any of the English reports there is no need to include "England" in any citation. The only exceptions are appeals originating from outside England to the House of Lords and to the Judicial Committee of the Privy Council. If one of these outside appeals is cited, the jurisdiction of law involved should be indicated.

Examples:

Grand Centre (Town) v. *Dalbar Feeders Ltd.* (1984), 31 L.C.R. 255 (Alta. L.C.B.).
Jiwa v. *Jiwa* (1992), 12 C.C.L.I. (2d) 54 (B.C.C.A.).
R. v. *Wholesale Travel Group Inc.*, [1991] 3 S.C.R. 154, 84 D.L.R. (4th) 161, 49 O.A.C. 161, 67 C.C.C. (3d) 193.
Alberta (A.G.) v. *Cook*, [1926] A.C. 444 (P.C. Alta.).
Raso v. *Dionigi* (1993), 62 O.A.C. 228 (C.A.).
Vandewall v. *Faria* (1993), 62 O.A.C. 266 (Gen. Div.).
United Lands Corp. v. *Mississauga (City)* (1993), 28 O.M.B.R. 279 (O.M.B.).

Ram Forest Products v. *Ont. Reg. Assess. Comm. No. 14* (1993), 28 O.M.B.R. 138 (Gen. Div.).

Rule 10: Page Reference

The first page of a reported case is included in a case citation and follows the abbreviation of the law report or, where applicable, the series number.

Example:

Clarkson, Gordon Inc. v. *United States Fire Insurance Co.* (1990), 67 D.L.R. (4th) 436 (N.S.S.C., T.D.).

A reference to a specific page number is prefaced with the word "at" as in *Carter* v. *Brooks* (1990), 77 D.L.R. (4th) 45 at 50 (Ont. C.A.); although usage varies. A specific reference to more than one page is abbreviated "ff" as in *R.* v. *Andrews* (1990), 77 D.L.R. (4th) 128 at 135ff (S.C.C.).

Rule 11: Order of Alternative or Parallel Citations

Where more than one report is cited in reference to a case the following is recommended.

(i)　　General Priority

First, official reports.

Examples:

Supreme Court Reports and *Federal Court Reports.*

Second, semi-official reports.

Examples:

Ontario Reports, Northwest Territories Reports, New Brunswick Reports (2d) and *Newfoundland and Prince Edward Island Reports.*

Third, unofficial reports.

Examples:

Dominion Law Reports, National Reporter, Western Weekly Reports, Manitoba Reports (2d), Saskatchewan Reports and *Ontario Appeal Cases.*

(ii)   Priority amongst unofficial reports

There is no unanimity on the correct order if all the reports referred to are unofficial.

(a)   Reports with larger geographical coverage have priority over reports covering smaller areas.

Example:

The *Dominion Law Reports* are cited before the *Manitoba Reports*:

Re Bateman and Association of Professional Engineers of Manitoba (1984), 9 D.L.R. (4th) 373, 28 Man. R. (2d) 264 (Q.B.).

(b)   General law reports have priority over subject reports.

Example:

New Brunswick Broadcasting Co. v. *C.R.T.C.* (1984), 13 D.L.R. (4th) 77, 55 N.R. 143, 2 C.P.R. (3d) 433, 12 C.R.R. 249 (F.C.A.).

NOTE: See Appendix VII for a list of official, semi-official, and unofficial reporters.

Rule 12: History of a Case

Where reference is made to more than one court which decided a case, there is no unanimity on the correct order of citation. The order recommended is the highest court followed by the lower court, or courts, in reverse chronological order.[57]

Examples:

R. v. *Skinner* (1985), 58 N.R. 240 (S.C.C.); ref'g leave to appeal (1984), 65 N.S.R. (2d) 313 (S.C., A.D.).
Xerox of Canada Ltd. v. *Regional Assessment Commissioners Region No. 10*, [1981] 2 S.C.R. 137; rev'g (1980), 30 O.R. (2d) 90 (C.A.); aff'g (1979), 27 O.R. (2d) 269 (Div. Ct.); aff'g (1978), 9 O.M.B.R. 330 (O.M.B.).

---

[57]   The form of citation may be varied so that the court level relevant to a point under discussion is cited first and previous decisions may be then given in chronological order.

In the first example, leave to appeal from a decision of the Nova Scotia Supreme Court of Appeal Division was refused.

In the second example, the Supreme Court of Canada reversed a decision of the Ontario Municipal Board which had been affirmed by both the Court of Appeal and the Divisional Court.

7. Exceptions to the General Rules

(A) UNREPORTED DECISIONS

The form of citation for unreported decisions consists of:

(i)   the name of the parties in italics;
(ii)   "v." separating the names of the opposing parties, not italicized;
(iii)   the date of the decision;
(iv)   the name of the judicial district;
(v)   the docket number; and
(vi)   the abbreviated name of the Court.

Examples:

R. v. *Perry* (6 December 1988), Antigonish, 61457 (N.S. Prov. Ct.) [unreported].

Draney v. *Yeungi* (7 September 1990), Vancouver, B891310 (B.C.S.C.) [unreported].

Some authors include a reference to a digest series in a citation to an unreported decision, as in the following example:

Accord Mortgage Corp. v. *Bolton* (19 October 1988), Vancouver Registry, C860976 (B.C.S.C.), (1989), 8 L.W.C.D. 118 (827-004) [unreported].

Decisions which have not been reported as of the date of the student's report or memorandum are cited in the same manner as unreported decisions with the addition of the notation "as yet unreported" or "not yet reported", as in the following example:

Dawe v. *Cypress Bowl Recreations* (24 November 1993), Nanaimo, 01933 (B.C.S.C.) [as yet unreported].

(B)   CASES VIEWED OR PRINTED FROM COMPUTERIZED DATABASES (COMPUTER CASES)

The form of citation for cases retrieved from a legal database consists of:

(i)   the name of the parties in italics (often the italicized words are high-lighted in bold letters);
(ii)   "v." separating the names of the opposing parties, not italicized;
(iii) the year of the decision in square brackets;
(iv)   the database in abbreviated form;
(v)   the number of the decision; and
(vi)   a reference to the database provider in round brackets.

Example:

Ashdown v. *Jumbo Video Inc.*, [1993] O.J. No. 1169 (QL).

CHAPTER 2

Secondary Legal Materials

Secondary legal materials are preliminary research tools that assist the student in finding, evaluating, and understanding primary materials such as statutes and case law. For general research the most important secondary tools are legal encyclopedias and digests. Other useful finding aids include citators, annotators, legal dictionaries, periodical articles, treatises and textbooks.

Encyclopedias are comprehensive multi-volume reference works containing up to date statements of the law in essay form. Digests and abridgments are comprehensive, multi-volume reference works which provide digests or summaries of cases.

There are two basic types of legal citators: statute citators and case citators. Statute citators contain the titles of all the statutes for a selected province or for Canada and indicate whether the statutes have been amended or judicially considered. This is illustrated in Table III which is taken from the *Ontario Statute Citator*, R.S.O. 1990 edition. (See also a companion work, *Ontario Statute Annotations*, R.S.O. 1990 edition.)

TABLE III

LAW SOCIETY ACT

R.S.O. 1990, Chap. L.8

Amendments

1991, Vol. 2, c. 41; in force November 25, 1991

1992, c. 7; proclaimed in force January 1, 1993

Section 29

Milligan (Re) (1991), I C.P.C. (3d) 12 (Gen. Div.). It is implicit in this provision that a member of the bar in good standing has the right to appear in any court in Ontario. The inherent right of a trial judge to control his own court process does not carry with it the right to choose which counsel are to appear before him.

Section 50

Subsec. (1) repealed and the following substituted [S.O.] 1991, Vol. 2, c. 41, s. 4:

(1)　Except where otherwise provided by law,

TABLE III (cont'd)

(a)   no person, other than a member whose rights and privileges are not suspended, shall act as a barrister or solicitor or hold himself or herself out as or represent himself or herself to be a barrister or solicitor or practise as a barrister or solicitor; and

(b)   no temporary member shall act as a barrister or solicitor or practise as a barrister or solicitor except to the extent permitted by subsection 28.1(3).

Source: *Ontario Statute Citator*, April 1993 (Aurora, Ontario: Canada Law Book Inc., 1993).

In the illustration, section 29 is shown as having received judicial consideration, while section 50 is shown as having been amended.

Case citators provide lists of cases and indicate subsequent judicial consideration. For example, *The Canadian Abridgment's Revised Second Edition* (cited Can. Abr. (2nd)) - *Canadian Case Citations* is a multi-volume set (with hardbound and softcover supplements) which contains lists of all the cases digested in *The Abridgment* which have been applied, considered, distinguished, followed, overruled, referred to, affirmed, reversed, set aside, varied, or, from which leave to appeal was refused or granted in a later decision.

Annotators are similar to case citators in that they indicate subsequent judicial consideration, including the disposition of all leaves to appeal, but they differ from citators in that the cases cited are indexed according to volume and page numbers rather than by case name. See, for example, the *Dominion Law Reports'* .... "Table of Annotations".

Words and Phrases are works which provide citations to cases (and sometimes to statutes) which contain definitions of selected words and/or phrases. Often they include extracts from the actual decision. Legal dictionaries provide definitions of legal terms and common words with special meanings at law, often with reference to judicial authority. The distinction between a dictionary and words and phrases is that the latter provides definitions from the courts (and sometimes from statutes) while the former attempts to define all legal terms whether or not they have been the subject of judicial definition.

Textbooks and treatises are comprehensive studies of particular areas of the law and often include tables of cases, tables of statutes, as well as case and statute references. Legal periodicals are regularly published collections of articles, case notes, and book reviews.

The following outline covers the major sources of secondary materials in a law library. The discussion of each major Canadian and English encyclopedia and/or digest is in five parts.

1. Scope
2. Time-Frame
3. Format
4. Finding Aids
5. Research Techniques

A. ENCYCLOPEDIAS

1. Canadian

(A) THE CANADIAN ENCYCLOPEDIC DIGEST THIRD EDITION

There are two parts to *The Canadian Encyclopedic Digest*. The first part covers matters relating to Ontario (cited C.E.D. (Ont. 3d)) and the second concerns the prairies and British Columbia (cited C.E.D. (West 3d)).

Scope

The C.E.D. (Ont. 3d) contains a general statement of all the provincial laws of Ontario and the federal laws of Canada. It also includes selected case law from the other common law provinces, England and other common law jurisdictions.

The C.E.D. (West 3d) is identical in scope, but covers provincial legislation for Alberta, British Columbia, Manitoba and Saskatchewan.[1]

Time-Frame

The first edition of *The Canadian Encyclopedic Digest* was published in 1926 and covered then current case and statute law, as well as a selection of earlier laws which the publishers believed were still relevant and would be usefully included in the second edition. The third edition was published between 1973 and 1986 in a looseleaf format. Individual looseleaf volumes are supplied with monthly inserts and provide a continuing present statement of the law. The cut-off date for material included in the various parts of individual volumes is noted on the front of each looseleaf sheet.

Format

The third edition of *The Canadian Encyclopedic Digest* (Ontario) consists of 34 main volumes and a one-volume *Research Guide and Key*. The *Statutes Concordance* volumes (which include an "Alphabetical Table of Revised Statutes of Ontario") has been published in conjunction with C.E.D. (Ont. 3d).[2] The main

---

[1] Territorial information is occasionally included.
[2] The C.E.D. (West 3d) consists of 35 volumes.

volumes contain a statement of law in narrative form, organized under 151 subject titles and alphabetically arranged, and they are annotated with footnote references to case and statute citations.

The arrangement under each subject title in each looseleaf binder is as follows:

1. Yellow Pages

(a)   "Pending Legislation" - This is a new section which replaces "Recent Legislation". This new section appears on the first page of the body of the yellow pages. It notifies the reader of any bills or acts subject to proclamation which have a direct bearing on a title. This section is updated with the supplement and to keep track of bills or provisions which are in force the reader should refer to *Canadian Current Law - Legislation* issues.

(b)   Notes - These constitute the body of the yellow pages. They serve to inform the reader of any additions, changes, and deletions relating to specific paragraph numbers of the main text (white pages).

(c)   "Table of Cases" - This section gives citations for cases that are dealt with in the supplement.

(d)   "Table of Statutes" (*i.e.*, R.S.C. 1985 and R.S.O. 1990) - Reference to this table helps to update a statement of law which includes references to the specific sections of the statute and paragraph numbers.

(e)   "Table of Regulations" - This provides supplementary regulation citations for the main text.

NOTE: These sections are omitted when there has been no change since the last revision.

2. White Pages

Each title contains the following headings:

(a)   "Table of Classification" (otherwise known as "Table of Contents") - This untitled table is found at the beginning of each title. It provides an overview of all the subtopics covered by the given title. References are to paragraph numbers.

(b)   "Table of Cases" - This is a consolidation of all the case citations referred to in the main text, as well as to other cases from outside Ontario. References are to paragraph numbers.

(c)   "Table of Statutes" - This is a consolidation of all the federal, provincial, and territorial statutes referred to in the footnotes to the discussion of each title. The references are to sections of the statutes and paragraph numbers of the main text.

(d) "Table of Rules and Regulations" - Each main title may or may not include a "Table of Rules" and/or a "Table of Regulations". The references are to sections of the statutes and paragraph numbers of the main text.

(e) General statements of the law, identified by paragraph numbers, are drawn from case and statute law. Refer to the "Table of Classification" to locate the specific topic under the title.

(f) "Index" - This section provides the subject index to the main text, as well as a cross-reference to other relevant subject titles in the C.E.D. (Ont. 3d). Again, each subject can be found by locating the paragraph numbers.

NOTE: Some titles may use other primary sources, and therefore include other miscellaneous tables.

The C.E.D. is kept current by replacement of the looseleaf white pages and by the yellow-page supplements to each title within a volume; each title being updated approximately once a year. Individual titles in the C.E.D. may be brought forward from the cut-off date noted on the looseleaf sheets by referring to *Canadian Current Law - Case Law Digests* and *Canadian Current Law - Legislation*.

Finding Aids

The Canadian Encyclopedic Digest, Third Edition, Research Guide and Key (hereinafter referred to as *The Key*)

Both the Ontario and Western editions have a one-volume key. This work features five main parts - "Research Guide", "Contents Key", "Statutes Key", "Rules and Regulations Key", and "Index Key". The main text of *The Key* is printed on white pages and is consolidated and republished annually. Supplements to *The Key* are printed on yellow paper and are published throughout the current year. The "Index Key" is updated throughout the year.

CONTENTS KEY

This key contains a list of the subject titles, arranged alphabetically, used in the C.E.D. together with references to the volume and title numbers for each subject. Thus, if the title is known, the "Contents Key" provides a convenient entry point into the main set.

STATUTES KEY

This key contains a consolidation of all provincial, territorial, and federal statutes appearing in the individual "Table of Statutes" for all C.E.D. titles. The cut-off point for material included in the white pages of *The Key* is noted on the first page. New material is published in the yellow-page supplement to *The Key*.

Statutes are listed alphabetically, and references are to volume, title, and paragraph numbers, except for Income Tax and Labour Law which also include a reference to part numbers. The "Statutes Key" may assist the student to quickly find a statement of law and a case citation dealing with the desired statutory provision.

RULES AND REGULATIONS KEY
This key contains a consolidation of all provincial, territorial, and federal rules in the "Tables of Rules" with separate alphabetical listings of each, and provincial, territorial, and federal regulations in "Tables of Regulations" with separate alphabetical listings of each for all C.E.D. titles published up to the latest update. New material is published in the yellow-page supplement to *The Key*. The rules are listed alphabetically and references are to volumes, titles, and paragraph numbers within those titles, except for Income Tax and Labour Law which also include a reference to part numbers.

INDEX KEY
This index covers all titles published with cross-references to locate the appropriate entry in the "Index". References are to volume, title, and paragraph numbers within those titles. For new materials refer to the yellow-page supplement.

Research Techniques

First, consult the "Index" in *The Key* for the topic under investigation, unless you know the volume number and title under which your subtopic falls. If the latter, consult the "Index" at the back of the title for the selected volume. This provides a detailed list of subtopics, as well as the relevant paragraph numbers. Locate the relevant paragraph numbers in the white pages. Your research can be updated by referring to the same paragraph numbers in the yellow pages at the beginning of the title. If the paragraph numbers do not appear in this supplement, then there have been no changes to that point of law. Update further by researching current issues of *Canadian Current Law*. The title page to the supplement indicates the cut-off date for material collected from earlier issues of *Canadian Current Law*.

2. English

(A) HALSBURY'S LAWS OF ENGLAND, FOURTH EDITION (CITED AS HALSBURY)

Scope

This work contains a general statement of the laws of the United Kingdom and selected case and statute law of Commonwealth countries. In addition, the law of the European Communities is covered in detail in volumes 51 and 52.

Time-Frame

The first edition of *Halsbury's Laws of England* was published between 1907 and 1917 and consisted of 31 volumes; the second edition consisted of 37 volumes and was published between 1931 and 1942; and, the third edition consisted of 43 volumes published between 1952 and 1964. Canadian students often find this edition to be more useful than the fourth edition, published between 1973 and 1987. Each volume in the set provides a statement of the law current at the time of publication. The cut-off date for each volume is noted on the "List of Contributors" page. It is updated by the reissue of specific volumes, annually by the publication of the two-volume *Cumulative Supplement*, and monthly by the *Current Service*.

Format

The fourth edition consists of 52 main volumes and several volumes of tables and indices: volume 53 - *Consolidated Tables of Statutes and Statutory Instruments* and *Table of European Communities Material*, volume 54 - *Consolidated Table of Cases*; volumes 55 and 56 - *Consolidated Indexes A-I and J-Z*.

The text is arranged in numbered paragraphs, each of which states the law on a particular topic and provides footnote references to statutes, statutory instruments and case law which serve as authority for the statements made in the text. The main set is kept current by the *Cumulative Supplement* and the *Current Service*. Each volume contains some or all of the following tables: "Table of Statutes", "Table of Statutory Instruments", "Table of European Communities Legislation", "Table of Treaties, Conventions, etc.", "Table of Other Enactments" and "Table of Cases". Each separate title within a volume has a "Table of Contents" which provides subjects and subtopics with reference to paragraph numbers. At the back of each volume is a topical index, as well as an index for "Words and Phrases", and entries in both indices refer to paragraph numbers.

Finding Aids

There are six main finding aids for the fourth edition:
  (*i*)   *Consolidated Index*;
  (*ii*) Indices to individual volumes;
  (*iii*) "Tables of Contents" for individual titles;
  (*iv*) *Cumulative Supplement*;
  (*v*)   *Current Service*; and
  (*vi*) *Canadian Converter, Third Edition*.

(i) Consolidated Index. This is a multi-volume work listing a great number of topical words which serve as an entry point to general areas of the law and to

particular volumes of the main set. References in the work are to volume and paragraph numbers.

(ii) Indices (to Individual Volumes). Individual volumes of the main set contain detailed topical indices to each title included in the volume. For example, the title "Contract" is indexed at the back of volume 9(1), beginning at page 890. References in the indices are to paragraph numbers.

(iii) Tables of Contents. Individual volumes of the main set contain a "Table of Contents" for each title included in the volume. The tables are arranged to emphasize the major subjects within each title. References in the tables are to paragraph numbers.

(iv) Cumulative Supplement. This publication serves as an annual encyclopedia and brings forward the information in the main work. Any changes or additions which affect or relate to a statement or citation in any particular paragraph or in a footnote thereto is noted in the *Supplement* under the same paragraph number and heading or, where it does not directly affect the paragraph of the main work, in a new paragraph placed so as to continue, as far as possible, the scheme of arrangement of the main work. Cases mentioned in the *Supplement* and decided after 1973 are summarized in *Halsbury's Laws of England Annual Abridgment.* The *Supplement* also includes a "Table of Cases", "Table of Statutes", and a "Cumulative Index" which refers to both volume and paragraph numbers. The *Supplement* brings the main work up to date to October 31st preceding its publication. Any developments in the law after this date are then noted in *Current Service* (see (*v*) below).

(v) Current Service. This is a multi-faceted looseleaf work which features a "Monthly Review" and a "Noter-Up". This two-volume work also includes alphabetical lists of "Abbreviations" and "Arrangement of Titles". There are also sections on "Cases", "Statutes", "Statutory Instruments", "Index", "Commencement of Statutes", "Destination Tables", "Personal Injury", "Practice", "Articles", "Words and Phrases" and "European Communities Material". The "Monthly Review" provides summaries of recent reported and unreported judgments and may be used to keep the main volumes up to date in so far as they are not already updated by the annual *Supplement,* as well as to update matters summarized in the *Supplement* itself.

    The "Noter-Up" completes the updating of the fourth edition and the *Cumulative Supplement* by supplying the many detailed annotations needed to maintain the accuracy of an encyclopedia. The order of the material is identical to that in the *Supplement* (*i.e.*, the same volume, title, and paragraph order of the main work), to which you should refer first for developments since publication of the original or reissued volumes. It is specified where the material in this "Noter-Up" updates paragraphs in the *Supplement* rather than in the main work.

Summaries of statutes, case law and other material are to be found in the "Monthly Reviews" in Binder No. 1, and these are fully tabled and indexed.

(vi) Canadian Converter to Halsbury's Laws of England, Third Edition. This is a multi-volume companion set to *Halsbury's Laws of England, Third Edition.* One volume of the *Canadian Converter* accompanies approximately every five volumes of the main set. The *Canadian Converter* provides Canadian annotations to the text of the main set by listing cases and statutes from the common law jurisdictions of Canada under the corresponding title and paragraph number of the main volumes. The *Canadian Converter* is kept up to date by periodic "replacement" editions.

Research Techniques

A. If the title or subject is unknown:

Step 1:
Consult volume 55 or 56 of the *Consolidated Index* and locate the topic under investigation. Note the relevant volume (in bold type) and paragraph numbers to the main set. Consult the "List of Volumes, Paragraph Numbers and Titles" to determine under which title the subject falls.

NOTE: The *Consolidated Index* is often outdated by reissue volumes. If the subject is not where the index indicated, refer to the "List of Volumes, Paragraph Numbers and Titles" in the *Cumulative Supplement* to find its new location.

Step 2:
Consult the given volume and paragraph numbers and note the references to the authorities which support the statements of law.

Step 3:
Consult the *Cumulative Supplement* and, if available, locate the given volume and the paragraph numbers of particular interest to the topic under investigation. Note any further textual or footnote information.

Step 4:
Consult the "Noter-Up" in the *Current Service* looseleaf binder for any new materials since the publication of the *Cumulative Supplement.*

Example:

To find English cases on the International Convention on Marine Pollution, refer first to volume 56 of the *Consolidated Index* to the fourth edition. There you will find the main heading "MARINE POLLUTION" and the subheading "International Convention". The index directs you to volume 52, paragraph 18.212n3 (found on page 828). Next, check the list of titles. The topic falls under the heading "European Community". Look up the paragraph in the main volume. When you next refer to the *Cumulative Supplement*, you will find (under the same volume and paragraph number as in the main set) that you should refer to EC Commission Regulation 2158/93 for the application of the Convention. Lastly, use the same number in the Noter-Up to find the most recent changes.

NOTE: the European Community materials have their own section in the Noter-Up Binder.

Step 5:
Consult the most recent "replacement" volume of the *Canadian Converter, Halsbury's Laws of England, Third Edition* (the green-band set). Subject titles are noted on the spine. Select the book which contains the given subject heading and scan the numbered paragraphs for desired subtopics. References are to the volume and paragraph numbers in the third edition of *Halsbury's Laws of England*. Note the references to case authorities and legislation.

B. If the title or subject is known:

Step 1:
Scan the title names on the spines of individual volumes for the desired title.

Step 2:
Consult the "Table of Contents" for that particular title in the volume and scan the headings and topic listings for the topic under investigation. Note and consult the appropriate paragraph number for the desired textual and footnote information.

Step 3:
Consult the *Cumulative Supplement* and *Current Service* to update the search following steps 3 and 4 in Research Technique "A" above.

Step 4:
Follow the procedure outlined in step 5 in Research Technique "A" above to find Canadian authorities on the topic under investigation.

B. DIGESTS

1. Canadian

The Canadian Abridgment Revised Second Edition (cited Can. Abr. (2nd)) is a comprehensive, seven-part work compiled to assist legal researchers locate cases by a variety of means.

Scope

The Case Digests (the red and black set) contain a digest of "Reported Decisions of Canadian courts, and tribunals since the beginning of law reporting; unreported decisions of courts of appeal since 1987."

Time-Frame

First published in 1809 and continues to date.

Format

The revised second edition of *The Case Digests* consists of an original set of multiple volumes each containing digests of case law. The set was published between 1981 and 1993 and is referred to as the "Main Work". The cut-off date for each "Main Work" volume is noted on the title page.

The digests of case law in *The Abridgment* are organized according to a comprehensive table of classification known as the *Canadian Abridgment Key & Research Guide*. This key is made up of subject titles from "Absentees and Missing Persons" to "Waters and Watercourses", broken down into subheadings. Table IV is an excerpt from the "Key Classification Table" located in *The Canadian Abridgment Key & Research Guide*, on page 2-171.

TABLE IV

CLASSIFICATION TABLE

I. NATURE OF CONTRACT

1. **What constitutes contract**
2. **Agreements between near relations**
   - *domestic contracts, see FAMILY LAW; recovery for benefits conferred between family members in anticipation of reward, see RESTITUTION V.5*
3. **Judgments as contracts of record**

II. PARTIES TO CONTRACT

1. **General**
2. **Joint, several, joint and several contracts**
3. **Capacity**
   - capacity of infants, see FAMILY LAW; capacity of directors and officers of corporations, see CORPORATIONS; partners, see PARTNERSHIP; capacity of agents, see AGENCY
   a. Drunkenness
   b. Mental incapacity
   c. Other disabilities
4. **Privity**
   - undisclosed principals, see AGENCY VII.2.e
   a. General
   b. Third party beneficiary
      i. General
      ii. Cestui que trust
         -formation and nature of trust relationship generally, see TRUST AND TRUSTEES

In the table above, the main headings under the subject title "CONTRACTS" are assigned large script roman numerals; the subheadings are assigned consecutive numbers and the most specific headings are assigned a letter or a small script roman numeral. These designations may be used to search for case digests in all parts of the set.

The "Main Work" volumes are updated on an ongoing basis by softcover supplements or by reissue volumes containing material not included in the main volumes. The earliest supplements for the revised second edition appeared in 1982. The subject "damage", for example, in volume R12A of the "Main Work", has been updated by a softcover supplement, R12A (supplement). The "Main Work" volumes R9-R11D and supplement volumes, R9-R11D (supplements) were published in May 1997 as reissue volumes R9-R11D. The cut-off date for each supplement or reissue volume is noted on the title page. New supplements are published every year and reissue volumes are released periodically.

The Canadian Current Law - Case Law Digests are monthly softcover volumes completing update searches past the end of the previous year.

Finding Aids and Research Techniques

The Canadian Abridgment Key & Research Guide (hereinafter referred to as the *Abridgment Key*)

This is a single-volume looseleaf finding aid to *The Case Digests*. It includes a classification key for all case law in this revised edition. The *Abridgment Key* may also be used as a table of contents to help students gain a perspective of the scope of the subject-matter covered in a selected area of the law, identify legal concepts, and locate case law under selected subject titles and subheadings in the main set.

Finding a Case by Legal Topic

Step 1:
Determine the appropriate subject title for your search by consulting the *Abridgment Key*. The *Abridgment Key* contains detailed entries so that you can find your title by looking up a term which best describes your issue. The "Subject Titles Table" is a useful entry point to the *Key*. The *Abridgment* overview classifies subjects by their umbrella areas of law (*i.e.* Criminal Law, Torts).

Step 2:
Ascertain that you have found the right subject area by checking the "Scope Note". The "Scope Note" describes the contents of the subject title and refers you to related subject titles that might be relevant. Narrow down the search to one or two specific classifications, and note the relevant classification numbers.

Step 3:
Consult the main revised or reissue volume of *The Case Digests* which contains the selected subject title. Scan the digests and note the names and citations of what would appear to be relevant cases. Next, consult the softcover supplement to the main volume, if one has been issued. The supplement covers digests from the cut-off date noted in the main volume to the end of the last year.

Step 4:
To update your research, past the end of the last year, refer to the monthly softcover issues of *Canadian Current Law - Case Law Digests*.

General Index

These looseleaf pages are ιʊund in the index binder along with "Words and Phrases", "Corrigenda", and "Case Law Update". The *General Index* is an alphabetically arranged subject index to the digest. The white pages of the *General Index* refer the user to digests in the main volumes while the yellow pages refer to the supplements.

Using the *Index* to Find Digests of Cases by Topic

Step 1:
Look up the selected legal word(s) in the white pages of the *General Index*. The entries use key words and phrases and are arranged from the general to the specific. The entry next to each subtopic directs the user to a volume and a digest

number in the "Main Work" and Supplement. The following is an excerpt from the "Key Classification Table" located in the *General Index* at page 80.

Example:

FORMATION OF CONTRACT
• acceptance
• • acceptance by conduct
• **R7B**Reiss. 744-788
    communication of acceptance
• **R7B**Reiss. 710-743

This tells the reader that case law digests dealing with the "acceptance of a contract" can be found in volume **R7B** Reissue of the "Main Work", digest numbers 744-788 and 710-743.

NOTE: The *Index* is alphabetized by main headings. Subheadings (indicated with one bullet) are also listed alphabetically. They are then broken down into two bullet headings and so on.

Step 2:
Note the title and Key Number of your topic. This number is found beside the digest number. It will look something like this: VIII.2.a.iii. Consult the back of the *General Index: Case Law Update*. The entries are listed alphabetically by title and are subdivided by key number. Note the digest number(s).

Consolidated Table of Cases

Using the *Table of Cases* to Find Legal Digests and Citations

To find a case by case name, refer to the *Consolidated Table of Cases*. This component of *The Abridgment* is the multi-volume gold and black set which arranges cases alphabetically by case name. This set consists of four hard-cover volumes, four annual soft-cover supplements, a quarterly soft-cover supplement and the monthly case law digests.

NOTE: The hard-cover volumes only contain cases dated 1995 or earlier. The soft-cover volumes are updated annually to reflect new cases. The most recent cases appear in the quarterly and monthly publications.

Step 1:
Refer to the hard-cover volume. Search for your case alphabetically. If the case was decided after 1995, searching the hard-cover volume is redundant.

Step 2:
Refer to the soft-cover volume. Search for your case alphabetically.

Step 3:
Refer to the quarterly issue. Search for your case alphabetically.

Step 4:
Refer to the table of cases in the monthly *Current Law - Case Digests* since the most recent quarterly publication. Search alphabetically.

The entry for each case in the table will give the case name (style of cause), any alternate style of cause, the year of the decision, citation(s), the court level of the decision, the result, court level of any higher decision, and the location of the digest. It should be noted that each case is cross-referenced according to the name of the defendant so, if one looked under *Chutorian* v. *Clark*, the table would direct the reader to see *Clark* v. *Chutorian*.

Canadian Case Citations

This is a multi-volume set which provides lists of cases showing, *inter alia*, how decisions have been dealt with in subsequent judgments. In particular, the lists show whether a decision has been affirmed, applied, considered, distinguished, followed, not followed or overruled, reversed, varied, referred to, set aside or quashed, or if leave to appeal was refused or granted.

A 22-volume consolidation of all material up until July 1998 has been published under the title *Canadian Case Citations, 1867- July 1998*. A cumulative supplement and monthly issues of *Canadian Case Citations* cover the period after July 1998.

Finding Cases Which Have Considered a Selected Earlier Case

If a case was decided before July 1998, refer to the main volume of *Canadian Case Citations*, and then refer to any subsequent volumes (including the soft-cover issues) to bring your research up to date. If the date of the case is known to be after July 1998, check only the appropriate supplement volume(s) and monthly issues of *Canadian Case Citations* after the cut-off date noted on the cover of the cumulative supplement to *Canadian Case Citations*.

NOTE: Law libraries which do not have the single-volume consolidation will usually have a 26-volume set referred to as *Cases Judicially Considered* covering the period 1867-1990.

Canadian Statute Citations

The *Canadian Statute Citations* is a multi-volume national statute citator, re-cording decisions of Canadian courts and tribunals, and noting the statutes and rules of court which have been interpreted or applied in them. This work is the continuation of the publication formerly called *Statutes Judicially Considered*. Bound volumes are issued for a year or for a number of years and the current year is serviced with a soft-cover supplement.

Finding Cases Which Have Considered a Statute or Section of a Statute for a Given Jurisdiction

Step 1:
Begin your search in the hard-cover volume which contains the relevant juris-diction.[3] The statutes are listed alphabetically by short title.

NOTE: The volumes list statutes considered generally first and then list specific sections of the legislation. As well, be certain that you have located the correct year or revision for your statute; statutes with multiple versions are listed chronologically.

Step 2:
Refer to the soft-cover supplement following the same steps as for the hard cover.

Step 3:
Refer to the quarterly supplement.

Step 4:
Refer to the monthly editions issued since the most recent quarterly publication.
This component of the *Abridgment* also contains a one-volume issue (sup-plemented by soft-cover updates) called *Rules Judicially Considered*. This work lists all Canadian jurisdictions alphabetically, and all the rules considered are listed alphabetically therein. A list of foreign rules considered can be found at the beginning of the volume.

NOTE: Foreign rules are listed alphabetically by their English titles.

---

[3]   There are separate volumes for federal legislation and for most provinces. As well, students can search international statutes which have been considered by Canadian courts.

Canadian Current Law - Legislation

Each issue of *Legislation* contains sections on "Progress of Bills", "Statutes Amended, Repealed or Proclaimed in Force" and "Regulations". Individual issues are collected into a *Legislation Annual*, which began in 1989. In order to track the progress of a bill, check the statutes enacted section of the most recent *Legislation Annual* to see if the desired bill has been enacted in the last year. Look first under a jurisdiction heading and then by name. Update the search by referring to the successive issues of *Canadian Current Law - Legislation* after the most recent *Legislation Annual*.

In order to see whether a selected statute has been amended, repealed, or proclaimed in force, refer to the "Statutes Amended, Repealed or Proclaimed in Force" section in the earliest relevant *Legislation Annual*. Look under the appropriate jurisdiction and statute name. Update the research in issues of *Canadian Current Law - Legislation* published after the most recent *Legislation Annual*.

In order to determine if a regulation has been made, repealed, or amended, consult the "Regulations" section in the earliest relevant *Legislation Annual*. Look for the regulation first by the jurisdiction and then by the name of its enabling statute. Update the research by referring to issues of *Canadian Current Law - Legislation* published after the most recent *Legislation Annual*.

Words and Phrases

The blue bound series of *The Abridgment* allows cases to be located by key words or phrases which have been considered or defined by Canadian courts. Each case listed includes an extract from the decision containing the particular word or phrase.

Step 1:
Consult the alphabetical listings in the hard-cover volumes. These volumes contain cases up to 1992.

Step 2:
Update your search in the soft-cover supplement.

Step 3:
Refer to the "Words and Phrases" section of *Canadian Current Law - Case Digests*.

Index to Canadian Legal Literature

The *Index to Canadian Legal Literature* is a multi-volume set which provides references to articles and books, as well as to annotations, case commentary on important judgments, and significant changes in statute law. The Index has five parts:

(1)   "Subject Index";
(2)   "Author Index";
(3)   "Tables of Cases";
(4)   "Table of Statutes"; and
(5)   "Book Review Index".

Using the Subject Index to Find Articles on a Selected Topic

Searching publications from 1985 onwards.

Step 1:
Search each volume alphabetically by Library of Congress[4] titles. Scan the columns for potentially helpful articles.

Step 2:
Update your search in the soft-cover issues of *Canadian Current Law - Canadian Legal Literature.*

NOTE: For a pre-1985 search, check the subject authorities table in volume 3 of the 1981-1984 series. Go to the *Table of Contents* in the three volumes to find the location of a list of publications.

Searching by statute[5]

Step 1:
Look for your statute under the relevant subject heading for literature written between 1981-1987. For 1988 onwards, consult the table of statutes in each volume.

Step 2:
To update your search, refer to the table of statutes in *Canadian Current Law - Canadian Legal Literature.*

Canadian Weekly Law Sheet (cited as C.W.L.S.)

The *Canadian Weekly Law Sheet* is a weekly publication providing digests of all Canadian cases reported during that week, some unreported cases, and notes from official gazettes on new statutes, regulations, Royal Assents and proclamations. There are citations to the full text of the cases digested.

---

4   These titles are more intuitive than those found in *The Abridgment.*
5   All other indices follow the same pattern as a search by subject.

All-Canada Weekly Summaries (cited as A.C.W.S.)

This is a weekly looseleaf service of case summaries in civil matters from every jurisdiction in Canada. Every summary is preceded by subject classification and key-word entries. There are no citations to the full text of the cases digested. Decisions are usually published within 8-14 weeks after they are rendered. The digests are collected in bound annual volumes, each served with a separate index. For the beginning student, the A.C.W.S. serves primarily as an updating tool in conventional library research. In addition, it may be used as a key-word glossary to prepare computer search strategies in general in the A.C.W.S. (Canada Law Book) database accessed through QUICKLAW.

2. English Digests

The Digest: Annotated British, Commonwealth and European Cases (hereinafter referred to as *The Digest*; formerly *The English and Empire Digest*)

Scope

This work provides, in digest form, all the case law of England, together with a considerable body of cases from the courts of Scotland, Ireland, Canada, Australia, New Zealand, and other countries of the British Commonwealth. It also contains extensive annotations denoting every instance in which the case digested was referred to in any subsequent judgment.

Time-Frame

The first edition of *The Digest* was published between 1919 and 1932 in 47 volumes. It was replaced by a 56-volume second (blue-band) edition during the period 1950 to 1970. A third (green-band) edition was started in 1971. The cut-off date for a volume is noted on the page following the title page.

The main volumes of *The Digest* are kept up to date by *Continuation* volumes and an annual *Cumulative Supplement*. The *Supplement* does this, first, by extending the *Consolidated Table of Cases* from the date of publication to the present; second, by indicating where the text of the various titles has been amended or changed by subsequent cases and developments in the law. The main part of the *Supplement* is a "Noter-Up" which contains new case digests and annotations relevant to the various titles in the main volume. The numbers used in the *Supplement* correspond with those in the main volumes. Small letter suffixes and roman numerals in brackets are appended to the numbers to show that a case or cases in the *Supplement* follow on naturally from the similarly numbered case in the main volumes. Where a new case appropriately appears at the beginning of a digest section, or before an existing case in the *Supplement*, the case is given a capital letter suffix.

Every few years the case digests in the annual *Supplements* are printed in a *Continuation* volume. Eventually, the materials in the latest *Supplement* and *Continuation* volumes are consolidated as reissued or new edition volumes. However, because at any given time only a limited number of titles are consolidated and reissued, all or parts of a *Continuation* volume may continue to be useful.

Format

The current green-band edition of *The Digest* consists of 51 main volumes, organized under 168 titles and several volumes of tables and indices. Each main volume includes:

(i)   a "Table of Contents" which follows the arrangement of the contents of the titles in *Halsbury's Laws of England, Fourth Edition*;

(ii)   cross-references to a general statement of the law in *Halsbury's Laws of England, Fourth Edition*, and to related titles and topics;

(iii)   digests of English cases in consecutively numbered paragraphs;

(iv)   annotations to the digest of English cases;

(v)   digests of "Scottish, Irish and Commonwealth [including Canada] Cases" (these form part of the consecutive numbering scheme adopted for the digests of English cases); and

(vi)   a "Table of Cases".

Finding Aids

There are four main finding aids for *The Digest* - the *Consolidated Index*, the *Consolidated Table of Cases*, the "Tables of Contents" for individual titles of *The Digest*, and the annual *Cumulative Supplement*.

Research Techniques

There are two ways to locate a case in *The Digest*: by subject matter; or by case name.

(i)   When the subject matter is known, scan the spines of the main volume (which are alphabetical) and select the appropriate volume or refer to the list of titles in the *Supplement* to point you to the relevant volume. The *Table of Contents* will help narrow your search within the broader headings.

Another approach is to consult the *Consolidated Index* and search by title. This table will list relevant volumes (in bold type), titles (in italics) and case numbers. This search method may be more helpful when the student has a more specific search topic such as "offer to consumers".

The index lists the word "**OFFER**" and contains "consumers" as a subheading. You are then directed to **12(1)** *Contr* 1059. After consulting the list of title abbreviations at the front of volume 12(1), you know to look to paragraph 1059 under the title Contracts.

(ii) To find a given case name, the digest of a case, and a citation to a report series, consult the *Consolidated Table of Cases*,[6] find the case name in the table, and obtain, as directed, the relevant title and volume number in the main volume:

Brixham Investments Ltd. v. Hansink (1971) (CAN) 12(1) Contr

Then, consult the "Table of Cases" in the main volume to find the case number, *e.g.*, 1504. Note the textual entry and citation.

In order to find cases that are more recent than the last main volume (which can lapse up to ten years), refer to the table of cases at the front of the *Cumulative Supplement*. There you will find the case name, the abbreviated title and a case number. Refer to the list of title abbreviations and turn to that case number for a summary. At the end of the summary, you will be directed to the long version of the decision in a case report series.

To find the various topics under which the case of *Barnett v. Sanker* has been classified, a digest of the case, and a citation to one or more report series, consult the *Consolidated Table of Cases* volume which includes the cases beginning with the letters A-F. At page 171, locate the case and note the references to **7(1) Betting**; **12(1) Contr** and **17(1) Custom**. Consult the "Table of Cases" in volume 12(1) and locate case number 3829 (referring to the *Barnett* case), on page 497; consult the "Table of Cases" in volume 17(1) and note that the reference to the *Barnett* case is page 99, turn to that page and locate the case at number 944; and then consult the "Table of Cases" in volume 7(1) and note the reference to the *Barnett* case, number 118. Turn to that case and you will find it on page 28, under the title "Betting, Gaming and Lotteries".

Current Law (cited C.L.)

Scope

This work contains a comprehensive statement of contemporary English law and a selection of laws from Commonwealth jurisdictions.[7] In addition, it provides

---

[6] The "Reference Adaptor", located at the back of each volume, shows the change in case numbering following the publication of a reissued volume.

[7] Prior to 1991, there was a separate edition called *Scottish Current Law Yearbook*.

an exhaustive compilation of lists of cases and statutes which have been published or referred to in court.

Time-Frame

Current Law has been published on a monthly basis since 1947 and has covered developments in the law from that date forward.

Format

Current Law is a multi-faceted paperback publication which includes digests of reported and unreported cases, digests of statutes and statutory instruments, commencement dates of statutes and statutory instruments, titles of new books, and citations to articles. The *Current Law Monthly Digests* are consolidated in an annual bound volume, the *Current Law Year Book*, which replaces the paper parts.

Finding Aids

As a first step, consult the "How to Use Current Law" pamphlet. It gives an overview of all the services which *Current Law* provides and instructions on how to use them.

Every issue of *Current Law Monthly Digest* contains a digest of cases, a "Cumulative Table of Cases", a "Cumulative (Subject) Index", a table of "Words and Phrases", a table of "Dates of Commencement - Statutes", a "Statute Citator" and an "Alphabetical Table of Statutory Instruments". The "Table of Cases" provides a list of the names of all the cases reported, judicially considered or otherwise commented upon, during the current year. The *Index* serves the digest portion of *Current Law*. Under each topic heading there is a reference to a month, and a paragraph where the digest of, or notes on, the topic may be found.

A *Current Law Year Book* incorporates each of these tables and finding aids, as well as an "Index of Articles", an "Index of Books" and a "Table of SR & O and SI Affected by Statutory Instruments of [year]". A year book also may contain an index which spans several years. For example, the index in the *1989 Year Book* consolidated the indices for the year books 1987 to 1989. There is also a "Cumulative Subject Index" in the *1976 Year Book* for the period 1947 to 1976, and one in the *1986 Year Book* for the year books 1972 to 1986. The index in the *1992 Year Book* is only for that year. In these indices reference is made to the year book and the paragraph number.

NOTE: When there is no date preceding the paragraph number, that reference is to be found in the *Current Law Consolidation 1947-1951.*

The *Current Law Case Citator* consists of three main volumes - 1947-1976, 1977-88 and 1989 to date. The *Current Law Legislation Citator* consists of three volumes - 1947-71, 1972-88 and 1989 to date. These services are updated by the *Current Law Monthly Digest*.

The *Current Law Case Citators* list the name of any case reported since 1947, excepting cases of the current year, and all the report series and journals, if any, in which the case is found. These case citators contain separate headings for England and Scotland. In addition, the case citators indicate, with respect to any case of any date:

(i)   the full name of any case reported between 1947 and 1993;

(ii)   an extensive list of references to the legal reports and journals of each case;

(iii)   the reference to the paragraph in the *Current Law Year Book* where a case is digested; and

(iv)   the history of any case which has been judicially considered, followed, overruled, distinguished or otherwise commented on from 1947 to 1998.

The *Current Law Legislation Citators* include a "Statute Citator", a "Table of Statutory Instruments Affected" and an "Alphabetical Table of Statutes". From the *Legislation Citators*, which have been arranged in chronological order, it can promptly be ascertained:

(i)   what public general acts have been passed since 1947;

(ii)   in respect of any act of any date whether it has been repealed, amended or otherwise modified since 1947;

(iii)   in respect of any act of any date, what cases have been decided on it since 1947;

(iv)   in respect of any statute passed between 1947 and 1959, where it is summarized in the *Current Law* volumes and, for any statutes thereafter, the date of the Royal Assent;

(v)   from the "Legislation Not Yet in Force" table it can be determined which acts or sections have received Royal Assent but have not yet been brought into force and for which no commencement date has been fixed; and

(vi)   in respect of any statutory provision, the details of any statutory instrument issued since 1947.

There are also additional services now being offered. The *Current Law Statutes Annotated*, the *European Current Law* which is a monthly guide to recent legal development throughout Europe, and the *Current Law Year Books* 1986 to date on CD ROM.

Research Techniques

(i) To find case and statute law on a topic under investigation, consult the "Index 1947-76" in the *Current Law Year Book 1976* and scan the columns for the topic under investigation. References in the index are to a paragraph number in a year book or to the *Current Law Consolidation 1947-1951*. Then, consult the year book or *Consolidation* as directed for case and statute notes, and case digests. Next, consult the "Index 1972-1986" in the *Current Law Year Book 1986*, followed by the "Index 1987-1989" in the *1989 Year Book*. Bring the research forward by means of the indices at the back of subsequent year books, as well as the "Cumulative Index" at the back of the most recent issue of *Current Law Monthly Digest*, which provides the month and paragraph references for locating particular cases and statute law.

(ii) To find a selected case name, in order to ascertain where it has been reported and whether the case has subsequently been judicially considered, refer to the relevant *Current Law Case Citator (i.e.*, 1947-1976, 1977-88, 1989 to date) and the "Cumulative Table of Cases" in the most recent issue of *Current Law Monthly Digest*.

(iii) To find a selected section of a statute, in order to determine if it has been modified or received judicial consideration, refer to the relevant *Current Law Legislation Citator (i.e.*, 1947-71, 1972-88 and 1989 to date) and to the "Statute Citator" section in the most recent issue of *Current Law Monthly Digest*. If the consolidation of *Current Law Legislation Citator* for the last calendar year is not published at the time of your research, consult the "Statute Citator" section in the December issue of *Current Law Monthly Digest* and then refer to the most recent monthly digest.

C. CASE CITATORS

1. Canadian

The Canadian Abridgment, Second Edition, Canadian Case Citations

The Abridgment provides an extensive citation service for Canadian cases. The work is described, *supra*, at page 97.

Dominion Law Reports, Annotation Service

This publication provides a table of cases which have been judicially considered or disposed of on appeal from any decision reported in the *Dominion Law Reports*. The period covered is noted on the title page. The annotations are listed under the D.L.R. volume and page number where the original case was reported. The nature of the disposition or consideration is indicated by abbreviations which are explained in the introduction. The work is described, *supra*, at page 50.

NOTE: Several other works offer citations or annotations to Canadian cases. These include:

(i)   the *All England Law Reports* index volumes;

(ii)   all the report series published by Maritime Law Book Company. Each volume of the individual report series (referred to on page 53) and;

(iii)   Western Legal Publication (W.L.P.) database on QUICKLAW.

2. English

There are a number of English publications which provide case citations and annotations, including the *All England Law Reports* index volumes, *The Law Reports* index volumes, *The Digest*, and *Current Law Case Citator*. These have been described in detail in the foregoing materials.

D. STATUTE CITATORS

Canada Statute Citator
British Columbia Statute Citator
New Brunswick Statute Citator
Nova Scotia Law News Statutes Judicially Noticed
Nova Scotia Statute Citator
Ontario Statute Citator and Annotations
Statutes of Alberta Judicially Considered
Statutes of British Columbia Judicially Considered
Statutes of Manitoba Judicially Considered
Statutes of Saskatchewan Judicially Considered

E. WORDS AND PHRASES

1. Canadian

The Encyclopedia of Words and Phrases, Legal Maxims

J. Gardner, ed., *Words and Phrases, Legal Maxims* (Toronto: Thomson Canada (Carswell), 1986).

The fourth edition of this work, in looseleaf binders, covers definitions provided by Canadian courts between 1825 and 1985. Under each word or phrase, definitions are listed according to the hierarchy of the courts. This work offers the most comprehensive coverage of Canadian judicial definitions. It is updated by cumulative supplements.

The Canadian Abridgment, Second Edition, Words and Phrases (Revised)

This is a compilation of individual words and phrases which have been defined or interpreted by a court. *Words and Phrases* are set out in alphabetical order, together with one or more citations to cases which have considered the word or phrase. For a full description on using *Words and Phrases*, see the section on *The Abridgment* in this Chapter.

NOTE: Other sources of words and phrases include the *Western Weekly Reports* and all the report series published by Maritime Law Book Company.

2. English

Words and Phrases Legally Defined

J.B. Saunders, ed., *Words and Phrases Legally Defined* (London: Butterworths, 1988).
Words and Phrases Legally Defined provides judicial definitions from decisions in the House of Lords, the Privy Council and the superior courts of England, Canada, Australia and New Zealand. Under each word or phrase, there is an explanatory note followed by extracts from cases. Where relevant, the reader is referred to *Halsbury's Laws of England*. The third edition consists of four main volumes, plus an annual *Cumulative Supplement*.

NOTE: Other sources of words and phrases include the *Current Law Year Book* and *Current Law Monthly Digest*, the index volumes to *The Law Reports*, the *All England Law Reports, Halsbury's Laws of England*, and *The Digest*.

F. DICTIONARIES

In addition to the standard dictionaries of the English language, a legal dictionary is invaluable to anyone involved in the law. Legal dictionaries provide definitions of legal words and phrases and ordinary words and phrases expressly defined by the courts. The following publications are usually available in a university law library:

Stroud's Judicial Dictionary of Words and Phrases

J.S. James, ed., *Stroud's Judicial Dictionary of Words and Phrases*, 5th ed. (London: Sweet & Maxwell, 1986).
Published in its fifth edition in 1986, it consists of five volumes. Definitions are annotated with references to English cases and statutes and to Commonwealth cases. The set is kept up to date by a soft-cover cumulative supplement.

Jowitt's Dictionary of English Law

J. Burke, ed., *Jowitt's Dictionary of English Law*, 2nd ed. (London: Sweet & Maxwell, 1977).
E. Williams, ed., *Second Supplement to Jowitt's Dictionary of English Law*, (London: Sweet & Maxwell, 1985).
Published in 1977, this is a two-volume work with annotations to English statutes, cases and standard textbooks. It is now in its second edition and is updated by a hard-cover cumulative supplement published in 1985.

Osborn's Concise Law Dictionary

L. Rutherford & S. Bone, eds., *Osborn's Concise Law Dictionary*, 8th ed. (London: Sweet & Maxwell, 1993).
Published in its eighth edition in 1993, this is a "user friendly" single-volume work which provides selected annotations to English statutes and cases.

Mozley & Whiteley's Law Dictionary

H.N. Mozley, *Mozley & Whiteley's Law Dictionary*, 11th ed. by E.R. Hardy Ivamy (London: Butterworth & Co., 1993).
This single-volume work is now in its 11th edition. It provides definitions of legal terms and phrases of the past and present, as well as expositions of the law.

Black's Law Dictionary

J.R. Nolan & J.M. Nolan-Haley, *Black's Law Dictionary*, 6th ed. by West Publishing Company Editorial Staff (St. Paul: West Publishing, 1990).
Published in its sixth edition in 1990, *Black's Law Dictionary* is an exhaustive one-volume work with annotations to American cases and to older English cases and commentaries.

Canadian Law Dictionaries

J. Yogis, *Canadian Law Dictionary*, 4th ed. (New York: Barron's Educational Series, 1998).

R.S. Vasan, ed., *The Canadian Law Dictionary* (Don Mills, Ontario: Law and Business Publications, 1980).

D.A. Dukelow & B. Nuse, *The Dictionary of Canadian Law*, 2nd ed. (Scarborough, Ontario: Thomson Professional Pub. Canada, 1994).

Published first in 1983, Yogis' dictionary is a small paperbound volume which provides annotations to Canadian statutes and cases.

There are two other useful Canadian law dictionaries. Vasan's dictionary contains definitions of both words and phrases as sanctioned by Canadian decisions. Dukelow's dictionary contains both word lists and definitions.

G. CITATION RULES FOR CANADIAN LEGAL MATERIALS

E.C. Maier, *How to Prepare a Legal Citation* (New York: Barron's Educational Series, 1986).

McGill Law Journal, *Canadian Guide to Uniform Legal Citation*, 4th ed. (Toronto: Thomson Canada (Carswell), 1998).

The Osgoode Hall Law Journal Citation Guide, rev. and expanded by Board of Editors (Toronto: Osgoode Hall Law School, 1984).

J.W. Samuels, *Legal Citation for Canadian Lawyers* (Toronto: Butterworth & Co. (Canada), 1968).

C. Tang, *Guide to Legal Citation & Sources of Citation Aid: A Canadian Perspective*, 2nd ed. (Toronto: Thomson Canada (Carswell), 1988).

H. RESEARCH GUIDES

M.A. Banks et al., *Banks on Using a Law Library: A Canadian Guide to Legal Research*, 6th ed. (Toronto: Thomson Canada (Carswell), 1994).

E.M. Campbell et al., *Legal Research Materials and Methods*, 4th ed. (Sydney: The Law Book, 1996).

J.R. Castel & O.K. Latchman, *The Practical Guide to Canadian Legal Research*, 2nd ed. (Toronto: Thomson Canada (Carswell), 1996).

P. Clinch, *Using a Law Library* (London: Blackstone Press, 1992).

J. Dane & P.A. Thomas, *How to Use a Law Library*, 3rd ed. (London: Sweet & Maxwell, 1996).

E.M.A. Kwaw, *The Guide to Legal Analysis, Legal Methodology and Legal Writing* (Toronto: Emond Montgomery Publications, 1992).

D.T. MacEllven & M.J. McGuire, *Legal Research Handbook*, 4th ed. (Markham, Ontario: Butterworths Canada Ltd., 1998).

I. LEGAL PERIODICALS

Legal periodicals contain collections of varied writings on the law published at regular intervals (monthly, quarterly, etc.). The typical periodical contains several articles on subjects of current interest (often in considerable detail) book reviews, and "comments" on important recent cases. There are two types of periodicals: those of a general nature covering any legal subject (*e.g.*, *The Canadian Bar Review*, *Yale Law Journal*) and those of a specialized nature (*e.g.*, *Criminal Law Quarterly*). Some periodicals devote whole issues to an exhaustive discussion of one subject in its various aspects, such as town planning or juvenile delinquency.

Although most periodicals publish their own indices, the search for periodical literature most usefully begins with a general index. The most comprehensive is the *Index to Legal Periodicals* published for the American Association of Law Libraries. Commencing in 1908, it covers major articles, notes, case comments, and book reviews from periodicals published in the United States, Canada, the United Kingdom, Australia and New Zealand. The work is indexed by subject and author and currently includes a table of case comments and a book review index. It appears monthly, with quarterly and annual cumulations since its commencement, and triennial cumulations beginning in 1926. Legal articles in non-legal journals may be located in the *Index to Periodical Articles Related to Law*, which has been published since 1958. In addition, there is an *Index to Foreign Legal Periodicals*, published annually since 1960.

There are three major Canadian sources of legal periodical literature: the *Index to Canadian Legal Literature*, the *Canadian Abridgment, Second Edition*, the *Index to Canadian Legal Periodical Literature* and *Current Law Index*.

J. TEXTBOOKS AND TREATISES

Textbooks and treatises are generally comprehensive studies of a particular area of the law. Usually the author will refer to the most important primary materials on the subject, leading cases, statutes and regulations. These works are the best means of acquiring a general view of the law before starting a major piece of research into primary materials. Often, too, they give excellent detailed analyses of specific problems. Texts are best discovered by working through the library's on-line catalogue, but first-year law students will soon learn the names of the standard texts in the major established fields of law.

K. INTERNET RESOURCES

Several general legal research Web sites provide many links that can help a legal researcher navigate the Internet. These sites, which defy traditional description, are usually a combination of encyclopedia , digest and legal magazine, providing updates on recent decisions of courts and tribunals, links to academic articles, and breaking legal news.

In Canada, the University of Toronto provides a search engine, domestic and international decisions from courts and tribunals, and links to law school Web pages (which, in turn, provide a wealth of other useful links) online: Jurist Canada <http://jurist.law.utoronto.ca>. Other useful sites include: Findlaw Canada, online: <http://www.findlaw.com/search/countries/ca.html> and Canadalegal, online: <http://www.canadalegal.com> are other popular starting points.

CHAPTER 3

Suggestions for Legal Research and Writing

In many Canadian law schools the beginning student is asked to cast himself or herself in the role of an articling student in a law firm and to prepare a memorandum setting out the state of the law relevant to a given factual situation. This chapter will, first, outline a procedure for researching a problem, second, suggest a method of preparing a memorandum and, third, prescribe general rules of style applicable to most forms of legal writing.

A. RESEARCH

Methods of research vary considerably according to the area of the law. For example, a problem in contract law is usually researched in a different manner than a problem in constitutional or criminal law. As well, the type and number of services consulted depends on the complexity of the problem, the extent of the information known to the researcher, and the instructions given by the person requesting the research and a memorandum. The procedure outlined below may be followed to research a broad range of legal problems. It assumes little prior knowledge of legal issues and particular case names or statutes.

1. Identifying the Legal Issues

The process of identifying the legal issues raised by a given set of facts often is not clear-cut. Sometimes it is only as research proceeds that the issues become clearly defined, and facts which at first appeared insignificant assume more importance. Early on, it may be helpful to recognize that the purpose of the process is, first, to formulate a set of questions and, second, to decide which questions are important and which questions should not be pursued any further.

The first step in the process is to review the facts several times, decide which are relevant, and make a list of them. Consider the following legal problem:

> During a two-day corporate conference at a Holiday Inn near the Toronto airport, a senior male office supervisor of a Canadian subsidiary of a well-known U.S. food giant asked his personal secretary if she was "in the mood for a late dinner with champagne in his executive suite". The "invitation" followed a series of remarks that he had made about her work habits, after-hour interests, previous marital status, and personal dress and grooming

habits. The comments had been made over a period of several months and were usually confined to so-called "neutral territories", *i.e.*, at the water cooler, in the elevator, or in the cafeteria located in the office building where they both worked. The secretary turned down the offer in disgust and has asked the Ontario Human Rights Commission to review a complaint pursuant to section 7(2) of the *Ontario Human Rights Code*.

"Office supervisor", remarks about her "previous marital status" and the statement "Are you in the mood for a late dinner with champagne in my executive suite" are relevant facts. "U.S. food giant", "Holiday Inn", and "a two-day corporate conference" would normally be viewed as irrelevant facts.

As the second step in the process, the student should consult a legal index. Refer to the "General Index" to *The Canadian Abridgment, Revised Second Edition*, or consult the online subject catalogue in your library and find a textbook or a specialized looseleaf service, which deals with human rights. Scan *all* the major headings (in the "General Index"), select the appropriate one and carefully read *all* the subheadings to find the words which most closely relate to the issues raised by the legal problem.

NOTE: A legal index is, in essence, a listing of the legal topics of a book, or set of books, arranged alphabetically according to the major areas of the law. As a result, before looking at an index, it may be helpful to make a list of the concepts, *e.g.*, human rights, employer, employee and sexual harassment, which best describe the given factual situation. Further, take a few moments to clarify and describe: (1) the nature of the activity or event (*i.e.*, a proposition or advance by a member of the opposite sex), (2) the relationship between the parties (*i.e.*, employer-employee), (3) the place where the event or activity took place (*i.e.*, hotel conference room), and (4) the general subject area (*i.e.*, human rights).

This exercise may make it easier for you to match the facts of your legal problem with the legal topics in an index so that it will help you better define the legal issues.

The third step, then, is to read the relevant passages of the text, look for any facts and ideas which seem to describe or relate to your problem and note any references to cases and statutes. Table V, below, reproduces portions of the index from W.S. Tarnopolsky and W.F. Pentney, *Discrimination and The Law* (Don Mills, Ontario: Richard De Boo, 1985), which is now a looseleaf service.

TABLE V

Discrimination and The Law

Employment
    advertising, 12-1-12-4
    affirmative action defined with reference to, 4-80-4-81
    age discrimination, 7-5-7-11
        occupational qualifications, 7-20

TABLE V (cont'd)

---

in U.S., 7-5-7-11
harassment
statutory reform, 8-40-8-41
...
Sex discrimination
ability to perform, 8-58-8-63
...
dictionary definitions of "sex", 8-1-8-2
...
personality reasons, 8-44-8-47
pregnancy, see **Pregnancy**
protective motive, 8-43
retirement policy, 4-33
sexual harassment, 8-18-8-42
sexual orientation, 8-2-8-4
...
Sexual harassment
amounted to disparate treatment, female victim won, 8-21
Canadian cases, 8-23-8-40
course of conduct, 8-32-8-33
Courts unsympathetic at first, 8-19-8-20
covered by prohibition of discrimination based on sex, 8-23-8-24
    distinction between "free speech" and, 8-24-8-25
employer's liability, 8-21, 8-25, 8-35-8-40
equal application of principles, 8-24
objective standard test, 8-31-8-32
poisoned environment, 8-26, 8-27-8-30, 8-33
preventive measures for employers, 8-21-8-22
prior complaint, 8-30-8-31
problems of proof, 8-33-8-35
quid pro quo, 8-25-8-27, 8-33
"reasonable" social interaction, evaluating limits of, 8-32
responsibility of employer for actions of supervisory personnel, 8-21, 8-25
statutory reform, 8-40-8-42
U.S. cases, 8-19-8-21
U.S. guidelines, 8-22-8-23

[Emphasis added]

Table V lists the most common issues within each major division and directs the user to the appropriate paragraph of the text.

Another useful source of ideas is *The Canadian Encyclopedic Digest (Ontario), Third Edition*. If you are uncertain of the subject title, refer first to the "Index

Key" in the *Research Guide and Key*. The entries in this key will help direct you to the appropriate volume and title. Turn to the "Table of Contents" or "Index" for that title. Scan all the major headings, select the appropriate one, and scan the subheadings for the appropriate word or words which relate to the problem. Consult the paragraph numbers as directed for a general statement of law. Make a note of references to cases and statutes, and check the supplement in the yellow pages preceding the main text for more recent entries. A companion volume to *The Canadian Abridgment, Second Edition*, entitled *Key and Research Guide* may be used for the same purposes.

While the procedure outlined above may help the genesis of a statement of issues, it is important to remember that the process is an ongoing one. Often, the issues will not be fully understood until the late stages of the research. This means that as the research proceeds the researcher will often need to expand the number of topics, key words or even titles investigated. For this reason, the student researcher should use work sheets to identify each library source and make notes of titles, topic headings, key words and/or numbers contained in each source. In addition, the researcher should record promising case citations throughout the research process and give a brief description of the facts and legal principle(s).

For certain areas of the law a more useful first step may be to consult an annotator or a topical law looseleaf service. To research criminal law problems, refer to one or more of the following criminal code annotators:

1. G.P. Rodrigues, ed., *Crankshaw's Criminal Code of Canada* (Toronto: Thomson Canada (Carswell), 1993-) (Supplemented by regular inserts).
2. E.L. Greenspan, ed., *Martin's Criminal Code of Canada* (Toronto: Canada Law Book, 1993-) (Supplemented by regular inserts).
3. R. Heather, ed., *Snow's Annotated Criminal Code* (Toronto: Carswell, 1989-) (Supplemented by regular inserts).
4. D. Watt & M. Fuerst, eds., *Tremeear's Annotated Criminal Code* (Toronto: Thomson Canada (Carswell), 1994-) (Supplemented by regular inserts).

To research problems involving the *Charter of Rights*, students may refer to the following:

1. J.B. Laskin et al., eds., *The Canadian Charter of Rights Annotated* (Aurora, Ontario: Canada Law Book, 1993-) (Supplemented by regular inserts).
2. R.M. McLeod et al., *Canadian Charter of Rights* (Toronto: Carswell, 1983-) (Supplemented by regular inserts).
3. D. Stratas, *The Charter of Rights in Litigation* (Aurora, Ontario: Canada Law Book, 1990-) (Supplemented by regular inserts).

To find material relating to the various Canadian constitutional documents, refer to P. Hogg, *Constitutional Law of Canada*, 3rd ed. (Toronto: Thomson Canada (Carswell), 1992-) (Supplemented by regular inserts).

To research specialized areas such as employment, tax, labour, health, or insurance law, consult the relevant looseleaf service offered by Commerce Clearing House (CCH) called *Topical Law Reports*. These include:

1. *Employment Benefits and Pension Guide;*
2. *Employment Safety and Health Guide;*
3. *Industrial Relations and Personnel Developments;*
4. *Insurance Law Reporter;* and
5. *Municipal Assessment and Taxation.*

2. Consulting the Primary Sources of Law

Once you have collected the first few citations from your readings, it is advisable to refer to the primary source materials. A reference to a provincial statute should be checked against the official text of the statutes, for example, in the 1990 *Revised Statutes of Ontario*, or in an annual volume of the *Statutes of Ontario* after 1990. If a federal statute is indicated, confirm its accuracy in the *Revised Statutes of Canada*, or in an annual volume published since the latest revision. Every statement of law of interest in the C.E.D. (Ont. 3d) should be checked against the original case report for accuracy and to make sure that you understand the context from which the statement was taken.

3. Checking for Amendments to Statutes and Finding Judicial Interpretations of Statutes

In order to bring the statute research forward from the latest supplement insert for the desired title in the C.E.D. (Ont. 3d), refer to the third column of the "Table of Public Statutes" in the most recent volume of the *Statutes of Ontario*. Consult the *Ontario Statute Citator* and annotations for the text of amendments, as well as for the most recent legislative activity. It may be prudent, as well, to check the heading "The Following Legislation is Pending" on the first page of the body of the yellow-page supplement, under the appropriate title in the C.E.D. (Ont. 3d) — changes subsequent to the stated cut-off of the supplement are easily tracked by reference to *Canadian Current Law - Legislation*.

NOTE: The cover page of the "Supplement" states: "This supplement contains...statutory material drawn from...statutes up to and including [year] *C.C.L. Legislation* No. [n.]". With this information the student need only check those parts of *Canadian Current Law - Legislation* which were published after the date indicated in the supplement.

Once you have discerned whether the desired statute or section of the statute has been changed, refer again to the *Ontario Statute Citator* and a companion volume, *Ontario Statute Annotations*, to determine if it has been judicially interpreted. It may be wise, as well, to refer to *Canadian Citations (Statutes Judicially Considered)* and check for the desired section of the statute in relevant bound and looseleaf volumes of the set. If the research uncovers a federal statute in the C.E.D. (Ont. 3d) (white or yellow pages), confirm the entry in the "Table of Public Statutes" in the latest annual volume of the *Statutes of Canada*, or in the most recent cumulative table in the *Canada Gazette, Part III*. Check for amendments and read the relevant statute in the appropriate statute volume. Next, examine the *Canada Statute Citator* (for the text of amendments) and a companion volume, *Canada Statute Annotations* (to determine how the amendments have been judicially treated). Consult, as well, the relevant volumes of *Canadian Citations (Statutes Judicially Considered)* under the applicable statute.

4. Expanding the Research to All Canadian Jurisdictions and Finding Judicial Consideration of Cases

Once you have collected and read the relevant case authorities from the sources noted above, consult the Can. Abr. (2nd) for digests of cases from other Canadian jurisdictions. An entry at the end of the "Table of Contents" for the selected title in the C.E.D. (Ont. 3d) may help direct you to the appropriate volume and page reference in the Can. Abr. (2nd). Alternatively, scan the spines of the jackets for the equivalent title in the Can. Abr. (2nd), or refer to the "Subject Titles Table" in *The Canadian Abridgment Key and Research Guide*. Next, turn to the "Table of Classification" in the main volume for the selected subject title, scan the classification headings, locate the relevant topics, and record the key classification entry. For example, the key classification "Contracts III.2.e" covers cases classified under: "Contracts - Formation of Contract - Offer Withdrawal of Offer".

After this is completed, refer to the appropriate pages for the digests relating to the selected topic. Bring the research forward (using the key classification entry) by referring to a supplement, if one is available, and *Canadian Current Law - Case Law Digests*. Every promising case culled from these sources should be checked against the original case report.

At the completion of this stage of the research, it is advisable to determine whether any case that you plan to rely on has been considered in a later case or if it is under appeal. Consult the soft-cover supplement and/or the bound volumes of *The Canadian Abridgment - Canadian Case Citations* beginning with the volume which includes the year (if it is known to you) of the desired case. Complete this part of the research by referring to the cumulative supplement and the monthly paper parts of *Canadian Case Citations*.

NOTE: If the problem under investigation involves one of the four Western provinces or the Territories, begin the search in the *Canadian Encyclopedic Digest*

(Western), *Third Edition*, and check any statement or textual reference against an official source. If a statute is noted, consult the appropriate services for amendments and judicial consideration, and then expand the research as outlined directly above. If the problem involves one of the Atlantic provinces (and the encyclopedic research indicates that the given legal issue is governed by Ontario statute law), consult the "Table of Public Statutes" in the most recent statute volume to determine if there is equivalent legislation for the selected jurisdiction.

If there is equivalent legislation, refer to the appropriate statute volume and decide whether or not the language of the relevant provision is similar to that of the corresponding provision in the Ontario statute. If it is relevant, check a statute citator (*e.g.*, *Nova Scotia Reports* (2d), *Digest and Consolidated Index to Statutes Judicially Noticed*, or *Canadian Citations (Statutes Judicially Considered)*) for a relevant case authority.

5. Computer Research

The completion of the basic encyclopedic research is an opportune time to conduct a computer search. Complete a search planner by using the key legal concepts or words (*e.g.*, sexual harassment) found in the cases retrieved during the manual search. The computer will search for case or statute law containing the word or word combinations entered by the operator. For example, the query "sex!/1 harassment" will retrieve cases (full text or headnote only), in the selected database, in which the word "sex" or its natural derivatives ("sexual" or "sexually") appears within one word of the term "harassment".

Computer research for a major assignment will usually be conducted in several steps. A good starting point is to search the DRS database on Q.L. since it contains only brief summaries of reported cases, and it will be more forgiving of a novice's inexperience with formulating efficient search queries. Once the issues are better defined and the student has gathered leading or other applicable cases, it may be useful to expand the computer search to include a regional (*i.e.*, Western Weekly Report (WWR)) or provincial database (*i.e.*, Ontario Reports (OR) and Ontario Judgments (OJ)), or a database for a particular court (*i.e.*, Supreme Court of Canada (SCC)), or a subject report database (*i.e.*, Canadian Criminal Cases (CCC)).

A student may wish to do a final update to determine whether a particular case has been appealed or considered elsewhere or to see if there has been a very recent unreported judgment. For example, Supreme Court of Canada Judgments (SCR) may be available in QUICKLAW's SCJ database on the same day of the decision and on the Supreme Court of Canada's Web site.

6. Supplementary Manual Research

Computer searching may not always be a useful first, or even second, step in the research process. Faced with a complex legal problem, the beginning student may be unable to sufficiently develop the issues early on in the research process to justify a computer search. When this happens, a student is advised to do additional background research. The "Table of Subject Authorities" or "Subject Index" to the *Index to Canadian Legal Literature* (part of *The Abridgment*) will permit the student to access journal articles and case commentary. These may give a perspective, or overview, of a particular legal issue, together with citations to case and statute law not uncovered from the preliminary research.

Once the basic manual and computer research is completed it may be wise to examine other sources of law for the elusive case on point or to make sure that no important cases may have been omitted. Students may wish to check digests such as the *All-Canada Weekly Summaries* (civil), *Weekly Criminal Bulletin* (criminal), *Canadian Weekly Law Sheet*, *Canadian Current Law - Case Law Digests* and *The Lawyer's Weekly*.

In addition, the student may research an appropriate provincial publication: (1) *Alberta Weekly Law Digest*; (2) *Alberta Decisions*; (3) *British Columbia Weekly Law Digest*; (4) *British Columbia Decisions*; (5) *Manitoba Decisions*; (6) *Nova Scotia Law News*; (7) *Ontario Decisions* (criminal); and (8) *Saskatchewan Decisions*.

NOTE: Some students may wish to begin their research with *The Abridgment* rather than with the C.E.D. (Ont. 3d). If so, it is important to know that generally *The Abridgment* does not note the legislative provisions relevant to the legal issues under consideration. For this reason, before undertaking a search in *The Abridgment*, consult the appropriate "Table of Public Statutes" to see if the legal issue is covered by legislation.

7. Expanding the Research to U.K. Case Authorities

When the law in a Canadian jurisdiction is unclear on any point, English law may become important. In some instances, particularly having regard to Charter rights, insurance law and aviation law, to mention only a few areas, American material may be relevant.

A good general statement of English law is found in *Halsbury's Laws of England, Fourth Edition*, or in *Halsbury's Laws of England, Third Edition*, with *Canadian Converters*. As most of the changes in the fourth edition are to statutory law, the third edition may be a more useful tool for a Canadian student than the fourth edition. Refer directly to the volume which contains the title under investigation (*e.g.*, CONTRACT, volume 8 in the third edition, and volume 9 in the fourth edition). Scan the table of contents for references to relevant paragraph numbers where you will find a statement of the law supported by references to cases and statutes. Alternatively, refer to the *Consolidated Index* for the set as a means of entry to the main volumes. For references to cases following the cut-off date for the main volumes, consult the *Cumulative Supplement* and the *Current Service* looseleaf binder. Complete this segment of the research by consulting the appropriate *Canadian Converter* volume. After reading *Halsbury's*, it may be useful to consult the *Current Law Year Book* (each volume contains an annual index, the *1976 Year Book* contains a 30-year index from 1947-76 and the *1986 Year Book* contains a cumulative index for the years 1972-86) and the *Current Law Monthly Digest* for December of the last calendar year, as well as the most recent issue for the current year (each *Monthly Digest* contains a "Cumulative Index") and perhaps find a hitherto undiscovered case reference on the selected topic. *The Digest* is also a very valuable tool, particularly since statements of law are often footnoted with Canadian annotations.

B. WRITING A MEMORANDUM

In many law offices the first test of an articling clerk will be his or her ability to write a clear and useful memorandum of law. This is no less true for the beginning law student. Often, the beginning clerk or student will have great difficulty in arranging legal material in the order that will be most helpful to the reader. Indeed, in some instances, the considerable efforts expended in the research process are wasted because of a poorly presented paper. Where there is a deficiency, it can be mastered only with a great deal of practice.

No one can lay down a detailed formula for presenting materials. The organization of a paper will vary depending on the nature of the problem. Also, since an office memorandum is written for the use of another member of the firm, its form will depend, in part, on the instructions given by the person concerned. Typically, the paper will be informal and structured with headings and subheadings to enable the reader to quickly find a discussion of a particular question. The following suggested scheme may serve as a model of an office memorandum of law.

1. Title

If litigation has commenced, use the title of the proceedings, *e.g.*,
Between
　　John Fisher

Plaintiff

　　-and-
　　General Motors Corporation, a body corporate

Defendant

If litigation has not yet commenced, use the following title:............................

TO:　　Senior Partner
FROM:　Articling Clerk
DATE:　April 1, 1993
RE:　　Joe Lord's arrest for selling obscene material

2. Facts

State the most material facts in one or two short paragraphs. The finer details should be discussed in the main body of the memorandum as the student applies the principles of law, culled from the research, to the particular facts of the problem under investigation.

3. Statement of the Questions Presented or Raised by the Facts

This part of the memorandum should give a clear statement of the main issues to be resolved. A statement of the narrower issues will normally be included in the body of the paper at the beginning of each new section.

4. Introduction

This is usually one or two paragraphs long and serves to orient the reader to the general field or fields of law to be discussed. It may also include a brief statement of the answer. Further, when there is concern about the exclusion of a discussion of a particular topic (which does not directly help to resolve the problem), it may be useful to explain your reasons in the introduction.

5. Discussion

Each issue formulated (under 3, above) should be developed in sequence. Present the authorities on which the conclusion rests, remembering that the purpose of the memorandum is to explore and evaluate both sides of a question. Therefore, the student should give equal attention to cases and other authorities that tend to support the client's position as to those cases and authorities that do not. The main purpose of a memorandum is to provide a reliable statement of law. It is not generally conceived as a forum for opinion, persuasive argument, or the writer's notions about what the law should be. It does, however, require the student to distinguish cases and to draw inferences from particular cases to the problem under investigation. As well, it may, when the authorities are in conflict or when little or no law can be found, require commentary on social or policy considerations.

6. Conclusion

The conclusion should include a brief summary of the main points and an evaluation of the strengths and weaknesses of the case law in terms of providing an answer to the legal issues of the question you have been asked to answer. If the research suggests that the law is unclear on a point, this should be acknowledged.

7. Recommendations

In some instances, it is appropriate for a memorandum to include a recommendation of action to be taken or strategy to be pursued. Usually, this relates directly to the contemplated litigation and may include commentary on the need for more information or on how to support the client's position. It may also include a suggestion to guide the future conduct or policies of the client.

C. SAMPLE MEMORANDUM

To: Senior Partner
From: Articling Clerk
Date: April 1, 1993
Re: Joe Lord's arrest for selling obscene material

Statement of Facts

Two R.C.M.P. officers purchased several magazines at Mr. Lord's store in Herring Cove. As a result of this purchase he was charged with selling obscene material, contrary to s. 163(2)(a) of the *Criminal Code*. Joe claims that, although he was familiar with the contents of the magazines, he did not know they were legally obscene.

Statement of Issues Raised by the Facts

1.   Are Joe's magazines obscene?
2.   What defences are available to him?

Introduction

Joe has been charged with selling obscene material contrary to s. 163(2)(a) of the *Criminal Code* which reads:

> Every one commits an offence who knowingly, without lawful justification or excuse,
> (a) sells, exposes to public view or has in his possession for such a purpose any obscene written matter, picture, model, phonograph record or other thing whatever;

This is a hybrid offence and the Crown may treat it either as an indictable offence or a summary offence matter. A conviction pursuant to an indictable count would attract a term of imprisonment for up to two years [s. 169(a)]. Alternatively, a summary conviction would make the accused liable to a fine of up to $2,000, or six months' imprisonment, or both [ss. 169(b) and 787(1)].

This memorandum is in three parts. The first contains an examination of the essential elements of the offence. The second examines the judicial interpretation of "obscene". The third discusses the defences available to our client. This analysis is followed by a conclusion and recommendations.

Discussion

I. ELEMENTS OF THE OFFENCE

The onus is on the Crown to prove all of the elements of the offence beyond a reasonable doubt. The *actus reus* consists of the sale of obscene magazines without lawful justification or excuse. The *mens rea* is expressed in the term "knowingly". The Crown must prove the magazines were "knowingly sold"; the absence of lawful excuse; and that the magazines were "obscene".

(i) "Knowingly sold"

The obscene material must be "knowingly sold". Both the Ontario Court of Appeal and the British Columbia Court of Appeal have said that sexual material may be obscene, even though the person who sold the material was unaware that the material was legally obscene. *R.* v. *Cameron*[1] and *R.* v. *McFall*[2] both make it clear that the prosecutor need only prove that the accused knew or was generally aware of the sexual nature of the subject-matter of the magazines.

The R.C.M.P. officers purchased the magazines at our client's newsstand and Joe has admitted that he knew of the contents of the magazines. It would appear that the Crown will be able to establish that he "knowingly sold" the magazines.

(ii) The absence of lawful excuse

The Crown must also prove that the obscene material was sold "without lawful justification or excuse".

A review of the cases reveals that the following may not constitute a "lawful justification or excuse":

1) the fact that a provincial censor board has approved a film;[3]
2) the fact that the material has been approved by customs officials;[4] and

---

[1] (1966), 49 C.R. 49 (Ont. C.A.); leave to appeal refused (1967), 1 C.R. (N.S.) 227 (S.C.C.) [hereinafter *Cameron*].

[2] (1975), 26 C.C.C. (2d) 181 (B.C.C.A.).

[3] *R.* v. *McFall, supra* note 2, and *R.* v. *Cinemas Québécois*, [1982] R.L. 180 (C.M.M.). *But see R.* v. *Bachand*, [1984] C.S.P. 1139 (Qué.) (holding that the accused had a lawful excuse for thinking that [a film] was not obscene because it had received approval from the Québec Censure Bureau and had been shown for seven weeks before being seized).

[4] *R.* v. *Regina News Ltd.* (1987), 39 C.C.C. (3d) 170 (Sask. C.A.) and *R.* v. *Prairie Schooner News Ltd.* (1970), 1 C.C.C. (2d) 251 (Man. C.A.); leave to appeal to S.C.C. refused, [1970] S.C.R. x.

3)   the fact that access to the materials was restricted to adults only.[5]

It should be noted that these factors were found to be relevant in assessing whether or not the subject-matter was obscene as discussed later in Part II. However, once the court determines the material is obscene, these factors usually will not provide a lawful justification or excuse. The authorities are unclear as to what will constitute same.

II. THE OBSCENITY REQUIREMENT

The Crown must prove the subject-matter is obscene. The question of what is obscene is governed by s. 163(8) of the *Criminal Code*. It provides:

(8)   For the purposes of this Act, any publication a dominant characteristic of which is the undue exploitation of sex, or of sex and any one or more of the following subjects, namely, crime, horror, cruelty and violence, shall be deemed to be obscene.

Prior to 1959, the *Criminal Code* contained no definition of "obscene". Canadian courts relied on the common law definition of obscenity formulated by Cockburn C.J. in *R. v. Hicklin*, who stated: "I think the test of obscenity is this, whether the tendency of the matter charged as obscenity is to deprave and corrupt those whose minds are open to such immoral influences, and into whose hands a publication of this sort may fall."[6]

The difficulty involved in interpretation may best be summarized by the remarks of Struble J. in *State v. Lerner* where he stated: "'Obscenity' is not a legal term. It cannot be defined so that it will mean the same thing to all people all the time, everywhere. 'Obscenity' is very much a figment of the imagination."[7]

In 1959, Parliament amended the *Criminal Code* and added the definition which now appears at s. 163(8).[8] Its wording has not changed since that time.

The *Hicklin* test was rejected by the Supreme Court of Canada in *R. v. Brodie*[9] and *Dechow v. R.*[10] It is now clear that the statutory definition is exhaustive. As discussed below, the *Hicklin* test has been replaced by a series of rules developed by the courts. The provision will be examined in light of these tests.

The Supreme Court of Canada first considered, what is now s. 163(8) in *R. v. Brodie*.[11] The majority found that the novel *Lady Chatterly's Lover* was not ob-

---

5
   Towne Cinema Theatres Ltd. v. R. (1985), 18 C.C.C. (3d) 193 (S.C.C.)[hereinafter *Towne Cinema Theatres*].
6
   (1868), L.R. 3 Q.B. 360 at 371.
7
   (1948), 81 N.E. 2d 282 at 286 (Ohio C.P.).
8
   S.C. 1953-54, c. 51, s. 150(8).
9
   (1962), 132 C.C.C. 161.
10
   (1977), 35 C.C.C. (2d) 22 [hereinafter *Dechow*].
11
   Supra note 9.

scene within the meaning of the provision. The Court recognized a need to test for obscenity on the basis of some objective criteria. It was held that to convict someone of obscenity the material must have as a dominant characteristic the undue exploitation of sex, or sex and any one of the subjects listed in s. 163(8). First, the Court indicated that if the material has several themes the Crown must prove that the sexual theme is the dominant one and that if the sexual theme is dominant it is without artistic relevance or merit, that it is not art.

Secondly, the Supreme Court of Canada pointed out that the material should be measured against community standards. The test for "undueness" was to be found by looking at community standards. That is, would the community find the material acceptable? If not, according to our highest Court, at least in 1962, the material would be deemed to be obscene.

The relation between sex and obscenity is developed further in *R. v. Odeon Morton Theatres Ltd.*[12] This case asks (i) whether or not sexual episodes play a legitimate role in the development of the theme or purpose of the work, and (ii) are the episodes justified by what has been called the "internal necessities" of the theme?

In most cases, whether or not sex is a dominant characteristic has not been a contentious issue. On the other hand, whether or not the Crown can prove beyond a reasonable doubt that the use or exploitation of sex is "undue" has been anything but a settled issue. The Court in *R. v. Brodie*[13] sets out what is meant by "undue". Judson J.A. in delivering the majority decision stated:

> Surely the choice of courses is clear-cut. Either the Judge instructs himself or the jury that undueness is to be measured by his or their personal opinion - and even that must be subject to some influence from contemporary standards - or the instruction must be that the tribunal of fact should consciously attempt to apply these standards. Of the two. I think the second is the better choice.[14]

A review of the numerous cases which applied the community standards test reveals a number of principles. It is the standards of the community as a whole which must be considered and not the standards of a small segment of that community, such as a city, where a picture was exposed.[15] It is a national standard which must be applied.[16] Community standards must be contemporary and respond to changing mores.[17] The test for "undueness" must be based on the community standard of tolerance, not taste. That is, what should be ascertained

---

[12] (1974), 16 C.C.C. (2d) 185 (Man. C.A.).
[13] *Supra* note 9.
[14] *Supra* note 9 at 182.
[15] *R. v. Kiverago* (1973), 11 C.C.C. (2d) 463 (Ont. C.A.).
[16] *Cameron, supra* note 1, and *R. v. Ariadne Developments Ltd.* (1974), 19 C.C.C. (2d) 49 (N.S.S.C., A.D.) [hereinafter *Ariadne Developments Ltd.*].
[17] *R. v. Dominion News & Gifts (1962) Ltd.*, [1964] S.C.R. 251 (adopting, in its entirety, the dissenting decision of Freedman J.A. of the Manitoba Court of Appeal (1963), 42 W.W.R. 65.).

is not what Canadians think is right for themselves to see but rather what they would tolerate other Canadians seeing.[18]

The test to determine what is "undue exploitation of sex" was expanded in recent years to include films containing scenes showing violence and cruelty in conjunction with sex, particularly where the depictions degrade and dehumanize the persons portrayed. Under this test, material which exploits sex in a degrading or dehumanizing manner would exceed the level of tolerance and would also fail the community standards rule.[19] In defining what falls within a definition of "undueness" a line must be drawn between that which is a portrayal of human sexual acts and that which dehumanizes and is intolerable to the victims and the community as a whole,[20] but "[t]here is nothing wrong in the treatment of sex *per se* ..."[21]

In *Towne Cinema Theatres Ltd.* v. *R.* Madam Justice Wilson asked: "How is 'undueness' to be measured?" and, following this question, stated:

> The standard we are concerned with, it seems to me, is the degree of exploitation of sex which the Canadian community at any given point of time is prepared to accept in its movies. This is sometimes referred to as the Canadian standard of tolerance.
>
> ....
>
> I think we have to approach the question more directly and ask: do Canadians today accept this degree of exploitation of sex in their movies? If they do, then the movie is not obscene. If they do not, then the exploitation is "undue" and, if it is a dominant characteristic of the movie, the movie is deemed to be obscene under the section.[22]

Wilson J. provided the following guidelines to assist courts in making a determination under s. 159(8):

> [T]he undue exploitation of sex at which s. 159(8) is aimed is the treatment of sex which in some fundamental way dehumanizes the persons portrayed and, as a consequence, the viewers themselves. There is nothing wrong in the treatment of sex *per se* but there may be something wrong in the manner of its treatment. It may be presented brutally, salaciously and in a degrading manner, and would thus be dehumanizing and intolerable not only to the individuals or groups who are victimized by it but to society at large. On the other hand, it may be presented in a way which harms no one in that it depicts nothing more than non-violent sexual activity in a manner which neither degrades nor dehumanizes any particular individuals or groups. It is this line between the mere portrayal of human sexual acts and the dehumanization of people that must be reflected in the definition of "undueness".[23]

---

18 *Towne Cinema Theatres, supra* note 5, and *Dechow, supra* note 10.

19 *R.* v. *Doug Rankine Co.* (1983), 9 C.C.C. (3d) 53 (Ont. Co. Ct.).

20 *Towne Cinema Theatres, supra* note 5.

21 *Ibid.* at 216.

22 *Ibid.* at 214.

23 *Towne Cinema Theatres, supra* note 5 at 216-217.

In two subsequent decisions, *R.* v. *Ramsingh*[24] and *R.* v. *Wagner,*[25] violence and cruelty were thought to be unnecessary for degrading or dehumanizing acts to exceed community tolerance standards. The type of materials falling into this category has been described by Ferg J. in *R.* v. *Ramsingh*:

> [Women] are exploited, portrayed as desiring pleasure from pain, by being humiliated and treated only as an object of male domination sexually, or in cruel or violent bondage. Women are portrayed in these films as pining away their lives waiting for a huge male penis to come along, on the person of a so-called sex therapist, or window washer, supposedly to transport them into complete sexual ecstasy. Or even more false and degrading one is led to believe their raison d'être is to savour semen as a life elixir, or that they secretly desire to be forcefully taken by a male.
>
> ...
>
> [W]here violence is portrayed with sex, or where there are people, particularly women, subject to anything which degrades or dehumanizes them, the community standard is exceeded, even when the viewing may occur in one's private home.[26]

In the 1980s, there were still courts which adhered to a rather narrow threshold of community tolerance. The Court in *Re Luscher and Deputy Minister, Revenue Canada Customs and Excise*, found that the lawful and natural relations of a man and woman engaged in sexual relations exceeded the community standard with regards to the magazine "concerned with the sexual activity of a man and a woman from foreplay to orgasm...accompanied by...text, in narrative form, explicitly describing in grossly vulgar language the actions depicted in the photographs".[27] Similarly, in *R.* v. *St. John News Co.* the Court found that the following exceeded the community standards test:

> The magazines are most explicit and depict sexual conduct, not merely nudity. The conduct shows lesbianism, homosexuality and heterosexuality. Male and female genitalia are explicitly photographed....There were no pictures depicting sex and 'the subject crime, horror, cruelty or violence' as set out in s. 159(8). The picutres [*sic*] appear to be of adults consenting to the sexual acts of the other(s).[28]

The authority on this issue is the decision of the Supreme Court of Canada in *R.* v. *Butler*.[29] Sopinka J. writing for the majority reviewed the community standards and degradation or dehumanization tests, and found that the determination

---

[24] (1984), 14 C.C.C. (3d) 230 (Man. Q.B.).

[25] (1985), 43 C.R. (3d) 318 (Alta. Q.B.).

[26] *Supra* note 24 at 239-240.

[27] (1983), 149 D.L.R. (3d) 243 at 245 (B.C. Co. Ct.).

[28] (1982), 47 N.B.R. (2d) 91 at 100 (N.B.Q.B., T.D.).

[29] (1992), 70 C.C.C. (3d) 129. See also *R.* v. *Pelletier* found online: <www.droit.umontreal.ca/doc/csc-scc/en/index.html>.

of what the community will tolerate others being exposed to should be based on the degree of harm that may result from such exposure. He stated in the decision:

> The courts must determine as best they can what the community would tolerate others being exposed to on the basis of the degree of harm that may flow from such exposure. Harm in this context means that it predisposes persons to act in an antisocial manner, as, for example, the physical or mental mistreatment of women by men, or, what is perhaps debatable, the reverse. Antisocial conduct for this purpose is conduct which society formally recognizes as incompatible with its proper functioning. The stronger the inference of a risk of harm the lesser the likelihood of tolerance.[30]

Sopinka J. in *R.* v. *Butler* divided pornography into three categories: "(1) explicit sex with violence, (2) explicit sex without violence but which subjects people to treatment that is degrading or dehumanizing, and (3) explicit sex without violence that is neither degrading nor dehumanizing. Violence in this context includes both actual physical violence and threats of physical violence".[31]

Sopinka J. concluded that the portrayal of sex coupled with violence will almost always amount to the undue exploitation of sex. Material in the second category may be undue if there is a substantial risk of harm. As to the third category, the Court held that sexually explicit material which is not violent and does not degrade or dehumanize will not be found to unduly exploit sex unless it involves children.

The highest court ruling, since the Supreme Court of Canada's pronouncements, on the question of what constitutes obscenity is found in *R.* v. *Hawkins*,[32] a decision of the Ontario Court of Appeal. In five separate appeals, involving such films as "Lawyers in Heat", "Pink 'n Pretty" and "Dr. Butts", the Crown argued that if the material was not violent but subjected persons to degrading or dehumanizing treatment, it can be inferred that the impugned films created a substantial risk of societal harm. Robins J. disagreed and observed that since 1990 the province's film board had approved such films for exhibition and distribution and this was clearly evidence of contemporary Canadian standards of tolerance. Robins J. found that the only obscene videos under s. 163(8) of the *Criminal Code* were those which coupled graphic sex with violence and coercion or subordination.

Robins J. also said that he did not accept the Crown's submission, that "once the portrayal of sexually explicit acts was found to be degrading or dehumanizing, it necessarily followed that the films were harmful and therefore obscene" and indicated that "[j]ust as there is a range of opinion as to what is degrading or

---

[30] (1992), 70 C.C.C. (2d) 129 at 150-151 (S.C.C.).
[31] *Ibid.* at 150.
[32] (1993), 15 O.R. (3d) 549.

dehumanizing, there is a range of opinion as to whether such material causes social harm or the risk of such harm".[33]

Robins J. noted that none of the films, with certain exceptions, combined sex with crime, horror, cruelty or violence, involved children or indicated lack of consent, even though their context was devoid of any loving or affectionate relationship. There was also no plot of any meaningful value.

I have not had the benefit of examining the seized magazines. Therefore, it is impossible to give an opinion as to whether or not they are likely to be found to be obscene. In their absence, I will summarize from previously decided cases what the courts have decided will, or will not, be tolerated by the contemporary Canadian community. It is unclear whether or not cases decided prior to *R. v. Butler*[34] would be still relevant as precedents, but some are included in this discussion.

Borins Co. Ct. J. in *R. v. Doug Rankine Co.* found that the contemporary community would tolerate "the distribution of films which consist substantially of scenes of people engaged in sexual intercourse...the distribution of films which consist of scenes of group sex, [l]esbianism, *fellatio, cunnilingus*, and anal sex".[35] He found that violence and cruelty coupled with sex, particularly where people are degraded or dehumanized, would not be tolerated.

Several courts have held that books or magazines whose dominant theme is primarily incest or bestiality are obscene.[36] In *R. v. Red Hot Video Ltd.*[37] the British Columbia Court of Appeal held that material which portrayed (i) violence coupled with explicit sex in an excessive degree; (ii) explicit sex involving the participation of children; and (iii) people as having animal characteristics was found to be obscene.

In *R. v. Ronish*[38] the Court found that sexually explicit films which portrayed heterosexual and lesbian behaviour, ejaculation onto the face, into the mouth and onto the body, and anal intercourse were not obscene.

In *R. v. Arena Recreations (Toronto) Ltd.*[39] the accused company was acquitted on a charge of distributing obscene material. The magazines contained photographs depicting nude and semi-nude females, tied with ropes. It should be noted that the acquittal was based on the Crown's failure to prove the magazines were obscene. The Crown did not lead any expert evidence and relied only on the photographs themselves, while the defence called three expert witnesses and established that the magazines had been passed by Canada Customs and by a

---

[33] *Ibid.* at 567.

[34] *Supra* note 29.

[35] *Supra* note 19 at 70.

[36] *Ariadne Developments Ltd., supra* note 16, and *R. v. McDougall's Drug Store* (1982), 53 N.S.R. (2d) 463 (Co. Ct.).

[37] (1985), 45 C.R. (2d) 36 (B.C.C.A.).

[38] (1993), 18 C.R. (4th) 165 (Ont. C.J. (Prov. Div.)).

[39] (1987), 56 C.R. (3d) 118 (Man. Q.B.).

committee established by the distributors. As a result, it cannot be said that the Court found the magazines were not obscene.

III. DEFENCES

The magazines were bought at our client's store and he is aware of their contents. As discussed previously, it appears the Crown will be able to establish that Mr. Lord "knowingly sold" the magazines.

Section 163(3) of the *Criminal Code* provides for a defence of public good. It reads:

> (3) No person shall be convicted of an offence under this section if he establishes that the public good was served by the acts that are alleged to constitute the offence and that the acts alleged did not extend beyond what served the public good.

Laskin J.A. in *R. v. Cameron* noted that the public good is to be measured "in terms of what is 'necessary or advantageous to religion or morality, to the administration of justice, the pursuit of science, literature or art, or other objects of general interest,' so long as there was no excess in the particular publication beyond what the public good required".[40] Laskin J. also remarked that "[t]he Canadian limitation of the defence to acts that do not extend beyond what serves the public good means simply that excessive obscenity will vitiate the defence of public good even if public good is established".[41]

In *R. v. Sutherland*[42] Hogg J. heard evidence on charges of possession of obscene articles for the purpose of distribution and sale, contrary to s. 159 of the *Criminal Code*, in respect of sexual aids, such as vibrators, items to assist in achieving an erection and creams and jellies for use in sexual intercourse, and he concluded that "it serves the public good to make available to those persons that so desire aids so that they may enjoy or further enjoy legitimate sexual acts and sexual harmony".[43]

The notion of public good was not included in the initial interview materials from our client and we would need more facts to determine if this defence applies.

Conclusion

The question of whether or not Mr. Lord's magazines are obscene cannot be answered until they have been examined. However, if they are "cornerstore" magazines which contain sexually explicit scenes without any violence and do

---

[40] *Supra* note 1 at 92. Quoting Sir J.F. Stephen, *A Digest of the Criminal Law (Crimes and Punishments)*, 9th ed. (London: Macmillan and Co., 1950) at 173.
[41] *Supra* note 1.
[42] (1974), 18 C.C.C. (2d) 117 (Ont. Co. Ct.).
[43] *Ibid.* at 124.

not dehumanize or degrade people, the case authorities suggest that they will not be found to be obscene, unless they involve children. It seems clear from the cases that if the material involves sex and children, or if it portrays violence coupled with sex, it will likely be found to be obscene. A difficulty arises, as indicated in *R. v. Hawkins*,[44] when the magazines portray explicit adult sex which is also alleged to be degrading or dehumanizing. Films of this *genre* will fall within the impugned section of the *Criminal Code* only if the trier of fact believes that they are also harmful.

Finally, as we were given a paucity of facts, I cannot comment extensively on how the cases may assist us in showing what defences are available to Mr. Lord. It seems clear, though, from the research that I conducted on the second issue, that the Defendant does not have an easy task if there is an attempt to show that the sale of sexually explicit magazines serves the public good since they do not easily fall into the category of sexual aids as described in *R. v. Sutherland*.[45]

Recommendations

It is clear from a number of cases that complaints on the part of the public are relevant in assessing the level of tolerance of the Canadian community. It would be important to ascertain whether the actions of the R.C.M.P. officers were based on a local complaint.

Notwithstanding that the burden is on the Crown to prove the magazines seized are obscene, if we do not lead some evidence on the issue we run the risk of a conviction. It also would be advisable to retain the services of someone who might be said to be an "expert" in this area. Some possibilities are: a sexologist, sociologist or someone from a civil libertarian organization that has done some research on pornography and its effects. Further, we should find out if the magazines were imported and approved by Canada Customs or approved by a provincial film board.

There is no possibility of challenging the constitutionality of s. 163(8) as being in violation of the *Charter*. The Supreme Court of Canada in *R. v. Butler*[46] ruled that while the section violated the guarantee of freedom of expression, it was a reasonable limit within the meaning of s. 1 of the *Charter*. As such, it would seem ill-advised to raise a new constitutional challenge of that point.

---

[44] *Supra* note 32.
[45] *Supra* note 42 at 119.
[46] *Supra* note 29.

D. GENERAL RULES OF STYLE

1. Citation

A citation is a reference to other published material and it is important that a student be able to cite legal materials without error. The need for accuracy is the primary reason for acquiring citing skills. A legal writer gives the citation of the material alluded to primarily to enable the reader to find that material and to personally examine it. This rationale leads to the oft-heard rule: a correct citation is one that leads, without ambiguity, to the primary source.

Students should follow a consistent method of citation. Certain guiding principles are laid down in this manual. (It is not suggested, however, that there is only one "correct" way to give a legal citation.) Whenever a point is not covered, the citation system used by the *Canadian Bar Review* is a good model. Reference may also be made to C. Tang, *Guide to Legal Citation and Sources of Citation Aid: A Canadian Perspective*, 2nd ed. (Scarborough, Ontario: Thomson Canada (Carswell), 1988); J.W. Samuels, *Legal Citation for Canadian Lawyers* (Toronto: Butterworth & Co. (Canada), 1968); and *Canadian Guide to Uniform Legal Citation*, 4th ed. (Scarborough, Ontario: Thomson Canada (Carswell), 1998). Useful information pertaining to the citation of books, periodicals, and American material generally may be found in the current (fifteenth) edition of Harvard Law Review's *The Bluebook: A Uniform System of Citation*.

When citing cases, statutes, regulations or other materials, a full citation is necessary. The citation for a case, statute or other legal material appears in a footnote or in the body of a memorandum. Always cite primary material before secondary material.

Never quote from secondary material when a primary source is available, except when you need a broad generalization to set the stage for detailed consideration. Unless you have no alternative, do not depend on a textbook or a legal periodical for a citation or for the interpretation of a case or statute. However, if you must do so, be sure to acknowledge the fact in a footnote.

2. Footnoting

Usually citations appear in footnotes. The general practice followed by most legal texts and law journals is to place footnotes at the bottom of each page. A few publications place citations at the end of chapters or articles (called "references" or "endnotes"). In many law offices it is common practice to include citations in the body of a memorandum, often in parenthesis, following a statement from the authority cited. Many Canadian law schools prefer the use of footnotes in student papers. If in doubt, assume that citations are to be placed in footnotes at the bottom of each page.

NOTE: The sample memorandum in this book uses parenthesis when adding information to the basic citation as shown on page 134, but not for the citation itself.

The most common practice is to raise the footnote number half a space in the text. Usually footnotes are numbered consecutively throughout an article, memorandum or each chapter of a book.

The names of cases and titles of books are usually italicized (and sometimes in bold-face type as well) in published text or underlined in typescript, as are the titles of statutes, although some publishers do not italicize titles of statutes. (Italicize references to the titles of all statutes in published material, even though the titles of acts appearing in the official statute volumes may not, themselves, be italicized.) The titles of periodical articles are usually placed in quotation marks, although sometimes titles are italicized in published material. This manual recommends placing the titles of articles in quotation marks.

If a particular passage in a case, article, or book is quoted or cited as authority, the page or pages on which it appears are indicated by the use of "at 00" or "at 00-00".

[11]   J.C. Smith, "The Unique Nature of the Concepts of Western Law" (1968), 46 Can. Bar Rev. 191, at 195.

[12]   *Osborne* v. *Canada (Treasury Board)* (1991), 82 D.L.R. (4th) 321, at 331 (S.C.C.).

[13]   M.P. Furmston, *Cheshire, Fifoot and Furmston's Law of Contract*, 12th ed. (London: Butterworths, 1991) at 115.

Legal writing of all kinds tends to be heavily footnoted. Since law is built on a system of authoritative pronouncements, propositions put forward are commonly supported by the citation of authority. However interesting a writer's opinions may be, a lawyer, because of his or her training, will want to assess the extent to which the ideas are based on authority, particularly when in the process of forming a professional opinion. Indeed, lawyers often use articles or memoranda merely as a means of discovering relevant cases or statutes. Thus, footnoting of authorities will make your legal writing more useful. Even more important, plagiarism must be carefully avoided. All direct quotes, paraphrases and borrowed ideas must be acknowledged by footnote references.

In legal writing, footnotes are frequently used for purposes other than the citation of authorities. They may be used to introduce subsidiary points, to deal with conflicting views, and generally, for the discussion of matters that interrupt the flow of the main argument.

3. Quotations

Quotation Marks and Indentation

Any passage quoted directly from other writings that is less than 50 words should normally be enclosed in quotation marks, but not set off from the text. If it is more than 50 words, (or if it is a legislative provision, irrespective of length) it should normally be indented on both sides of the page and single-spaced without quotation marks. (The latter is called a "block quote".) Where it is necessary to change the quotation for the flow of the argument, the altered portion should be placed in square brackets. Where only part of a passage is reproduced by the author, the first letter of the passage being quoted should be capitalized and placed in square brackets. If quoted material contains an error, place "sic" in square brackets (*i.e.*, [sic]) after the word(s).

Omissions

The omission of words from a quoted passage should be indicated by the ellipsis signal (three dots). The following rules will apply:

(1) The ellipsis is not used at the beginning of a sentence or after the period at the end of a final quoted sentence.

(2) When quoting a phrase from a text or when using quoted material as a phrase the ellipsis is not used before or after the phrase which is quoted.

Example:

The Supreme Court of Canada decided that the award of $300,000 arising out of a breach of the wrongful dismissal was not "[a debt]...for services performed for the corporation" for which the directors of Wabasso would be liable and that section 114 "is [there] to ensure that certain sums, including wages, are paid to employees in the event the corporation becomes bankrupt or insolvent". (*Crabtree* v. *Barrette* (1993), 10 B.L.R. 1 (S.C.C.), quoting A. Bohemier and A-M. Poliquin, "Réflexion sur la protection des salariés dans la cadre de la fuillite on de l'insolvabilité" (1988), 48 R. du B. 75, at 81).

(3) When omitting material from within a quoted phrase or sentence use an ellipsis.

Examples:

(i) Phrase

"[A]ccording to traditional wisdom, Parliament always was...concerned with protecting employees" where a company declared bankruptcy or insolvency.

(ii) Sentence

"The parameter which is at the heart of the appeal is therefore not the concept of wages, but the expression 'debts...for services performed by the corporation'."

(4)   When words are omitted from the beginning of a quoted sentence capitalize the first letter and place it in square brackets unless it is capitalized in the source text.

Example:

"[O]ne can see and read object code as a series of 0s and 1s when the same has been printed out by a computer...no programmer can find those 0s and 1s on looking at any part of the computer's hardware or software for they are but electrical impulse."

(5)   When words are omitted from the end of a quoted sentence the ellipsis is used following the final punctuation to show the omission.

Example:

"To the extent the individual features of the Macintosh interface are licensed or are unprotectible they are together...with the protectible features, claimed as copyrightable arrangement - a 'look and feel' which constitutes protectible expression apart from its individual elements...."

(6)   When words are omitted between the end of the sentence and additional quoted material the ellipsis is used together with punctuation at the end of a new sentence. An ellipsis is not used to indicate that the text which follows a period or other final punctuation that concludes a final quoted sentence was not included in the quoted passage.

Example:

"Southam has not denied that it failed to meet the delivery schedule stipulated in the contract....[T]here was a breach of the contract in this respect which frustrated the commercial purpose of the contract."

Paragraph Structure

In a block quote, the paragraph structure of the original material is retained by indenting the first sentence of each paragraph. If the first word of the quoted paragraph is not the first word of the original paragraph, however, no indentation is shown. Also, if material is omitted at the beginning of the first paragraph, no indentation or ellipsis should occur. If material is omitted from the beginning of the second or subsequent paragraphs, this is indicated by indentation and by an ellipsis.

If there is a substantial omission of a paragraph or more, four dots should be inserted in its place, leaving a double space between the dots and the paragraphs above and below.

Example:

"Defamation can be conveyed in any number of styles. What matters is the tendency of the utterance, not its form. Ridicule, *e.g.*, is a familiar weapon for attacking reputation, as by juxtaposing the plaintiff's portrait with that of a gorilla in a magazine article or by publishing a photo of him in what appears to be an obscene posture. On the other hand, if a statement is made as a harmless joke and so understood, its defamatory barb may thereby disappear.

. . .

[D]efamation is confined to only those that strike at character or reputation."

If you wish to draw attention to certain words in a quoted passage, you should italicize those words and include the explanation "[Emphasis added]" at the end of the passage. Any other modifications (such as a change from upper to lower case or vice versa or the substitution of one or more words) in the quoted passage should likewise be noted.

Example:

The report goes on to say that "drastic changes to the current procedure are *not* necessary at this time". [Emphasis added]

4. Introductory Signals

"Introductory Signals" is the term applied, in the Harvard Law Review's *A Uniform System of Citation*, to words or symbols used to introduce the citation of an authority in a footnote. The signal indicates the degree of support afforded the proposition in the text by the authority cited. No signal is used where the footnote simply identifies the source of a quote or gives the citations of the case or statute named in the text, nor is the signal used where the cited authority directly supports the proposition in the text.

The signals set out in *A Uniform System of Citation* to support a proposition advanced are the following:

[No signal necessary]

Example:

The doctrine of ancient lights is worthy of examination as it does demonstrate that "the law can recognize and protect a natural resource that supplies significant benefits to individuals". M. Freeman, "Securing Solar Access in Maine" (1980), 32 Me. L. Rev. 439, at 440.

NOTE: In the above example, no signal is required as the cited authority directly identifies the source of the quotation and states the proposition.

e.g.,   This indicates there are other authorities that state the proposition; "*e.g.,*" which is italicized and followed by a comma, is also frequently used in combination with other signals:

See, *e.g.*
But see, *e.g.*

Example:

The recognition by the Superior Courts in both British Columbia and Nova Scotia of the need for caution in dispensing with a parent's consent is consistent with recent developments in English law. *E.g.*, P. Seago & A. Bissett-Johnson, *Cases and Materials on Family Law* (London: Sweet and Maxwell, 1976), at 418-481; A. Bissett-Johnson, "Step-Parent Adoptions" (1978), 41 Mod. L. Rev. 96; B. Hoggett, "Adoption by Step-Parents" (1973), 117 Sol. J. 606.

Accord   "*Accord*" is used when two or more cases state or clearly support the statement, but the text quotes or refers to only one; the others are then introduced by "*accord*". "*Accord*" is also apt to show that the law of another jurisdiction is in accord with the law of the jurisdiction cited.

Example:

Contracting parties cannot exclude an antecedent right to sue in tort unless an intention to do so is clearly expressed in the contract. *Edgeworth Construction* v. *N.D. Lea & Assoc.* (1993), 17 C.C.L.T. (2d) 101 (S.C.C.). *Accord BG*

Checo Int'l v. B.C. Hydro (1993), 14 C.C.L.T. (2d) 233 (S.C.C.) and *Central Trust Co. v. Rafuse*, [1986] 2 S.C.R. 147.

See   This indicates that an examination of the material cited will support the proposition put forth, although the proposition is not put forth explicitly in that material.

Example:

Lord Denning's sometimes cavalier attitude to precedent and his attachment to general principles of fairness for resolving contractual disputes appear very attractive to trial judges. See *McKenzie* v. *Bank of Montreal* (1975), 55 D.L.R. (3d) 641 (Ont. H.C.).

See also   This indicates material that might profitably be examined by the reader because it provides additional support for the proposition in the text.

Example:

Despite the fact that several communities attempt to use zoning to "freeze" land, the practice has run into trouble in the courts. See *Re Corporation of District of North Vancouver Zoning ByLaw 4277*, [1973] 2 W.W.R. 260 (B.C.S.C.); see also *Regina Auto Court* v. *Regina (City)* (1958), 25 W.W.R. (N.S.) 167 (Sask. Q.B.).

Cf.   This indicates that the material cited lends support to the proposition in the text, although directed to a different point.

Example:

An obligation of confidence under the law relating to breach of confidence may arise from a condition precedent of confidentiality between a private company and the Crown to which the company has submitted a proposal to develop Alpine Ski facilities. *Pharand Ski Corp.* v. *Alberta* (1991), 7 C.C.L.T. (2d) 225 (Alta. Q.B.). *Cf. LAC Minerals Ltd.* v. *Int'l Corona Resources*, [1989] 2 S.C.R. 574 (holding that the acquisition of property by one company as a result of information given in contemplation of a possible joint venture amounted to a breach of confidence at common law).

The following signals contradict a proposition advanced:

Contra   This indicates that the material cited directly contradicts the proposition in the text.

Examples:

The application of the doctrine of *ex turpi causa non oritur actio* to tort actions was accepted by the British Columbia Court of Appeal in *Hall* v. *Hebert* (1991), 6 C.C.L.T. (2d) 294. *Contra Gala* v. *Preston* (1991), 172 C.L.R. 243 (Aust. H.C.) and *Pitts* v. *Hunt*, [1990] 3 All E.R. 344 (C.A.).

The Court of Appeal in *Metall and Rohstoff AG* v. *Donaldson Lufkin & Jenrette Inc.*, [1989] 3 All E.R. 14 (C.A.), gave a narrow application to the tort of civil conspiracy in requiring proof in every case that the predominant intention of the conspirators was to injure the plaintiff. See *Allied Arab Bank Ltd.* v. *Hajjar* (No. 2), [1988] 3 All E.R. 103 (Q.B.D.). *Contra Lonrho plc* v. *Fayed*, [1991] 3 All E.R. 303 (H.L.) (holding that if the conspirators used unlawful means to injure the business interests of the plaintiff it was no defence to say that their predominant purpose was to advance a legitimate business interest).

But see   This indicates that the cited authority supports a proposition contrary to the main proposition.

Example:

King v. *University of Saskatchewan*, [1969] S.C.R. 678, seems to lay down the general principle that a later, properly conducted appeal can cure an earlier defective hearing. But see *Leary* v. *National Union of Vehicle Builders*, [1971] 1 Ch. 34 (holding that, as a general rule, a failure of natural justice in the trial body cannot be cured by a sufficiency of natural justice in the appellate body).

But *cf.*   This indicates contradiction, but is not as strong as "but see". The cited authority supports a proposition analogous to the contrary of the main proposition.

Example:

These arguments seem strongly to support the idea that defects in a hearing should not be curable by properly conducted appeals. But *cf. Calvin* v. *Carr*, [1979] 2 W.L.R. 755 (P.C.) (suggesting that in some circumstances an appeal might cure an earlier defect).

In addition to the above signals, "see generally" is commonly used to indicate useful background material related to the proposition. "Compare" (which is used with the connectives "with" or "and") may also be used to contrast sources that support or illustrate a proposition in the text. "Compare" differs from "*cf.*" in that the former requires comparison of two or more references which, standing alone, could not support the proposition.

Examples:

For a good discussion of China's development in the late nineteenth century, see generally J. Chesneaux et al., *China from the Opium Wars to the 1911 Revolution* (New York: Pantheon Books, 1977).

Prior to the Court of Appeal's decision in *Lewis* v. *Averay*, [1972] 1 Q.B. 198, the English law on mistaken identity favoured a distinction between mistake as to identity and mistake as to attributes. However, in application the distinction often produced conflicting decisions in situations where the facts were clearly indistinguishable. Compare *Phillips* v. *Brooks Ltd.*, [1919] 2 K.B. 243, with *Ingram* v. *Little*, [1961] 1 Q.B. 31 (C.A.).

5. Repeated References

One source or authority may be cited more than once. In fact, it is common in legal writing to refer repeatedly to the same case or other source referring, perhaps, to different pages each time. The first reference to a source is given a full citation in a footnote. A subsequent footnote reference to that source is not given a full citation. It merely refers back to the initial footnote citation.

A citation to a repeated reference consists of the name of the source, or a shortened version of the name, and a cross-referencing signal, such as *supra* or *ibid.*, to direct the reader to the footnote giving the full citation of the source. If a shortened version of the source is to be used, the reader should indicate this in square brackets at the end of the full citation by the use of the word "hereinafter" for legislation or cases.

Examples:

Alberta Oil Sands Technology and Research Authority Act, R.S.A. 1980, c. O-6 [hereinafter *Oil Sands Act*].
Rights of the Aboriginal Peoples of Canada, Part II of the *Constitution Act 1982* (U.K.), being Schedule B to the *Canada Act, 1982*, R.S.C. 1985, App. II, c. 44 [hereinafter cited as *Aboriginal Rights*].
R. v. *Skinner* (1985), 58 N.R. 240 (S.C.C.) [hereinafter cited as *Skinner*].
A.G. Guest, ed., *Chitty on Contracts*, 26th ed. (London: Sweet & Maxwell, 1989) [hereinafter cited as *Chitty*].

Where the citation includes parallel references to other cases, it may be useful to indicate which source is being referred to in subsequent footnote references with the use of the expression "cited to...".

Taylor v. *Co-operative Fire & Casualty Co.* (1984), 35 Alta. L.R. (2d) 77, 57 A.R. 328, 10 C.C.L.I. 284 (Q.B.) [hereinafter *Co-op* cited to Alta. L.R.].

If a secondary source is referred to more than once, the shortened citation may refer to the author's name, in which case the writer need not indicate "hereinafter" or "hereinafter cited as". Alternatively, the writer may refer to the shortened version of the title of the work.

Examples:

¹ S.M. Waddams, *The Law of Damages* (Toronto: Canada Law Book, 1983).
⁵ S.M. Waddams, *supra* note 1 at 36.
or
² R.M. Fernandes, *Marine Insurance Law of Canada* (Toronto: Butterworths, 1987) [hereinafter *Marine*].
⁶ *Marine, supra* note 2, at 45.

The simplest way to cross-reference is by using, in footnotes, the words "*supra*" for that which has gone before and "*infra*" for that which comes after. Note that the words are italicized.

Examples:

⁷ *R.* v. *Skinner* (1985), 58 N.R. 240 (S.C.C.).
¹² *Skinner, supra* note 7, at 243.

Where the author is directing the reader to a footnote appearing later in the work, the footnote might state:

¹ *Infra* note 6.

In some instances the writer may simply wish to refer to material discussed later in the work. In this instance, the term "below" should be used.

² For a discussion of the citation and footnoting of legal literature see Section 6, below.

"*Ibid.*" (*Ibidem*, in the same place) may be used where there is no intervening footnote between the first and second references to a source. It takes the place of the name and citation of a case, or of the author, title and citation of an article or book. "*Ibid.*" can appear after the original full citation, or after the use of "*supra*", or following the use of another "*ibid.*" in a footnote. It should not be used as the first citation on a page. If the writer directs the reader to a page reference which is not the same as the preceding note, this must be indicated.

Examples:

[16] *McLean* v. *Pettigrew*, [1945] S.C.R. 62, at 63.
[17] *Ibid.*

or

[33] *Watteau* v. *Fenwick*, [1893] 1 Q.B. 346.
[34] *Ibid.* at 348-350.

6. The Citation and Footnoting of Legal Literature

By the time most students enter law school they have adopted a workable system of footnoting material derived from periodicals, books and other sources. Legal citation, however, may differ in some respects from the practice recommended in other disciplines. The following examples are representative of common usage in Canada for the citation of books and articles.

Books

With respect to both books and articles do not capitalize all the letters in the title. It is common in Canada to use upper and lower case letters. Titles of books are italicized (and may also appear in bold-face) in printed text. Normally, a subtitle need not be cited as part of a title unless it imparts clarifying substantive information. Abbreviations are not acceptable unless employed in the actual text.

When citing a book in a piece of legal writing, it is helpful to place in brackets, before the date of publication, the place of publication, as well as the publisher's name. Generally, references to definite articles, abbreviations such as "Inc.", "Ltd.", "Co.", and, also, the words "publishing" or "publisher", which may appear on the title page, are omitted.

Example:

G.J. Borrie, *Elements of Public Law* (London: Sweet & Maxwell, 1967).

When there are two or three authors, list the initials and surnames of each separating the last two with an ampersand (&).

Examples:

D.A. Dukelow & B. Nuse, *Dictionary of Canadian Law* (Scarborough, Ontario: Thomson Canada (Carswell), 1991).
M.O. Price, H. Bitner & S.R. Bysiewicz, *Effective Legal Research*, 4th ed. (Boston: Little, Brown and Co., 1979).

A work of more than three authors may be designated by the initials and surname of the first author followed by "et al.", which is followed by a comma:

B. Cass et al., *Why So Few? Women Academics in Australian Universities* (Sydney: Sydney University Press, 1983).

In Canadian legal writing it is the usual practice to include a reference to the name of an editor or editors, followed by the abbreviation "ed." or "eds." and a comma.

Example:

R. St. J. Macdonald, G.L. Morris & D.M. Johnston, eds., *Canadian Perspectives on International Law and Organization* (Toronto: University of Toronto Press, 1974).

In some books, the name of the original author has become part of the title. Reference should be made also to the current editor or editors.

Example:

A.G. Guest, ed., *Chitty on Contracts*, 26th ed. (London: Sweet & Maxwell, 1989).

Where the name of the original author is retained, separate from the title, the name of the editor is commonly placed after the edition reference.

Example:

R.E. Megarry, *Manual of the Law of Real Property*, 6th ed. by D.F. Hayton (London: Stevens & Sons, 1982).

Periodical Articles

In citing articles appearing in periodicals, the year of the volume (in round brackets) is placed immediately after the name of the article and before the volume number, name of the periodical and page number. It is common to give the author's initials and last name in citing articles, as is the case with books. The title of an article is often placed in quotation marks (unlike the title of a book which is italicized in printed text) and many publishers place a comma after the title if the year appears in square brackets and omit the comma if the year appears in round brackets. The abbreviations for legal periodicals are not italicized. Information on the details of publication are not included when referring to a periodical.

The major legal periodicals are contained in several sources; consult the *Index to Canadian Legal Literature*, the *Index to Canadian Periodical Literature*, *Black's Law Dictionary*, *Osborn's Concise Oxford Law Dictionary* and the latest edition of *The Bluebook: A Uniform System of Citation*.

Examples:

C. Boyle, "The Battered Wife Syndrome and Self-Defence: *Lavallee* v. *R* ." (1990), 9 Can. J. of Fam. L. 171.

S. Boyd, "Child Custody and Working Mothers" in K. Mahoney & S. Martin, eds., *Equality and Judicial Neutrality* (Toronto: Carswell, 1987) at 168.

If a particular periodical employs a calendar year system rather than a volume number, the year is placed in square brackets.

Examples:

T.R.S. Allan, "Legislative Supremacy and the Rule of Law", [1985] Camb. L.J. 111 at 113.

P. Birks, "Personal Restitution in Equity", [1988] Lloyd's Mar. and Com. Quart. 128 at 132.

The rules governing multiple authors are the same for periodicals as for textbooks.

Examples:

E. Abner, M.J. Mossman & E. Pickett, "A Matter of Simple Justice: Assessing the Report of the Royal Commission on the Status of Women in Canada" (1990), 22 Ottawa L. Rev.573.

J. Bonta et al., "The Characteristics of Aboriginal Recidivists" (1992), 34 Can. J. Crim. 15.

CHAPTER 4

American Legal Materials

American and Canadian legal materials are essentially similar as both legal systems have their common origin in English law. Canadian students, therefore, should find little difficulty in adapting themselves to American materials. However, the sheer volume of primary materials emanating from the multitude of American jurisdictions has generated a corresponding volume of secondary materials which appears, at first sight, to be a labyrinth of annotations and cross-references. Contrary to this first impression, research into American law is greatly simplified by the existence of several comprehensive systems of interrelated legal materials. In particular, the West Publishing Company employs "Key Numbers" to correlate its editions of annotated statutes, case reports, encyclopedias, digests, words and phrases, and rules of practice and procedure. Also, there is an exhaustive citation service collectively entitled *Shepard's Citations*. A familiarity with these systems will greatly expedite research.

This chapter attempts only to introduce the reader to the most useful American materials. The section on primary materials deals with the United States Constitution, federal statutes, and federal and regional case reports. The section on secondary materials describes the most important digest, encyclopedic and citator services. For greater detail, consult the following publications:

M.L. Cohen & R.C. Berring, *How to Find the Law*, 9th ed. (St. Paul: West Publishing, 1989).

M.L. Cohen & K.C. Olson, *Legal Research in a Nutshell*, 6th ed. (St. Paul: West Publishing, 1996).

How to Use Shepard's Citations (Colorado Springs, Colo.: Shepard's, 1984).

J.M. Jacobstein & R.M. Mersky, *Fundamentals of Legal Research*, 5th ed. (Westbury, N.Y.: Foundation Press, 1990).

Legal Research Illustrated, An Abridgment of Fundamentals of Legal Research, 5th ed., (Westbury, N.Y.: The Foundation Press, 1990).

M.O. Price, H. Bitner & S.R. Bysiewicz, *Effective Legal Research*, 4th ed. (Boston: Little, Brown and Co., 1979).

W.P. Slatsky, *Legal Research and Writing: Some Starting Points*, 4th ed. (St. Paul: West Publishing, 1993).

West's Law Finder: A Legal Research Manual (St. Paul: West Publishing, 1991).

A. PRIMARY MATERIALS

1. The United States Constitution

The text of the Constitution may be found in almost all compilations of federal, state and municipal laws. However, the following annotated editions are recommended:

The Constitution of the United States of America; Analysis and Interpretation (Library of Congress ed. 1987)

This is a convenient compendium of the U.S. Constitution, bringing together historical and contemporary commentary, as well as summaries of judicial interpretations of each clause of the U.S. Constitution. There are extensive annotations of major constitutional decisions, including footnotes which may be particularly useful for Canadian students researching material related to the *Canadian Charter of Rights and Freedoms*. An index covers both the text and the annotations. It is kept up to date by pocket supplements.

United States Code Annotated, Constitution Volumes (cited as U.S.C.A.)

A West publication, this unofficial set includes several volumes devoted entirely to the U.S. Constitution. The text is annotated, including assigned key numbers, with federal and state decisions that deal with each article or amendment of the U.S. Constitution. There is an index to the U.S. Constitution in the last volume of the set. This multi-volume set is kept current with cumulative annual pocket parts and supplement pamphlets.

United States Code Service, Constitution Volumes (cited as U.S.C.S.)

The U.S.C.S. also publishes several constitutional volumes. Each section of text is annotated with court decisions, and there are cross-references to *American Law Reports* (A.L.R.) and other Lawyers Co-op Practice publications. There is an index to the U.S. Constitution in the last volume of the set. This set is supplemented by annual pocket parts and by *Later Case and Statutory Service* pamphlets.

Shepard's United States Citations — Statute Editions

This work provides ready access to federal court decisions which have considered selected clauses of the U.S. Constitution. It provides citations to the U.S. Constitution and state constitutions; the *United States Code* and acts of Congress (not included in the *United States Code*); various state codes, legislative enactments and court rules; and various municipal charters and ordinances.

Additional judicial interpretations of the U.S. Constitution can be found in digests of federal cases, such as the *Digest of United States Supreme Court Reports*, *United States Supreme Court Digest* and *Federal Digest*, and in annotations in the *American Law Reports Federal Annotated* and the *United States Supreme Court Reports, Lawyers' Edition*.

2. Federal Statutes

United States Code (cited as U.S.C.)

United States Statutes at Large

The earliest official print of a federal statute is known as a "slip law". At the end of each congressional session, the slip laws are cumulated and bound, in numerical and chronological order, in a set entitled *United States Statutes at Large*. The *Statutes at Large* are the official text of federal statutes. They include public and private laws, as well as an index for each session. Amendments appear in subsequent laws, which can be located by referring to the tables in each volume. These tables list how each public law affects previous public acts. The public laws of general interest are printed later in a subject arrangement of statutes called the *United States Code*, printed by the U.S. Government Printing Office. Sections of statutes are referenced to the original text in the official *Statutes at Large*. A citation to the U.S.C. can be located in either the *United States Code Annotated* or the *United States Code Service*, both of which are discussed below. Each contains the exact text of the *Code*, as found in the official U.S.C., but, in addition, each contains annotations of court decisions that have cited or interpreted a section of the U.S.C. The *Code* is published in a revised edition every six years and is served by annual cumulative bound supplements. LEXIS and WESTLAW have the current text of the U.S.C. in their databases.

United States Code Annotated (cited as U.S.C.A.)

This is a privately published annotated edition of the official text of United States statutes. It gives references to amendments, case notes and secondary sources which assist the user in interpreting the *Code*. A subject index to the annotations directs the user to abstracts related to particular sections of statutes. The set is served by a multi-volume general index, in paperback, which is issued annually, annual pocket part supplements located at the back of each volume and monthly advance pamphlets, indicating changes in the law. This is now available on CD-ROM.

United States Code Service (cited as U.S.C.S.)

A publication of Lawyers Co-operative Publishing Co., this unofficial set is similar in format to the official *Code*. It contains authority references, historical notes, cross-references and other research aids in a section entitled "History; Ancillary Laws and Directives", case annotations in a section entitled "Interpretive Notes and Decisions", and a "Research Guide". This set is served by a multi-volume general index, several volumes of tables and a two-volume *United States Code Guide*. The *United States Code Service* is kept up to date with cumulative annual pocket parts, a cumulative quarterly *Later Case and Statutory Service* and monthly *Advance* pamphlets.

U.S. Federal Statutes on the Internet

The *U.S. Code* is available online: Legal Information Institute <http://www.law.cornell.edu:80/uscode/>.

The site provides a Table of Contents by title listing, and allows for searching within each title.

3. State Statutes

The organization and publication of state statutes is similar to that of federal statutes. All states publish and index laws enacted by their legislatures. There are annotated "codes" for every state and both the law and annotations are kept up to date by annual pocket parts and pamphlet supplements. Each state annotated "code" is served by a general index for all the volumes of the set. Two other useful sources are the *Constitutions of the United States, National and State*, 2nd ed. (1974 to date), which publishes the state constitutions in looseleaf format, and the *Statute Editions* and state citators published as parts of *Shepard's Citations*. Many state constitutions can be retrieved from WESTLAW and LEXIS.

4. Federal Case Reports

United States Reports (cited as U.S.)
West's Supreme Court Reporter (cited as S. Ct. or Sup. Ct.)
United States Supreme Court Reports. Lawyers' Edition (cited as L. Ed. and
   L. Ed. 2d) (hereinafter referred to as *Lawyers' Edition*)[1]

The official source of Supreme Court judgments is the *United States Reports*, printed by the U.S. Government Printing Office. Each decision is issued first as a "slip opinion"; next, it is reproduced in an advance sheet (called a "preliminary print"), and then, perhaps as much as 12 months later, is published in a bound

---

[1] This edition is also known as *Rose's Notes* edition.

volume. There are two unofficial Supreme Court reporters: *West's Supreme Court Reporter* and the *United States Supreme Court Reports, Lawyers' Edition*, both of which publish cases before the *United States Reports*. These two report series have cross-reference tables listing the cases in the *United States Reports*.

West's Supreme Court Reporter, a part of its *National Reporter System*, begins its coverage with the October Term in 1882. It is available in advance sheet form, biweekly, and then as one or two bound annual volumes. Each decision contains a "synopsis" (a summary) and extensive headnoting furnished with West's "Key Number" classification system. Refer to the discussion of this system provided below.

The *Lawyers' Edition*, a publication of Lexis Law Publishing Co.[2], has been available since 1882 and it is now in its second series. It includes all cases from the *United States Reports*, summaries of each case, annotations and summaries of the briefs of counsel. This latter feature is useful as a learning aid for the beginning student. Headnotes are classified according to topic and section numbers. Since volume 32[3], each volume has pocket part supplements at the back which have a *Citator Service*, consisting of brief summaries from Supreme Court opinions subsequent to those reported in the volume and a *Later Case Service* which supplements the annotations in the volume. This set has two useful companions, the *United States Supreme Court Digest, Lawyers' Edition*, and a *Desk Book to the United States Supreme Court Reports, Lawyers' Edition*. The latter was first published in 1978 and has been updated by supplements since then. It contains several tables, as well as an index to all annotations in L. Ed. 2d and A.L.R. Fed.

United States Law Week (cited as U.S.L.W.)

This unofficial weekly publication of United States Supreme Court decisions is from the Bureau of National Affairs. It is published in two or more looseleaf volumes which may be available to subscribers within a matter of days after decisions are rendered.

The first two pages of the binder contain the section called "Case Alert". This section details the contents of the issue in topical abstracts. The second section provides one-paragraph summaries of selected cases. The full text can be accessed through the Bureau of National Affairs Webpage online: <http://www.bna.com/index.html>. A general topical index is compiled for the first two sections.

The third section, "Supreme Court Today", contains Supreme Court proceedings and opinions. This section is indexed separately and has the following features: summary of orders; journal proceedings; cases docketed; summary of

---

[2]   This series was formerly published by the Lawyers Co-op Publishing.
[3]   There are two-volume sets for volumes 1-31.

cases recently filed; hearings scheduled; arguments before the court; table of cases and case status report; and a topical index.

WESTLAW and LEXIS

These two computer research services, referred to in Chapter 5, allow access to the full text of all Supreme Court decisions within 72 hours after they are rendered. LEXIS also provides Supreme Court briefs.

NOTE: The LEXIS network currently provides a computerized source for American citations and Shepardizing. One can access both cases and statutes with the system, as well as track their legislative histories and bring them up to date with the Shepardizing function.

Federal Reporter (cited as F., or Fed. in some older cases, or F. 2d)
Federal Supplement (cited as F. Supp.)

The *Federal Reporter* (1880 to date), now in its second series, is part of the *National Reporter System*. Until 1932, it included opinions from Circuit and District Courts, but it now reports, primarily, cases from the intermediate U.S. Courts of Appeal. It has also published decisions from various federal courts, *i.e.*, U.S. Commerce Court, U.S. Court of Patent Appeals, U.S. Court of Appeals, and Temporary Emergency Court of Appeals. From time to time, the *Federal Reporter* also includes a list of "Decisions without Published Opinions".

The *Federal Supplement*, also a West Publication, began in 1932, and publishes, *inter alia*, selected decisions of the federal district courts, as well as decisions and rulings from other special courts, *i.e.*, U.S. Court of Claims, Court of International Trade, Special Court of the Regional Rail Reorganization Act, and Judicial Panel on Multidistrict Litigation. Published decisions from the Court of International Trade may be of particular value to Canadian researchers. Both of these sets are published in advance sheets and then in bound volumes.

Two other useful sources of decisions of federal courts are *Federal Cases* (for cases prior to 1880) and *Federal Rules Decisions*.

5. Regional Case Reports

West's National Reporter System

The decisions of the courts of individual states are published in official or unofficial reporters, or in both. The most widely used unofficial source of state case reporting is known as *West's National Reporter System*, which began in 1879 with the *North Western Reporter*. The system includes seven regional reporters, and two state reporters, namely, the *California Reporter* and *New York Supplement*. The *National Reporter System* contains opinions of state, federal and special courts, and covers all state intermediate appellate court decisions, as well as selected trial court decisions. The reporters publish weekly advance paper parts which are bound later in hard-cover volumes. The regional reporters are:

Atlantic Reporter, 1885 to date; Conn., Del., Me., Md., N.H., N.J., Pa., R.I., Vt., D.C. (cited as A. and A.2d);
North Eastern Reporter, 1885 to date; Ill., Ind., Mass., N.Y., Ohio (cited as N.E. and N.E.2d);
North Western Reporter, 1879 to date; Iowa, Mich., Minn., Neb., N.D., S.D., Wis. (cited as N.W. and N.W.2d);
Pacific Reporter, 1883 to date; Alaska, Ariz., Cal., Colo., Hawaii, Idaho, Kan., Mont., Nev., N.M., Okla., Or., Utah, Wash., Wyo. (cited as P. and P.2d);
Southern Reporter, 1887 to date; Ala., Fla., La., Miss. (cited as So. and So.2d);
South Eastern Reporter, 1887 to date; Ga., N.C., S.C., Va., W. Va. (cited as S.E. and S.E.2d); and
South Western Reporter, 1886 to date; Ark., Ky., Mo., Tenn., Tex. (cited as S.W. and S.W.2d).

These nine reporters, together with other West publications, comprise a uniform system bound together by a topic and key number indexing and digesting scheme (*American Digest* classification scheme). The basic unit of the system is known as an "abstract" or "headnote". This is a one-sentence summary of each principle of law dealt with in a case, prepared by the publisher's editorial staff. A case has as many headnotes as there are points of law in a decision and each abstract appears under a key number and one of West's 400 topic headings. The key number is assigned and fixed to a particular point of case law. Every point of case law has its own key number.

Example:

Contracts  9

Certainty as to subject-matter

West's Key Number System is used in all West's reporters covering state and federal courts. The system is of significant practical value because all cases classified under the same key number may be easily retrieved and one case on point will readily lead to others which have the same key number. As well, it permits a relatively quick transfer from the report series of the researcher's own jurisdiction to the report series of many other jurisdictions.

The key number system and headnotes from the decisions in a West reporter are brought together to form another component of the West system known as "Key Number Digests" or simply as "case law indices". These are published for jurisdictional (*e.g.*, *New York Digest*, *Pacific Digest*) and court (*e.g.*, *Federal*

Digest) report series, and each serves as an index to all the cases published in its report series.

All individual digests, such as the *North Eastern Digest* and the *United States Supreme Court Digest*, are consolidated into a master index to all the case law of the United States. This is called the *American Digest System*[4]. Thus, while the *North Eastern Digest* covers all the cases reported in the *North Eastern Reporter*, the various units of the *American Digest System* cover all decisions published in all West's report series. The units of the system are described, *infra*, at 168.

Cases in WESTLAW contain not only the actual text for each case, but also all of the additional editorial features in the reporters of the *National Reporter System* (the "synopsis", the headnotes, and the Key Numbers).

WESTLAW and LEXIS

These two computer services allow access to full text and/or headnotes of state appellate court decisions. Law librarians usually have various pamphlets available which describe each of these services in detail.

American Law Reports Annotated (cited as A.L.R.)
American Law Reports Federal Annotated (cited as A.L.R. Fed.)

American Law Reports, now in its fifth series, offers a small selection of cases, primarily appellate decisions, from all jurisdictions in the United States based on their usefulness to the practising lawyer. This is the descendant of *Lawyers' Annotated* (L.R.A.), published from 1888 to 1918, and forms part of *The Total Client-Service Library* (TCSL). Each case is printed in full and followed by an annotation. In legal research, A.L.R. Annotated is not used for the reported decisions but rather for subsequent annotations.

An annotation may run to well over 100 pages and consists of an encyclopedic treatment of the issues involved, footnoted to other cases on point, other annotations, and the encyclopedia Am. Jur. 2d. A case often appears in this series a year after the decision is handed down because of the time necessary to prepare the annotations. The *American Law Reports* include the following: First Series, 1918-1948 (175 vols.); Second Series, 1948-1965 (100 vols.); Third Series, 1965-1980 (100 vols.); Fourth Series, 1980-1991 (90 vols.); and Fifth Series, 1992 to date. As well, since 1969, selected federal decisions have been published in a parallel series called *American Law Reports Federal Annotated*.

A.L.R. and A.L.R. Fed. collect, organize, and analyze all the case law relevant to various specific points of law and fact situations. What A.L.R. designates as an annotation is in fact a legal memorandum on a particular aspect of the law that covers all sides of every question, presents general principles deduced from

---

[4]   Every 10 years, these are compiled to form *Decennial Digests*.

the cases, and gives their exceptions, qualifications, distinctions, and applications.

Access to the subject-matter of the annotations may be obtained through the *Quick Index*, a single-volume soft-cover publication for the third, fourth and fifth series which is periodically replaced or supplemented. There is more detailed coverage, however, in the six-volume *Index to Annotations* (covering the 2d, 3d, 4th, 5th, Fed.). It also provides entry into the annotations in the *Lawyers' Edition*, which was an integral part of the L.R.A. This six-volume *Index* replaces the five-volume *Index to Annotations* published in 1986. The A.L.R. Annotated also allows access to full text of cases by reference to a table of cases in the "digest" volumes of the first and second series of A.L.R. There is also a one-volume *Quick Index*, and separate *Table of Cases* volume for the federal series which is kept current by annual pocket supplements.

Once the title and section are located, the user can proceed from one digest to another. There is a 12-volume permanent digest set for A.L.R. (First Series) Annotated, which includes digests of all the material, both decisions and annotations, with "scope notes". A seven-volume digest set covers the second series. This digest service is continued by the nine-volume digest set for the third, fourth, fifth and federal series. This new digest is divided into over 400 topics. A "Table of Contents" for each topic is provided as a guide. Within each title, text references, practice references, annotations and case notes can be obtained. This digest series is kept up to date with periodic pocket supplements.

Annotations in the first series that are supplemented or superseded in subsequent series can be found in the *Blue Book of Supplemental Decisions*, which also lists citations to all decisions on the same topic as the annotations. This eight-volume set is updated by annual cumulative pamphlets. To find the most recent or supplementary annotations to the first series, consult the final volume.

The second series is supplemented by the *Later Case Service* and is a useful tool for reference to additional reported cases on point and for the further development of the law. A.L.R. 3d, A.L.R. 4th, A.L.R. 5th and A.L.R. Fed. are kept up to date by *Later Case Service* pocket supplements.

Any annotations replaced or substantially changed because of the effect of a new judgment are noted in the "Annotation History Table" in the *Index*. The pocket parts of the *Index* provide for later annotations in A.L.R. 5th, A.L.R. Fed. and L. Ed. 2d. The most up to date annotation in A.L.R. may be retrieved in LEXIS simply by entering the volume and page number of the selected annotation; any case citation can be checked through AUTO-CITE.

In addition, the second series has a *Word Index to Annotations*. Since it only covers the annotations, it is intended to be used in conjunction with the digests for the second series which covers the reported cases.

One further aid was introduced with *A.L.R. (Fifth Series) Annotated* in 1992. This is a soft-cover pamphlet entitled *Electronic Search Queries and West Digest Key Number for Annotations in A.L.R. 4th*, which has been since incorporated into the pocket supplements for the fourth series.

6. U.S. Decisions on the Internet

The following sites allow the researcher access to both federal and state court decisions via the Internet:

U.S. Supreme Court Decisions online: Findlaw <http://www.findlaw.com/casecode/>,

U.S. Circuit Court and U.S. State Court Decisions online: National Center for State Courts <http://www.ncsc.dni.us/court/sites/courts.htm>.

B. SECONDARY MATERIALS

1. Encyclopedias

At present, there are two major encyclopedias covering all American jurisdictions: *Corpus Juris Secundum* and *American Jurisprudence 2d.*

Corpus Juris Secundum (cited as volume C.J.S. title and section)

Corpus Juris Secundum, a West publication which supersedes *Corpus Juris*, purports to be based on all reported cases since 1658 from all federal and state jurisdictions. It consists of approximately 150 volumes, including the supplements. The footnotes in C.J.S. occasionally refer to C.J. rather than repeating the citations that appear in that set; therefore, the first series is a useful companion and, thus, it can be still found on law library shelves.

Titles are arranged alphabetically and major titles are subdivided. Each major title is preceded by a note on the scope of the text (the "scope note"). Each subdivision of a major title consists of a statement of the prevailing rule, in bold type, followed by a textual summary of the law on that point. The text is supplied with extensive footnotes to all significant decisions found in West reporters.

A general statement of the law may be found by going directly to the volume which covers the desired topic. At the front of each volume is a list of major titles to the whole set and a list of major titles to that particular volume. Alternatively, the user may refer to the appropriate volume of the three-volume softcover *General Index* to find the desired volume and topic. When a topic is located, either from the list of topics or the *General Index*, consult the detailed table of contents or the "scope note" preceding the topic or, if necessary, the index at the end of the volume for that topic. Cross-references also are included to corresponding West topics and key numbers, allowing access to the *American Digest System*. *Corpus Juris Secundum* is kept up to date by replacement volumes and cumulative annual pocket parts. The pocket parts include a "WESTLAW Electronic Research Guide".

American Jurisprudence 2d (cited as volume Am. Jur. 2d, title and section)

American Jurisprudence 2d provides a comprehensive statement of American law in 83 volumes. While resembling C.J.S. in subject coverage, arrangement, indexing and supplementation, Am. Jur. 2d differs substantially in its scope of citation. Am. Jur. 2d cites only selected decisions in support of its statement of the law and more attention is paid to statutes, especially the *U.S. Code* and *Uniform Laws*. There is a separate volume of *Tables of Statutes, Rules,* and *Regulations Cited* which covers the *United States Code Service*, federal regulations, "Federal Rules of Procedure", "Federal Rules of Evidence", and the "Uniform and Model Laws". The text provides direct leads to supporting cases, related annotations (*i.e.*, A.L.R., A.L.R. Fed. and L. Ed. and L. Ed. 2d), forms, proofs, and trial techniques. The main entry point to the set is the four-volume soft-cover *General Index*, which releases annual updates in soft-cover bound volumes. Am. Jur. 2d is kept up to date by annual pocket supplements and by a looseleaf *New Topic Service*. The series also has a *Desk Book* providing miscellaneous information, as well as useful research and practice aids. The *Desk Book* is updated by pocket supplements.

NOTE: *Corpus Juris Secundum* and *American Jurisprudence* are not authoritative and the user always should read the case reports cited in them. In addition, since individual volumes of these encyclopedias may be several years old, it is important to check the appropriate pocket parts to determine if the cases cited have been judicially considered elsewhere. The American term for this function is "Shepardizing".

2. Digests

American Digest System (cited as Am. Dig.)

The *American Digest System* is the most comprehensive digest service. It covers virtually all decisions from courts of every state and federal jurisdiction since 1658. It is described by West as a "master index to all of the case law of our country". It is an invaluable case finder for the beginning law student since it provides quick access to the *West National Reporter System*, described, *supra*, at 162.

The system is divided into separate units; each covers a ten-year period. These units are called "Decennial Digests". The ninth and succeeding digests appear in two parts, each a complete five-year unit. The *Decennial Digests* contain all headnotes, with corresponding topics and key numbers assigned to cases during a ten-year period. The most current part of the *American Digest System* is the *General Digest*, which is published in bound volumes on a monthly basis. It is, in effect, the advance part for the *Decennial Digest* unit. Every tenth volume of the *Digest* provides cumulative tables for those ten volumes.

Table VI shows the arrangement of the set.

	TABLE VI
1658 to 1896	*Century Digest* (50 vols.)
1897 to 1906	*First Decennial Digest* (1st D) (25 vols.)
1907 to 1916	*Second Decennial Digest* (2d D) (24 vols.)
1916 to 1926	*Third Decennial Digest* (3d D) (29 vols.)
1926 to 1936	*Fourth Decennial Digest* (4th D) (34 vols.)
1936 to 1946	*Fifth Decennial Digest* (5th D) (52 vols.)
1946 to 1956	*Sixth Decennial Digest* (6th D) (36 vols.)
1956 to 1966	*Seventh Decennial Digest* (7th D) (38 vols.)
1966 to 1976	*Eighth Decennial Digest* (8th D) (50 vols.)
1976 to 1981	*Ninth Decennial Digest, Part I* (9th D Pt 1) (38 vols.)
1981 to 1986	*Ninth Decennial Digest, Part II* (9th D Pt 2) (48 vols.)
1986 + 1991	*Tenth Decennial Digest, Part I* (10th D Pt 1) (44 vols.)
1991 - 1996	*Tenth Decennial Digest, Part II* (in progress)
1991 - 1996	*West's General Digest, Eighth Series* (Gen. Dig. 8th)
1996 - 2001	*West's General Digest, Ninth Series* (in progress)

Each *Decennial* unit and *General Digest* of the *American Digest System* has a *Descriptive Word Index*. It is the primary finding aid in all West digests. This *Index* contains lists of fact words from reported decisions and lists of words representing legal concepts in West's Key Number Classification System. It assists in locating relevant subjects and key numbers which may then be used to find cases on a selected problem in the given unit.

3. Citators

Shepard's Citations

This is the most comprehensive citation service in the United States. Its various units annotate, *inter alia*, virtually all statutes and appellate decisions at both the federal and state levels. It constitutes an invaluable aid in assessing the current authority of American primary material. The annotations to cases include parallel citations, judicial histories and construction, articles in periodicals, and other cases on point. A separate set of *Shepard's Citations* is published for each set of court reports, *i.e.*, sets for each of the 50 states, the District of Columbia, and Puerto Rico; separate sets for each of the regional reporters of the *National Reporter System*; one set for the *Federal Reporter* and the *Federal Supplement*; and one for the *American Law Reports Annotated*.

  Shepard's Citations consist of a number of distinct units including:

(i)   *Shepard's Northwestern Reporter Citations*;

(ii)   *Shepard's Atlantic Reporter Citations*;
(iii) *Shepard's Northeastern Reporter Citations*;
(iv)   *Shepard's Pacific Reporter Citations*;
(v)   *Shepard's Southern Reporter Citations*;
(vi)   *Shepard's Southwestern Reporter Citations*;
(vii) *Shepard's Southeastern Reporter Citations*; and
(viii) *Shepard's New York Supplement Reporter Citations*.

A detailed explanation of the process of "Shepardizing" a case or statute is available at the beginning of any volume of *Shepard's Citations* and in the publisher's pamphlet, *How to Use Shepard's Citations*. Shepard's case citators are available online in WESTLAW or LEXIS.

National Reporter Blue Book

This set, published in conjunction with the *National Reporter System*, provides a series of tables showing the *National Reporter Blue Book* citation for every case that appears in the state reports. It is useful for two reasons: (1) many Canadian libraries hold the *National Reporter* but not the state reports; and (2) it is correct form to cite both the official state report and the *National Reporter*, in that order. All state citations are listed alphabetically by state, and parallel citations in the *National Reporter* are also listed. The set consists of the original volume, permanent supplements dated 1936, 1948, 1960, 1970, 1980 and 1990, and annual cumulative supplements.

Corresponding sets for each state, called *Blue and White Books*, provide tables translating citations from the *National Reporter* to the state reports, as well as from the state reports to the *National Reporter*.

4. Words and Phrases

The West Publishing Company's *Words and Phrases* provides all judicial construction and definitions of words and phrases by state and federal courts from 1658. The set is arranged in alphabetical order, like a dictionary. Any word or phrase that appears in several different legal contexts (for example, the heading "Abandon, Abandonment") is broken down into numerous subdivisions and listed immediately after the main heading. Each definition is supplied with a citation to the case report and enough of the context to be easily followed. In addition, cross-references are supplied to synonymous or analogous definitions under other headings. The set is updated annually by cumulative pocket supplements[5] which are further supplemented by "Words and Phrases Tables" in the current volumes and advance sheets of the various units of the *National Reporter System*.

---

[5] The series occasionally issues replacement volumes.

5. Dictionaries

Black's Law Dictionary has been considered a standard for students in both Canada and the United States for many years. It is available in every Canadian law school library.

J.R. Nolan & J.M. Nolan-Haley, *Black's Law Dictionary*, 6th ed. by West Publishing Co. Editorial Staff (St. Paul: West Publishing, 1990).

Some other American law dictionaries are:

W.S. Anderson, ed., *Ballentines' Law Dictionary with Pronunciations*, 3rd ed. (San Francisco: Bancroft-Whitney, 1969).

B. Garner, *A Dictionary of Modern Legal Usage*, 2d ed. (Oxford: Oxford University Press, 1995).

R. Max, *Law Dictionary*, 2nd ed. rev. and expanded by M.O. Price and Oceana Editorial Staff (Dobbs Ferry, N.Y.: Oceana Publications, 1970).

D. Mellinkoff, *Mellinkoff's Dictionary of American Legal Usage* (St. Paul: West Publishing, 1992).

M.M. Prince, ed., *Bieber's Dictionary of Legal Abbreviations*, 4th ed. (Buffalo: W.S. Hein & Co., 1993).

K. Redden & E.L. Veron, *Modern Legal Glossary* (Charlottesville, Va.: Michie, 1980).

P.G. Renstrom, *The American Law Dictionary* (Santa Barbara, Calif.: ABC-CLIO, 1991).

6. Citation Rules for American Legal Materials

American legal materials demand special rules of citation. Follow the rules set down in one of the following manuals:

The Bluebook: A Uniform System of Citation, 15th ed. (Cambridge, Mass.: The Harvard Law Review Association, 1991).

A. Dworsky, *A User's Guide to the Bluebook*, rev. for the 15th ed. of *The Bluebook* (Littleton, Colo.: F.B. Rothman & Co., 1991).

E. Good, *Citing and Typing the Law: A Guide to Legal Citation & Style*, 3rd ed. (Charlottesville, Va.: LEL Enterprises, 1992).

M.O. Price, *A Practical Manual of Standard Legal Citations*, 2nd ed., rev. and expanded (Dobbs Ferry, N.Y.: Oceana Publications, 1970).

M.M. Prince, ed., *Bieber's Dictionary of Legal Citations*, 5th ed. (Buffalo: W.S. Hein & Co., 1997).

7. Research Guides

G. Block, *Effective Legal Writing for Law Students and Lawyers*, 4th ed. (Westbury, N.Y.: Foundation Press, 1992).

M.L. Cohen & R.C. Berring, *Finding the Law: An Abridged Edition of How to Find the Law*, 9th ed., (St. Paul: West Publishing, 1989).

M.L. Cohen & K.C. Olson, *Legal Research in a Nutshell*, 6th ed. (St. Paul: West Publishing, 1996).

S. Elias, *Legal Research: How to Find and Understand the Law*, 4th National ed. (Berkeley, Calif.: Nolo Press, 1995).

J.M. Jacobstein & R.M. Mersky, *Fundamentals of Legal Research*, 7th ed. (Westbury, N.Y.: Foundation Press, 1998).

J.M. Jacobstein & D. Dunn, *Legal Research Illustrated: An Abridgment of Fundamentals of Legal Research*, 5th ed. (Westbury, N.Y.: Foundation Press, 1990).

W.P. Statsky, *Legal Research and Writing: Some Starting Points*, 4th ed. (St. Paul: West Publishing, 1993).

W.P. Statsky et al., *West Legal Desk Reference* (St. Paul: West Publishing, 1990).

L. Teply, *Legal Research & Citation*, 4th ed. (St. Paul: West Publishing, 1992).

CHAPTER 5

Computerized Legal Research

Computerized legal research has established its value as a research tool and in many instances is bringing about fundamental changes in research methods. In a short time, it has lost its reputation as an "interesting novelty" and has become an important component of the law school and law office library. More and more students and lawyers are recognizing that almost every legal research problem has some aspect which can be usefully investigated by computer. At the same time, there is a growing awareness that in order to effectively use a computerized legal research system it is important to understand its limitations and to know how to prepare intelligent search requests. Used effectively, the computer will allow the user to research even complex legal problems and achieve superior results in less time than would normally be possible with entirely manual methods of research.

The computer offers the contemporary researcher five important features:

(i)   speed of retrieval;
(ii) accuracy;
(iii) a substantial data bank;
(iv) currency; and
(v)   new or enhanced opportunities for research.

The single most important component of any computerized legal retrieval system is speed. For example, in less than one minute, LEXIS can search for a phrase in more than one million cases stored in the North Eastern Reporter database. By contrast, an equivalent search in the American Digest System by conventional library methods could take up to three hours.

In recent years, there has been an impressive growth in the number and types of legal databases available in Canada. The advent of the internet has also provided a wealth of legal resources, many of which are freely accessible (see previous chapters), and user-friendly springboards to commercial database providers.

While the computer's speed and accuracy in gathering information will readily be apparent to the beginning student, its value in expanding traditional research techniques will be less evident. The following provides several examples of research options and capabilities that are currently available for computerized legal research.

A. LEXIS-NEXIS

LEXIS-NEXIS provides enhanced information services and management tools to the legal, business, government and academic markets. Through LEXIS-CANADA services, professionals have access to over 6,000 authoritative sources of legal information and over 18,000 sources of news and business information. Users are aided by full text descriptions and several straightforward icons to assist in narrowing their search.

The NEXIS databases contain a wide variety of public records information, company and financial information.

LEXIS-NEXIS Canada contains the statutes and regulations consolidated for each of the following jurisdictions: federal, Ontario, Alberta and British Columbia. It contains numerous reports received directly from courts and boards, including the *Supreme Court Reports*, *Federal Court Reports* and *Canada Industrial Relations Board Reports*. It offers comprehensive case law reporting, through the inclusion of Canada Law Book's summary services (*All Canada Weekly Summaries*, *Weekly Criminal Bulletin* and *Canadian Labour Arbitration Summaries*) linked to the full text of the judgments. It is the only online source for the complete Maritime Law Book National Reporter System, containing over 90,000 decisions from across Canada.

In terms of U.S. content, LEXIS-NEXIS offers the largest selection of online U.S. legal materials available. It is the only online provider to offer Shepard's Citations Service. It also offers international content, much of which is provided in its original language.

Access to LEXIS-NEXIS is available through the Internet and the lexis.comSM interface or via LEXIS-NEXIS traditional proprietary research software and a direct-dial connection. Users can research through the lexis.comSM easy-to-use browser-based interface.

Canadians can now subscribe to LEXIS-NEXIS Advantage packages, offering a variety of legal resources bundled into content packages tailored to regional needs.

LEXIS-NEXIS can be contacted online: <http://www.lexis-nexis-canada.com>.

B. E-CARSWELL

The Carswell/Thomson Publication company has created its own computerized research database. Though this system, one can search "Family.Pro", "Insolvency.Pro" or "Securities.Pro". These sites contain both case law and all Canadian legislation relevant to those specific areas of law. For a more general approach to case law research, "Law.Pro" contains all Carswell publications as well as all officially reported cases since 1986 and unreported decisions from 1996 onward.

E-Carswell has also acquired the rights to distribute Westlaw, a major American resource, in Canada.

E-Carswell can be found online: <http://www.ecarswell.com>. Westlaw also has a website at: <http://www.westlaw.com>.

C. MARITIME LAW BOOK

Maritime Law Book has provided computerized research capabilities along with its bound editions. In addition, the Maritime Law Book Web site contains three series which are not available in hard-copy: British Columbia Trial Cases; New Brunswick Reports (2d) Supplement; and Ontario Trial Cases.

This search tool can be found online: <http://www.mlb.nb.ca>.

D. QUICKLAW

QuickLaw, one of the first computerized legal research databases, has undergone major changes. Although QuickLaw has lost Westlaw, a major link to American legal research, it has retained 36 topical databases which provide both case summaries and links to full text case decisions. As well, one can update the status of a case using the QuickCite option.

QuickLaw is available commercially, but offers its services free of charge to law students while they are in school.

QuickLaw can be contacted online: <http://www.quicklaw.com>.

Recommended Methods of Citation for Federal and Provincial Statutes and Regulations

A. FEDERAL

1. Statutes

A reference to a statute in the 1985 *Revised Statutes of Canada* should appear in the following form:

Postal Services Interruption Relief Act, R.S.C. 1985, c. P-16, s. 4(1).

The example citation contains:

(i)   the title, which is italicized,
(ii)   a designation by the abbreviation "R.S.C." for *Revised Statutes of Canada*,
(iii) a reference to the year of the revised statutes, and
(iv)   the abbreviations "c." for chapter and "s." for section.

A reference to a statute in an annual volume should appear in the following form:

Health of Animals Act, S.C. 1990, c. 21, s. 1.

The example citation contains:

(i)   the title of the act, which is italicized,
(ii)   a designation by the abbreviation "S.C." for *Statutes of Canada*,
(iii) a reference to the year of the annual volume of the *Statutes of Canada*, and
(iv)   the abbreviations "c." for chapter and "s." for section.

Statutes which have been amended may be cited as follows:

Diplomatic Service (Special) Superannuation Act, R.S.C. 1985, c. D-2 as am. by S.C. 1989, c. 6, s. 14.

Crop Insurance Act, R.S.C. 1985, c. C-48, as am. by S.C. 1990, c. 9.

Criminal Records Act, R.S.C. 1985, c. C-47, s. 2, as am. by R.S.C. 1985, c. 1 (4th Supp.), s. 45.

Canadian Wheat Board Act, R.S.C. 1985, c. C-24, s. 8, as am. by R.S.C., c. 38 (4th Supp.), s. 3.

In these examples the volume and chapter number in which the statute was initially published is cited first. The first example citation shows that the *Diplomatic Service (Special) Superannuation Act* was amended in the 1989 volume of the *Statutes of Canada*. The reference to section 14 following the chapter reference is included because the amendment is part of an "omnibus statute"; if the amending statute had amended this Act alone, the section number would have been omitted. Generally, a reference to the amending section is omitted, unless the writer wishes to draw particular attention to the amended section.

The second example shows that c. C-48, the *Crop Insurance Act*, was amended by chapter 9 of the 1990 *Statutes of Canada*. The third example indicates that section 2 of the *Criminal Records Act* was amended by chapter 1, section 45, in the 4th Supplement to the *Revised Statutes of Canada*, which in this case is an "omnibus act", referred to as the *Miscellaneous Statute Law Amendment Act, 1987*. The fourth example indicates that a particular section (*i.e.*, section 8) of the *Canadian Wheat Board Act* was amended by chapter 38, section 3, in the 4th Supplement to the *Revised Statutes of Canada*.

A history of amendments to the revision, other acts included in the supplement volumes, and new acts in the annual volumes of *Statutes of Canada*, may be cited as follows:

Governor General's Act, R.S.C. 1985, c. G-9 as am. by R.S.C. 1985, c. 50 (Supp.), ss. 1-2; S.C. 1990, c. 5, ss. 1-2; 1993, c. 13, s. 9.

Merchant Seamen Compensation Act, R.S.C. 1985, c. M-6 as am. by R.S.C. 1985, c. 31 (Supp.), ss. 81-84; c. 1 (2nd Supp.), s. 213(1) (Sch. I, item 8); c. 3 (2nd Supp.), s. 30(F); c. 27 (2nd Supp.), s. 10 (Sch., item 16); S.C. 1990, c. 16, s. 17; c. 17, s. 35; 1992, c. 51, s. 57.

NOTE: The abbreviations "S.C." and "R.S.C." need not be repeated if the source is evident from the description of amendments. Also, the year need not be repeated.

In both examples the order of citation is as follows:

(i)   *Revised Statutes of Canada*,

(ii) *Revised Statutes of Canada, 1st Supplement,*
(iii) *Revised Statutes of Canada, 2nd Supplement,* and
(iv) *Statutes of Canada*, annual volumes.

NOTE: It is not necessary to indicate an amendment to a statute unless it is relevant to a point or a specific section under discussion, nor is it correct to simply put the reference "as am. by" in a citation. Citations are presumed to be to the statute as amended. Exception: the citation "R.S.Q. 1977" refers to the unamended statutes published in bound volumes. (The citation "R.S.Q. c. 20" refers to the updated looseleaf set.)

2. Regulations

A reference to a regulation in the 1978 *Consolidated Regulations of Canada* should appear in the following form:

Civilian Dental Treatment Regulations, C.R.C., c. 682 (1978).

A reference to a regulation published after the consolidation should appear in the following form:

Patent Cooperation Treaty Regulations, SOR/89-453.

Regulations which have been amended are cited as follows:

Pesticide Residue Compensation Regulations, C.R.C., c. 1254 (1978) as am. by SOR/78-865.
Potato Production and Sale (Central Saanich) Restriction Regulations, SOR/82-186 as am. by 82-612; 83-294.
Physical Security Regulations, SOR/83-77 as am. by 84-81; 85-1016; 91-585.

B. ALBERTA

1. Statutes

The citation of a revised statute should be made to the *Revised Statutes of Alberta*.

Example:

Students Loan Guarantee Act, R.S.A. 1980, c. S-25.

The example citation contains the title of the revised statute, the abbreviation for *Revised Statutes of Alberta*, the year of the revision and the chapter number of the act.

Citation of an amendment to the revision is made, first, to the revised statute and, second, to the bound volume of the *Statutes of Alberta*.

Example:

Boilers and Pressure Vessels Act, R.S.A. 1980, c. B-8 as am. by S.A. 1983, c. 37, s. 7; 1992, c. M-20.1, s. 62.

The example citation contains the title of the revised statute, the abbreviation for *Revised Statutes of Alberta*, the year of the revision, the chapter number of the Act, the abbreviation for *Statutes of Alberta*, the year of the bound volume, and the chapter and section numbers of the amending statute. This reference to an amending statute is followed by a reference to another amending statute (where the abbreviation S.A. is optional), the year of the bound volume, the chapter number and the section number.

Citation of a new act or an amendment to a new act since the revision is made to the *Statutes of Alberta*.

Examples:

Fisheries (Alberta) Act, S.A. 1992, c. F-12.2.
Alberta Mortgage and Housing Corporation Act, S.A. 1984, c. A-32.5 as am. by S.A. 1984, c. P-35.1, s. 51(2); c. 43; 1985, c. 3; 1986, c. D-25.1, s. 21(2); 1987, c. 29, s. 3.

NOTE: A reference to an entry in the looseleaf consolidation of the *Statutes of Alberta* is cited in the same manner as in the above examples and includes the same chapter designation.

2. Regulations

Individual regulations are cited to their regulation number in *The Alberta Gazette, Part II*:

Certification of Teachers Regulation, Alta. Reg. 261/90.

Amendments to regulations are cited, first, to the original regulation number, followed by a reference to the regulation number of the amending regulation(s). No other information is required.

Marriage Act Regulation, Alta. Reg. 111/85 as am. by 33/88; 209/89; 88/90; 412/91; 194/92.

C. BRITISH COLUMBIA

1. Statutes

The citation of a revised statute may be made to the bound or the looseleaf edition of the *Revised Statutes of British Columbia*. In either case the citation will be the same.

Example:

Gas Utility Act, R.S.B.C. 1996, c. 170.

The example citation contains the title of the revised statute, the abbreviation for *Revised Statutes of British Columbia*, the year of the revision and the chapter number of the Act.

Citation of an amendment to the revision is made, first, to the revised statute and, second, to the sessional volume of the *Statutes of British Columbia*.

Example:

Dentists Act, R.S.B.C. 1996, c. 94 as am. by R.S. (Supp.), c. 94.1.

The example citation contains the title of the revised statute, the abbreviation for *Revised Statutes of British Columbia*, the year of the revision, the chapter number of the Act, the abbreviation for *Statutes of British Columbia*, the years of the sessional volumes, and chapter and section numbers (in the case of an "omnibus act") of the amending statutes.

Citation of a new act may be made to the *Statutes of British Columbia* with the addition of the chapter designation in the looseleaf consolidation of the *Revised Statutes of British Columbia*.

Example:

Supply Act (No.1), 1997, S.B.C. 1997, c. 1.

Citation of an amendment to a new act passed since the revision should be made to the bound volume of the *Statutes of British Columbia* with the addition of a reference to the chapter designation of the act in the consolidation.

Example:

Mineral Tax Act, S.B.C. 1989, c. 55 (c. 263.1), as am. by S.B.C. 1990, c. 56.

2. Regulations

Individual regulations are cited with reference to their regulation number printed in *The British Columbia Gazette, Part II*:

Assisted Adoption Regulation, B.C. Reg. 372/89.
Egg Product Regulation, B.C. Reg. 99/78 as am. by 139/88; 479/90.

D. MANITOBA

1. Statutes

The generally accepted citation of a re-enacted statute will direct the user to the *Continuing Consolidation of the Statutes of Manitoba*, and to the bound *Re-enacted Statutes of Manitoba*.[1]

Example:

The Fatal Accidents Act, R.S.M. 1987, c. F50, C.C.S.M. c. F50.

The less commonly adopted method of citing a statute will direct the user to either the looseleaf consolidation or to the bound volume of re-enacted acts.

Examples:

The Age of Majority Act, C.C.S.M., c. A7,
or *The Age of Majority Act*, R.S.M. 1987, c. A7.

The first example citation gives the name of the re-enacted statute, the abbreviation for the *Re-enacted Statutes of Manitoba*, the year of the re-enactment and the chapter of the Act, followed by the abbreviation for the *Continuing Consolidation of the Statutes of Manitoba* and the chapter number. The second example citation contains the name of the re-enacted statute, the abbreviation for the *Consolidation* and the chapter number of the Act. The third example includes the abbreviation for the *Re-enacted Statutes of Manitoba*, the year of the re-enactment and the chapter number of the Act.

Citation of an amendment to the re-enactment is made, first, to the re-enacted statute and, second, to the bound annual volume of the *Statutes of Manitoba*, with the addition of a reference to the *Consolidation*.

---

[1] The *Re-enacted Statutes of Manitoba*, in bilingual versions, were published in bound and looseleaf formats, commencing in 1987.

Example:

The Garage Keepers Act, R.S.M. 1987, c. G10 as am. by S.M. 1989-90, c. 91, s. 6, C.C.S.M. c. G10.

The example citation contains the title of the re-enacted statute, the abbreviation for the *Re-enacted Statutes of Manitoba*, the year of the re-enactment, the chapter number of the Act, the abbreviation for *Statutes of Manitoba*, the year of the bound volume, the chapter and section numbers of the amending statute with the addition of a reference to the *Consolidation*.

Citation of a new act, an amendment to a new act since the re-enactment, an act which was passed before the re-enactment began but which was not included in the re-enactment and an amendment to such an act may be made to the bound annual volume of statutes and to the *Consolidation*.

Examples:

The Pharmaceutical Act, S.M. 1991-92, c. 28 C.C.S.M. c. P80.

The Economic Innovation and Technology Council Act, S.M. 1992, c. 7, C.C.S.M. c. E7.

The Rural Development Bonds Act, S.M. 1991-92, c. 47 as am. by S.M. 1992, c. 58, s. 31, C.C.S.M. c. R175.

The Freedom of Information Act, S.M. 1985-86, c. 6, C.C.S.M. c. F175.

The Infants' Estates Act, S.M. 1985-86, c. 19, as am. by S.M. 1986-87, c. 19, s. 24, C.C.S.M. c. I35.

NOTE: The information tables in the bound *Statutes of Manitoba* include "Acts in the *Continuing Consolidation of the Statutes of Manitoba*", *i.e.*, re-enacted statutes and other public acts, "Public General Acts not included in the C.C.S.M." and "Acts and Parts of Acts Enacted Subject to Proclamation".

2. Regulations

Individual regulations are cited to the regulation number in *The Manitoba Gazette, Part II*:

Ambulance Services and Licenses Regulation, Man. Reg. 62/93.

Anatomy Regulation, Man. Reg. 309/88 R.

The "R" in the second example indicates that the regulation was re-enacted in English and French.

Amendments to Manitoba regulations are cited as follows:

Election Fees, Expenses and Rentals Regulation, Man. Reg. 168/88 as am. by 183/90.
Barbers Regulation, Man. Reg. 93/87 R as am. by 8/88.

NOTE: Each re-enacted regulation is a revision and consolidation of amendments up to the date of the re-enactment of the particular regulation.

E. NEW BRUNSWICK

1. Statutes

The citation of a revised statute is made to the *Revised Statutes of New Brunswick* whether it appears in the bound volume or the continuing consolidation.

Example:

Change of Name Act, R.S.N.B. 1973, c. C-2.

The example citation contains the title of the revised statute, the abbreviation for *Revised Statutes of New Brunswick*, the year of the revision and the chapter number of the Act.

Citation of an amendment to the revision is made, first, to the revised statute and, second, to the bound sessional volume of the *Statutes of New Brunswick*.

Example:

Health Services Act, R.S.N.B. 1973, c. H-3 as am. by S.N.B. 1982, c. 29; 1990, c. 61; 1992, c. 52.

The example citation includes the title of the revised statute, the abbreviation for *Revised Statutes of New Brunswick*, the year of the revision, the chapter number of the Act, the abbreviation for *Statutes of New Brunswick*, the years of the bound volumes and the chapter numbers of the amending statutes.

Citation of a new act or an amendment to a new act should be made to the bound volume of the *Statutes of New Brunswick*.

Examples:

Charitable Donation of Food Act, S.N.B. 1992, c. C-2.002.
Custody and Detention of Young Persons Act, S.N.B. 1985, c. C-40 as am. by S.N.B. 1988, c. 11, s. 17; c. 13, s. 9; 1992, c. 52, s. 7.

NOTE: The chapter designations of acts will be the same in the continuing consolidation and in the bound statute volumes.

2. Regulations

Individual regulations are cited with reference to a regulation number, which appears in *The Royal Gazette*:

> *Protected Area Exemption Regulation - Clean Water Act*, N.B. Reg. 90-120.
> *General Regulation - Credit Unions Act*, N.B. Reg. 94-5.
> *Fees Regulation - All-Terrain Vehicle Act*, N.B. Reg. 85-202 as am. by 88-272; 91-72; 92-64.

F. NEWFOUNDLAND

1. Statutes

The citation of a revised statute should be made to the *Revised Statutes of Newfoundland*.

Example:

Commemoration Day Act, R.S.N. 1990, c. C-24.

The example citation contains the title of the revised statute, the abbreviation for *Revised Statutes of Newfoundland*, the year of the revision and the chapter number of the Act.

Citation of an amendment to the revision is made, first, to the revised statute and, second, to the annual volume of the *Statutes of Newfoundland*.

Examples:

Evidence Act, R.S.N. 1990, c. E-16 as am. by S.N. 1991, c. 13.
Human Rights Code, R.S.N. 1990, c. H-14 as am. by S.N. 1992, c. 48, s. 13.

The example citations contain the titles of the revised statutes, the abbreviation for *Revised Statutes of Newfoundland*, the year of the revision, the chapter numbers of the acts, the abbreviation for *Statutes of Newfoundland*, the years of the bound volumes, and the chapter and section numbers of the amending statutes.

Citation of a new act or an amendment to a new act since the revision is made to the bound volumes of the *Statutes of Newfoundland*.

Example:

Jury Act, 1991, S.N. 1991 as am. by S.N. 1992, c. 52, s. 6.

2. Regulations

Individual regulations are cited with reference to a regulation number, which appears in *The Newfoundland Gazette, Part II*:

> *The Aquaculture Regulations, 1988*, Nfld. Reg. 113/88.
> *The Day Care and Homemaker Services Regulations, 1982*, Nfld. Reg. 219/82, as am. by 9/91.

G. NORTHWEST TERRITORIES

1. Statutes

The citation of a revised statute should be made to the *Revised Statutes of Northwest Territories*.

Example:

Arbitration Act, R.S.N.W.T. 1988, c. A-5.

The example citation contains the title of the revised statute, the abbreviation for *Revised Statutes of Northwest Territories*, the year of the revision and the chapter number of the act.

Citation of an amendment to the revision is made, first, to the revised statute and, second, to the bound volumes of the *Statutes of Northwest Territories*.

Example:

Income Tax Act, R.S.N.W.T. 1988, c. I-1 as am. by R.S.N.W.T. 1988, c. 19 (Supp. vol. I); c. 58 (Supp. vol. II); c. 87 (Supp. vol. III); c. 118 (Supp. vol. III); S.N.W.T. 1989, c. 3; 1990, c. 10; 1992, c. 37.

The example citation contains the title of the revised statute, the abbreviation for *Revised Statutes of Northwest Territories*, the year of the revision, the chapter number of the Act (followed by similar citations for the three supplements to the revision), the abbreviation for *Statutes of Northwest Territories*, the years of the bound volumes, and the chapter numbers of the amending statutes.

Citation of a new act or unrevised act is made to the annual bound volumes of the *Statutes of Northwest Territories*.

Examples:

Northwest Territories Development Corporation Act, S.N.W.T. 1990, c. 12.
Statute Revision Act, S.N.W.T. 1987, c. 32 as am. by S.N.W.T. 1988, c. 19.

2. Regulations

Revised regulations are cited to the 1990 bound volumes of *Revised Regulations of the Northwest Territories*:

Whale Cove Liquor Prohibition Regulations, R.R.N.W.T. 1990, c. L-48.

Amendments to revised regulations are cited as follows:

Social Assistance Regulations, R.R.N.W.T. 1990, c. S-16 as am. by N.W.T. Reg. R-083-92.

Amendments contained in the supplement and in the *Northwest Territories Gazette, Part II*, are cited as follows:

Electrical Protection Regulations, R.R.N.W.T. 1990, c. E-21, as am. by R.R.N.W.T. 1990, c. E-21 (Supp.); N.W.T. Reg. R-098.92.

New regulations are cited with reference to their regulation number in the *Northwest Territories Gazette, Part II*:

Hours of Service Regulations, N.W.T. Reg. R-001-92.

H. NOVA SCOTIA

1. Statutes

The citation of a revised statute should be made to the *Revised Statutes of Nova Scotia* which are available in a consolidated looseleaf form.

Example:

Guardianship Act, R.S.N.S. 1989, c. 189.

The example citation contains the title of the revised statute, the abbreviation for *Revised Statutes of Nova Scotia*, the year of the revision and the chapter number of the Act.

Citation of an amendment to the revision is made, first, to the revised statute and, second, to the bound volume of the *Statutes of Nova Scotia*.

Example:

Metropolitan Authority Act, R.S.N.S. 1989, c. 285 as am. by S.N.S. 1990, c. 19, ss. 46-49.

The example citation contains the title of the revised statute, the abbreviation for *Revised Statutes of Nova Scotia*, the year of the revision, the chapter number of the Act, the abbreviation for *Statutes of Nova Scotia*, the year of the bound volume, the chapter number and section numbers of the amending statute.

Citation of a new act or an amendment to a new act since the revision is made to the bound volumes of the *Statutes of Nova Scotia*.

Example:

Kings Regional Rehabilitation Centre Act, S.N.S. 1990, c. 16, as am. by S.N.S. 1991, c. 17.

2. Regulations

Nova Scotia Regulations are all cited in the same manner, as follows:

Health Services Tax Flea Market Regulations, N.S. Reg. 146/91.

I. NUNAVUT

At the time of publication, the newly created Government of Nunavut had not yet selected an official printer. As a result, all new legislation passed in that territory has been distributed to municipalities within that jurisdiction.

Pursuant to the *Nunavut Act*, S.C. 1993, c. 28, all legislation which was in effect as of March 31, 1999 and related to the Northwest Territories was duplicated for Nunavut.

The government is planning to release a consolidation of its legislation on CD-ROM in 2000-2001.

J. ONTARIO

1. Statutes

The citation of a revised statute should be made to the *Revised Statutes of Ontario*.

Example:

Mining Tax Act, R.S.O. 1990, c. M.15.

The example citation contains the title of the revised statute, the abbreviation for *Revised Statutes of Ontario*, the year of the revision and the chapter number of the Act.

Citation of an amendment to the revision is made, first, to the revised statute and, second, to the bound volume of the *Statutes of Ontario*.

Example:

Absentees Act, R.S.O. 1990, c. A.3 as am. by S.O. 1992, c. 32, s. 1.

The example citation contains the title of the revised statute, the abbreviation for *Revised Statutes of Ontario*, the year of the revision, the chapter number of the Act, the abbreviation for *Statutes of Ontario*, the year of the bound volume, and the chapter and section numbers of the amending statute.

Citation of a new act or an amendment to a new act since the revision is made to the annual volumes of the *Statutes of Ontario*.

Examples:

Waste Management Act, 1992, S.O. 1992, c. 1.
County of Simcoe Act, 1990, S.O. 1990, c. 16 as am. by S.O. 1991, c. 15, s. 35.

2. Regulations

Regulations published in the latest *Revised Regulations of Ontario* are cited as follows:

First Aid Requirements Regulation, R.R.O. 1990, Reg. 1101.
General Regulations - Workers' Compensation Act, R.R.O. 1990, Reg. 1102.

Amendments to the revision are cited, first, to the revised regulations and, second, to the regulation number in *The Ontario Gazette*:

General Regulation - Child and Family Services Act, R.R.O. 1990, Reg. 70 as am. by O. Reg. 139/91; 239/92; 683/92; 161/93; 400/93.

New regulations are cited to a regulation number in *The Ontario Gazette*:

Recycling and Composting of Municipal Waste Regulation, O. Reg. 101/94.

K. PRINCE EDWARD ISLAND

1. Statutes

The citation of a revised statute is made to the *Revised Statutes of Prince Edward Island*. The reference may be used to locate an act in the bound volume or in the continuing consolidation which is referred to as "The Revised Statutes of Prince Edward Island 1988 ([year] up-date)".

Example:

Judicial Review Act, R.S.P.E.I. 1988, c. J-3.

The example citation contains the title of the revised statute, the abbreviation for *Revised Statutes of Prince Edward Island*, the year of the revision and the chapter number of the Act.

Citation of an amendment to the revision is made, first, to the revised statute and, second, to the bound volume of the *Statutes of Prince Edward Island*.

Example:

Garnishee Act, R.S.P.E.I. 1988, c. G-2 as am. by S.P.E.I. 1989, c. 3; 1991, c. 42, s. 3.

NOTE: Users of the consolidation would naturally look for c. G-2 which will include amendments in the latest update.

The example citation contains the title of the revised statute, the abbreviation for *Revised Statutes of Prince Edward Island*, the year of the revision, the chapter number of the Act, the abbreviation for *Statutes of Prince Edward Island*, the year of the bound volume and the chapter number of the amending statute (followed by a similar citation of another amending statute).

Citation of a new act or an amendment to a new act since the revision is made to the *Statutes of Prince Edward Island*, with further reference to the chapter number in the looseleaf consolidation, if available.

Examples:

Environment Tax Act, S.P.E.I. 1991, c. 9 (c. E-8.3).
Correctional Services Act, S.P.E.I. 1992, c. 13 (c. C-26.1).
Petroleum Products Act, S.P.E.I. 1990, c. 43 as am. by S.P.E.I. 1991, c. 18, Sch. (c. P-5.1).

2. Regulations

Regulations that have been consolidated are cited to *The Revised Regulations of Prince Edward Island* with reference to the regulation number in the "Table of Regulations" (blue pages at the back of the revision):

Schools of Nursing Regulations, R.R.P.E.I. EC 333/76.

Regulations published after the revision are cited to their regulation number in the *Royal Gazette, Part II*:

Trout and Salmon Regulations, EC 105/92.

Amendments to revised regulations are cited:

Arterial Highways Regulations, R.R.P.E.I. EC 163/92 as am. by EC 470/92; 634/92.

L. QUÉBEC

1. Statutes

The citation of a revised statute can be made to the looseleaf edition of the *Revised Statutes of Québec* or to the bound revision of the *Statutes of Québec*.

Examples:

Lands and Forests Act, R.S.Q., c. T-9.
Lands and Forests Act, R.S.Q. 1977, c. T-9.

The first example citation contains the title of the revised statute, the abbreviation for *Revised Statutes of Québec* and the chapter number of the act in the looseleaf consolidation. The second example includes the same information as the first, as well as a reference to the date of the bound *Revised Statutes of Québec*.

Citation of an amendment to the revision is made, first, to the revised statute and, second, to the bound volume of the *Statutes of Québec*.

Example:

Business Concerns Records Act, R.S.Q. 1977, c. D-12 as am. by S.Q. 1990, c. 4, s. 388.

The example citation contains the title of the revised statute, the abbreviation for *Revised Statutes of Québec*, the year of the revision, the chapter number of the act, the abbreviation for *Statutes of Québec*, the year of the bound volume, and the chapter and section numbers of the amending statute.

Citation of a new act or an amendment to a new act since the revision is made to the annual *Statutes of Québec* or to the consolidation.[2]

Examples:

> *An Act respecting the Ordre National du Québec*, S.Q. 1984, c. 24 as am. by S.Q. 1985, c. 11,

or

> *An Act respecting the Ordre National du Québec*, R.S.Q., c. O-7.01.

NOTE: Acts passed after the revision have different chapter designations in the bound volumes and in the looseleaf revision.

2. Regulations

Regulations published in the revision are cited to the *Revised Regulations of Québec*, with reference to both their regulation number and to the chapter number of their enabling statute:

> *Regulation respecting the use of water for mining purposes*, R.R.Q. 1981, c. M-13, r. 13.

Amendments are cited with reference to the revised regulation number and the appropriate issue of the *Gazette officielle du Québec*:

> *Regulation respecting travel agents*, R.R.Q. 1981, c. A-10, r. 1, as am. by O.C. 994-86, 2 July 1986, G.O.Q. 1986.II.1361; 449-90, 4 April 1990, G.O.Q. 1990.II.697; 546-92, 8 April 1992, G.O.Q. 1992.II.2345.

M. SASKATCHEWAN

1. Statutes

The citation of a revised statute should be made to the *Revised Statutes of Saskatchewan*. "The" is part of all Saskatchewan titles.

---

[2] Reference should be made to the consolidation whenever possible.

Example:

The Grain and Fodder Conservation Act, R.S.S. 1978, c. G-7.

The example citation contains the title of the revised statute, the abbreviation for *Revised Statutes of Saskatchewan*, the year of the revision and the chapter number of the act.

Citation of an amendment to the revision is made, first, to the revised statute and, second, to the bound volume of the *Statutes of Saskatchewan*.

Example:

The Grain Charges Limitation Act, R.S.S. 1978, c. G-6 as am. by S.S. 1979-80, c. M-32.01, s. 14; 1983, c. 11, s. 30.

The example citation contains the title of the revised statute, the abbreviation for *Revised Statutes of Saskatchewan*, the year of the revision, the chapter number of the act, the abbreviation for *Statutes of Saskatchewan*, the year of the bound volume, and the chapter and section numbers of the amending statute. A semi-colon separates a reference to a second amending statute which, like the first reference to an amending statute, contains the year of the bound volume and the chapter and section numbers of the amending statute.

Citation of a new act or an amendment to a new act since the revision is made to the *Statutes of Saskatchewan*.

Examples:

The Crown Employment Contracts Act, S.S. 1991, c. C-50.11.
The Government Organization Act, S.S. 1986-87-88, c. G-5.1, as am. by S.S. 1989-90, c. 54 (Sch. I, Sch. II).

2. Regulations

Regulations that have been revised are cited to the *Revised Regulations of Saskatchewan*:

The Resource Lands Regulations, 1989, R.R.S., c. P-31, Reg. 3.

Amendments to the revision and unrevised regulations are cited with reference to their regulation number in *The Saskatchewan Gazette*.

The Direct Sellers Regulations, R.R.S., c. D-28, Reg. 1 as am. by Sask. Reg. 11/87; 24/93.

The Housing and Special-Care Homes Care and Rates Regulations, Sask. Reg. 132/81 as am. by 147/82; 173/83; 106/84; 36/86; 23/87; 101/92.

N. YUKON TERRITORY

1. Statutes

The citation of a revised statute should be made to the *Revised Statutes of Yukon Territory*.

Example:

Dental Profession Act, R.S.Y. 1986, c. 42.

The example citation contains the title of the revised statute, the abbreviation for *Revised Statutes of Yukon Territory*, the year of the revision and the chapter number of the act.

Citation of an amendment to the revision is made, first, to the revised statute and, second, to the bound volume of the *Statutes of Yukon Territory*.

Example:

Insurance Premium Tax Act, R.S.Y. 1986, c. 92 as am. by S.Y. 1988, c. 17, s. 4.

The example citation contains the title of the revised statute, the abbreviation for *Revised Statutes of Yukon Territory*, the year of the revision, the chapter number of the act, the abbreviation for *Statutes of Yukon Territory*, the year of the bound volume, and the chapter and section numbers of the amending statute (*i.e.*, *Miscellaneous Statute Law Amendment Act, 1988*).

Citation of a new act or an amendment to a new act since the revision is made to the *Statutes of Yukon Territory*.

Examples:

Intergovernmental Agreements Act, S.Y. 1989-90, c. 14.
Change of Name Act, S.Y. 1987, c. 25 as am. by S.Y. 1989-90, c. 16, s. 5.
Pesticides Control Act, S.Y. 1989-90, c. 20 as am. by S.Y. 1991, c. 5, s. 189.

2. Regulations

Regulations are cited to their year of registration and Order-in-Council number:

Agricultural Development Areas Regulations, Yukon O.I.C. 1989/79.
Equipment Regulations, Yukon O.I.C. 1987/86 as am. by 1987/191; 1988/131.

Shelving of Law Reports

ROW 1

Privy Council Appeals	Eng. & Irish Appeals	Sco. & Div. Appeals	Appeal Cases	Appeals Cases
(1865-75) Vols. 1-6 cited L.R.P.C.	(1866-75) Vols. 1-7 cited L.R.H.L.	(1866-75) Vols. 1-2 cited L.R. Sc. & Div.	(1875-90) Vols. 1-15 cited App. Cas.	(1891-date) Vols. 1-7 - - - [year] A.C.

ROW 2

Chancery Appeals	Equity Cases	Chancery Division	Chancery Division
(1865-75) Vols. 1-10 cited L.R.Ch.	(1865-75) Vols. 1-20 cited L.R.Eq.	(1875-90) Vols. 1-45 cited Ch.D.	(1891-date) - - - cited [year] Ch.

ROW 3

Court of Exchequer	Exchequer Division	Common Pleas	Common Pleas Division	Crown Cases
(1865-75) Vols. 1-10 cited L.R.Ex.	(1875-80) Vols. 1-5 cited Ex. D.	(1865-75) Vols. 1-10 cited L.R.C.P.	(1875-80) Vols. 1-5 cited C.P.D.	(1865-75) Vols. 1-2 cited L.R.C.C. or L.R.C.C.R.

Queen's Bench Cases	Queen's Bench Division	Queen's or King's Bench Division		
(1865-75) Vols. 1-10 cited L.R.Q.B.	(1875-90) Vols. 1-25 cited Q.B.D.	(1891-date) cited [year] Q.B. or K.B.		

ROW 4

Admiralty and Ecclesi- -astical	Probate and Divorce	Probate Division[1]	Probate Division[2]	Family Division[3]
(1865-75) Vols. 1-4 cited L.R.A. & E.	(1865-75) Vols. 1-3 cited L.R.P. & D.	(1876-90) Vols. 1-15 cited P.D.	(1891-1971) 80 Vols. cited [year] P.	(1972-date) cited [year] Fam.

[1] Includes decisions from the Probate, Divorce, Admiralty, Ecclesiastical courts and the Privy Council.

[2] Includes decisions from the Probate, Divorce, Admiralty and Ecclesiastical courts, the Court of Appeal and the Privy Council.

[3] Includes decisions from the Family and Ecclesiastical courts and the Court of Appeal.

NOTE: In some law libraries the order of shelving is reserved so that the *Chancery Division* reports and their predecessor sets appear first, followed by the *Queen's Bench Division* reports and their predecessors, *Family Division* reports and their predecessors, and the *Appeal Cases* reports and their predecessors.

Subject Reports – Publication Periods and Sample Citations

A. FAMILY LAW

Reports of Family Law, 1971 to 1978
  Rodrigue v. *Dufton* (1976), 30 R.F.L. 216 (Ont. H.C.J.).
Reports of Family Law (Second Series), 1978 to 1986
  Davies v. *Davies* (1985), 49 R.F.L. (2d) 108 (B.C.C.A.).
Reports of Family Law (Third Series), 1986 to 1994
  Lévesque v. *Lapointe* (1993), 44 R.F.L. (3d) 316 (B.C.C.A.).
Reports of Family Law (Fourth Series), 1994 to date
  Rice v. *Rice* (1996), 17 R.F.L. (4th) 328 (B.C.S.C.).

B. CRIMINAL LAW

Canadian Criminal Cases, 1893 to 1962
  R. v. *Plotsky* (1962), 133 Can. C.C. 41 (Alta. S.C., A.D.)
  or
  R. v. *Plotsky* (1962), 133 Can. Cr. Cas. 41 (Alta. S.C., A.D.).
Canadian Criminal Cases, 1963 to 1970
  R. v. *Ladelpha*, [1970] 5 C.C.C. 1 (Ont. Co. Ct.).
Canadian Criminal Cases (Second Series), 1971 to 1983
  R. v. *Giambalvo* (1982), 70 C.C.C. (2d) 324 (Ont. C.A.).
Canadian Criminal Cases (Third Series), 1983 to date
  R. v. *Crabe* (1993), 79 C.C.C. (3d) 323 (B.C.C.A.).
Criminal Reports, 1946 to 1967
  Hebert v. *A.G. Qué.* (1966), 50 C.R. 88 (Q.B.).
Criminal Reports (New Series), 1967 to 1978
  Imrich v. *R.* (1977), 39 C.R.N.S. 92 (S.C.C.).
Criminal Reports (Third Series), 1978 to 1991
  R. v. *Manuel* (1986), 50 C.R. (3d) 47 (C.S.P.).
Criminal Reports (Fourth Series), 1991 to 1996
  R. v. *Brown* (1993), 19 C.R. (4th) 140 (Man. C.A.).

Criminal Reports (Fifth Series) 1997 to date
  R. v. *Domm* (1997), 4 C.R. (5th) 61 (Ont. C.A.).
Motor Vehicle Reports, 1979 to 1988
  R. v. *Killen* (1985), 37 M.V.R. 190 (N.S.S.C., A.D.).
Motor Vehicle Reports (Second Series), 1988 to 1994
  R. v. *Chapman* (1992), 42 M.V.R. (2d) 296 (Nfld. S.C.).
Motor Vehicle Reports (Third Series) 1994 to date
  Villeneuve v. *Scott* (1998), 36 M.V.R. (3d) 147 (Ont. Gen. Div.).

C. TAXATION

Canada Tax Cases, 1917 to date
  Jean Lemelin Inc. v. *M.N.R.,* [1992] 2 C.T.C. 2832 (T.C.C.).
Dominion Tax Cases, 1920 to date
  Paquin v. *R.,* 90 D.T.C. 6663 (F.C., T.D.).

D. LABOUR

British Columbia Labour Relations Board Decisions, 1981 to date
  Turner Distribution Systems Ltd. v. *Teamsters Local Union No. 31,* [1994]
      B.C.L.R.B. 240-01.
Canadian Labour Law Cases, 1944 to date[1]
  Gauvreau v. *Banque Nationale du Canada,* 92 C.L.L.C. para. 17,018
      (C.H.R.T.).
Canadian Labour Relations Board Reports, 1974 to 1982
  Lester Drugs Ltd. v. *U.F.C.W.U.,* [1982] 3 Can. L.R.B.R. 233.
Canadian Labour Relations Board Reports (New Series), 1983 to 1989
  McCance v. *C.N.R.* (1985), 10 C.L.R.B.R. (N.S.) 23.
Canadian Labour Relations Board Reports (Second Series), 1989 to date
  Coull v. *Teamsters Local 880* (1992), 17 C.L.R.B.R. (2d) 301.
Labour Arbitration Cases, 1948 to 1972
  Re C.U.P.E. (1971), 23 L.A.C. 111 (Ont.).
Labour Arbitration Cases (Second Series), 1973 to 1981
  Re Air Canada and C.A.L.E.A. (1981), 30 L.A.C. (2d) 28 (Can.).
Labour Arbitration Cases (Third Series), 1982 to 1989
  Re City of Penticton and C.U.P.E. (1985), 21 L.A.C. (3d) 233 (B.C.).
Labour Arbitration Cases (Fourth Series), 1989 to date
  Re Fleet Industries and I.A.M., Loc 171 (1992), 30 L.A.C. (4th) 368 (Ont.).
Ontario Labour Relations Board Reports, 1944 to date

---

[1]   The current binder is titled *Canadian Labour Law Reporter.*

Int'l Bros. Elect. Wks., Local 894 v. *Ellis-Don Ltd.*, [1992] O.L.R.B. Rep. 147.
Western Labour Arbitration Cases, 1979 to 1985
B.C. Hydro v. *Int'l Bros. Elect. Wks.*, [1985] 2 W.L.A.C. 1 (B.C.).

E. HUMAN RIGHTS

Canadian Human Rights Reporter, 1980 to date
    Cremona v. *Wardair Canada Inc.* (1991), 14 C.H.R.R. D/262.
Canadian Rights Reporter, 1982 to 1991
    MacBain v. *Canadian Human Rights Comm.* (1985), 18 C.R.R. 165 (F.C.A.).
Canadian Rights Reporter (Second Series), 1991 to date
    R. v. *Simpson* (1993), 14 C.R.R. (2d) 388 (Ont. C.A.).
Charter of Rights Decisions, 1982 to date
    R. v. *Hill*, [1993] C.R.D. 725.1:20-02. (Alta. Q.B.).

F. OTHER

Administrative Law Reports, 1983 to 1991
    Gershman Produce Ltd. v. *Motor Trans. Bd.* (1985), 16 Admin. L.R. 1 (Man. C.A.).
Administrative Law Reports (Second Series), 1992 to 1998
    A.T.A. v. *Edmonton School Dist. No. 7* (1992), 9 Admin. L.R. (2d) 240 (Alta. C.A.).
Administrative Law Reports (Third Series), 1998 to date
    Khan v. *University of Ottawa* (1998), 2 Admin. L.R. (3d) 298 (Ont. C.A.).
Business Law Reports, 1977 to 1991
    Lake Mechanical Systems Co. v. *Crandell Mechanical Systems Inc.* (1985), 31 B.L.R. 113 (B.C.S.C.).
Business Law Reports (Second Series), 1991 to date
    Flandro v. *Mitha* (1992), 7 B.L.R. (2d) 280 (B.C.S.C.).
Canadian Bankruptcy Reports, 1920 to 1960
    Re Letovsky (1958), 37 C.B.R. 83 (Man. S.C.).
Canadian Bankruptcy Reports (New Series), 1960 to 1990
    Waverly Management Ltd. v. *Sobie* (1985), 58 C.B.R. (N.S.) 97 (Alta. Q.B.).
Canadian Bankruptcy Reports (Third Series), 1991 to date
    Royal Bank v. *Zutphen Brothers Construction Ltd.* (1993), 17 C.B.R. (3d) 314 (N.S.S.C.).
Canadian Cases on Employment Law, 1983 to 1994
    Niwranski v. *H.N. Helicopter Parts Int'l Corp.* (1992), 45 C.C.E.L. 303 (B.C.S.C.).
Canadian Cases on Employment Law (Second Series), 1994 to date

Crary v. *Royal Bank* (1997), 35 C.C.E.L. (2d) 289 (Ont. Gen. Div.).
Canadian Cases on the Law of Insurance, 1983 to 1991
   Matchett v. *London Life Insurance Co.* (1985), 14 C.C.L.I. 89 (Sask. C.A.).
Canadian Cases on the Law of Insurance (Second Series), 1991 to date
   Kuan v. *Insurance Corp. of British Columbia* (1992), 12 C.C.L.I. (2d) 155 (B.C.S.C.).
Canadian Cases on the Law of Torts, 1976 to 1990
   R. v. *The Ship Sun Diamond* (1983), 25 C.C.L.T. 19 (F.C., T.D.).
Canadian Cases on the Law of Torts (Second Series), 1990 to date
   Weber v. *Ontario Hydro* (1992), 13 C.C.L.T. (2d) 241 (Ont. C.A.).
Canadian Customs and Excise Reports, 1980 to 1989
   Apt Art Ltd. v. *Deputy M.N.R.* (1984), 8 C.E.R. 53 (Tar. Bd.).
Canadian Environmental Law News, 1972-1977
   R. v. *Lake Ontario Cement Ltd.*, [1973] 2 C.E.L.N. 23 (Ont. S.C.).
Canadian Environmental Law Reports, 1978 to 1986
   R. v. *Vandervoet* (1986), 14 C.E.L.R. 140 (Ont. Prov. Offences Ct.).
Canadian Environmental Law Reports (New Series), 1987 to date
   R. v. *Varnicolor Chemical Ltd.* (1992), 9 C.E.L.R. (N.S.) 176 (Ont. C.J. (Prov. Div.)).
Canadian Patent Reporter, 1942 to 1971
   Dupont of Canada Ltd. v. *Nomad Trading Co.* (1968), 55 C.P.R. 97 (Qué. S.C.).
Canadian Patent Reporter (Second Series), 1971 to 1984
   Corning Glass Works Co. v. *Canada Wire & Cable Ltd.* (1984), 81 C.P.R. (2d) 39 (F.C., T.D.).
Canadian Patent Reporter (Third Series), 1985 to date
   Business Depot Ltd. v. *Canadian Office Depot Inc.* (1993), 47 C.P.R. (3d) 325 (F.C., T.D.).
Carswell's Practice Cases, 1976 to 1985
   Continental Bank v. *Rizzo* (1985), 50 C.P.C. 56 (Ont. Dist. Ct.).
Carswell's Practice Cases (Second Series), 1985 to 1992
   Woolford v. *Lockhart* (1985), 2 C.P.C. (2d) 16 (Ont. H.C.J.).
Carswell's Practice Cases (Third Series), 1992 to 1997
   Abate v. *Borges* (1992), 12 C.P.C. (3d) 391 (Ont. C.J. (Gen. Div.)).
Carswell's Practice Cases (Fourth Series), 1997 to date
   Snowmount Investments Corp. v. *Elliott* (1998), 13 C.P.C. (4th) 305 (Ont. Gen. Div.).
Construction Law Reports, 1983 to 1992
   Meilleur v. *U.N.I. Crete Canada Ltd.* (1985), 15 C.L.R. 191 (Ont. H.C.J.).
Construction Law Reports (Second Series), 1993 to date
   Concord Construction Inc. v. *Camara* (1992), 4 C.L.R. (2d) 263 (Ont. C.J. (Gen. Div.)).
Estates and Trusts Reports, 1977 to 1994
   Ginsburg v. *M.N.R.* (1992), 46 E.T.R. 188 (T.C.C.).

Estates and Trusts Reports (Second Series), 1994 to date
Plantz v. Plantz (1995), 8 E.T.R. (2d) 235 (Sask. Q.B.).
Insurance Law Reporter, 1934 to date
Dale v. *Metropolitan Life Insurance Company*, [1990] I.L.R. 10,436 (Ont. S.C.).
Land Compensation Reports, 1971 to date
Metvedt v. *Credit Valley Conservation Authority* (1992), 48 L.C.R. 289 (O.M.Bd.).
Municipal and Planning Law Reports, 1976 to 1990
FoodCorp Ltd. v. *City of Brampton* (1984), 30 M.P.L.R. 39 (Ont. Co. Ct.).
Municipal and Planning Law Reports (Second Series), 1991 to date
Bell Canada v. *Olympia & York Developments Ltd.* (1992), 13 M.P.L.R. (2d) 161 (Ont. C.J. (Gen. Div.)).
Ontario Municipal Board Reports, 1973 to date
Green Road Developments Ltd. v. *City of Stoney Creek* (1991), 270 M.B.R. 327.
Real Property Reports, 1977 to 1989
Dominion Stores Ltd. v. *Bramalea Ltd.* (1985), 38 R.P.R. 12 (Ont. Dist. Ct.).
Real Property Reports (Second Series), 1989 to 1996
Dobson v. *Christoforatou* (1993), 29 R.P.R. (2d) 228 (Ont. C.J. (Gen. Div.)).
Real Property Reports (Third Series), 1996 to date
Frost v. *Stewart* (1999), 19 R.P.R. (3d) 281 (Ont. Gen. Div.).

Common Abbreviations of Courts and Jurisdictions

A. CANADA

A.D. .... Appeal Division
App. Div. .... Appellate Division
C.A. ....Court of Appeal
Co. Ct. .... County Court
Dist. Ct. .... District Court
Div. Ct. ....Divisional Court
F.C. ....Federal Court of Canada
Gen. Div. .... General Division
H.C. .... High Court
H.C.J. .... High Court of Justice
Prov. Div. .... Provincial Division
Q.B. (or K.B.) .... Queen's Bench (or King's Bench)
S.C. ....Supreme Court
S.C. *in banco* .... Supreme Court *in banco*
S.C.C. ....Supreme Court of Canada
T.D. .... Trial Division

B. PROVINCIAL COURTS

Alta. C.A. ....Alberta Court of Appeal
Alta. Q.B. .... Alberta Queen's Bench
B.C.C.A. ....British Columbia Court of Appeal
B.C.S.C. .... British Columbia Supreme Court
Man. C.A. .... Manitoba Court of Appeal
Man. Q.B. ....Manitoba Queen's Bench
N.B.C.A. ....New Brunswick Court of Appeal
N.B.Q.B. .... New Brunswick Queen's Bench
Nfld. S.C., A.D. ....Newfoundland Supreme Court, Appeal Division
Nfld. S.C., T.D. .... Newfoundland Supreme Court, Trial Division

N.W.T.S.C. ....Northwest Territories Supreme Court
N.W.T. Terr. Ct. .... Northwest Territories Territorial Court
N.S.C.A. .... Nova Scotia Court of Appeal
N.S.S.C. ....Nova Scotia Supreme Court
O.C.A. .... Ontario Court of Appeal
O.C.J. ....Ontario Court of Justice
P.E.I.S.C., A.D. .... Prince Edward Island Supreme Court, Appeal Division
P.E.I.S.C., T.D. ....Prince Edward Island Supreme Court, Trial Division
Q.C. or C.Q. ....Québec Court or Cour du Québec
Q.C.A. or C.A.Q. .... Québec Court of Appeal or Cour d'appel Québec
Q.S.C. or C.S.Q....................Québec Superior Court or Cour Supérieure Québec
Sask. C.A. .... Saskatchewan Court of Appeal
Sask. Q.B. ....Saskatchewan Queen's Bench
Sask. S.C. ....Saskatchewan Supreme Court
Y.C.A. .... Yukon Court of Appeal
Y.S.C. ....Yukon Supreme Court

C. ENGLAND

Ch.D. .... Chancery Division
C.A. ....Court of Appeal
Fam. Div. .... Family Division
H.L. .... House of Lords
P.C. ....Privy Council
Q.B.D.(or K.B.D.).............. Queen's Bench Division (or King's Bench Division)

D. CANADIAN JURISDICTIONS

Alta. .... Alberta
B.C. ....British Columbia
C.. Canada
Man. ....Manitoba
N.B. ....New Brunswick
Nfld. ....Newfoundland
N.S. ....Nova Scotia
N.W.T. .... Northwest Territories
Ont...Ontario
P.E.I. ....Prince Edward Island
Qué...Québec
Sask. ....Saskatchewan
Y. ....Yukon

Recommended Abbreviations for Major Canadian Report Series

Administrative Law Reports, 1983-1991 .... Admin. L.R.

Administrative Law Reports (Second Series), 1991 to date .... Admin. L.R. (2d)

Alberta Law Reports, 1908-1932 .... Alta. L.R.

Alberta Law Reports (Second Series), 1976-1992 .... Alta. L.R. (2d)

Alberta Law Reports (Third Series), 1992 to date .... Alta. L.R. (3d)

Alberta Reports, 1977 to date .... A.R.

All-Canada Weekly Summaries, 1977-1979 ....[] A.C.W.S.

All-Canada Weekly Summaries (Second Series), 1980-1986 .... A.C.W.S. (2d)

All-Canada Weekly Summaries (Third Series), 1986 to date............. A.C.W.S. (3d)

Atlantic Provinces Reports, 1975 to date .... A.P.R.

British Columbia Labour Relations Board Decisions,
  1981 to date ....[] B.C.L.R.B.

British Columbia Law Reports, 1976-1986 ...............................B.C.L.R.

British Columbia Law Reports (Second Series),
  1986 to date .... B.C.L.R. (2d)

British Columbia Reports, 1867-1947..................................... B.C.R.

Business Law Reports, 1977-1991 .... B.L.R.

Business Law Reports (Second Series), 1991 to date .......................B.L.R. (2d)

Canada Tax Cases, 1917 to date ....[] C.T.C.

Canadian Bankruptcy Reports, 1920-1960 ...............................C.B.R.

Canadian Bankruptcy Reports (New Series), 1960-1990 ...............C.B.R. (N.S.)

Canadian Bankruptcy Reports (Third Series), 1991 to date ..................C.B.R. (3d)

Canadian Cases on Employment Law, 1983 to date .... C.C.E.L.

Canadian Cases on the Law of Insurance, 1983-1991 .... C.C.L.I.

Canadian Cases on the Law of Insurance (Second Series),
  1991 to date.. C.C.L.I. (2d) 225

Canadian Cases on the Law of Torts, 1976-1990 .... C.C.L.T.

Canadian Cases on the Law of Torts (Second Series),
  1990 to date ....C.C.L.T.(2d)

Canadian Criminal Cases, 1893-1962 ....Can. C.C. or Can. Cr. Cas.

Canadian Criminal Cases, 1963-1970 ....[] C.C.C.

Canadian Criminal Cases (Second Series), 1971-1983 .... C.C.C. (2d)

Canadian Criminal Cases (Third Series), 1983 to date .... C.C.C. (3d)

Canadian Current Law..[] C.C.L.

Canadian Customs and Excise Reports, 1980-1989 .... C.E.R.

Canadian Environmental Law News, 1972-1977 .... [] C.E.L.N.
Canadian Environmental Law Reports, 1978-1986 .... C.E.L.R.
Canadian Environmental Law Reports (New Series),
    1987 to date .... C.E.L.R. (N.S.)
Canadian Human Rights Reporter, 1980 to date .... C.H.R.R.
Canadian Insurance Law Reporter, 1934 to date .... C.I.L.R.
Canadian Labour Law Cases, 1944 to date .... C.L.L.C.
Canadian Labour Relations Board Reports, 1974-1982 .... Can. L.R.B.R.
Canadian Labour Relations Board Reports (New Series),
    1983-1989 .... C.L.R.B.R. (N.S.)
Canadian Labour Relations Board Reports (Second Series),
    1989 to date .... C.L.R.B.R. (2d)
Canadian Native Law Bulletin, 1977-1978 .... [] C.N.L.B.
Canadian Native Law Cases, 1763-1975 .... C.N.L.C.
Canadian Native Law Reporter, 1979 to date .... [] C.N.L.R.
Canadian Patent Reporter, 1942-1971 .... C.P.R.
Canadian Patent Reporter (Second Series), 1971-1984 .... C.P.R. (2d)
Canadian Patent Reporter (Third Series), 1985 to date .... C.P.R. (3d)
Canadian Railway Cases, 1902-1939 .... C.R.C.
Canadian Railway and Transport Cases, 1940-1966 .... C.R.T.C.
Canadian Reports, Appeal Cases, 1828-1913 .... [] C.R.A.C.
Canadian Rights Reporter, 1982-1991 .... C.R.R.
Canadian Rights Reporter (Second Series), 1991 to date .... C.R.R. (2d)
Canadian Weekly Law Sheet .... C.W.L.S.
Carswell's Practice Cases, 1976-1985 .... C.P.C.
Carswell's Practice Cases (Second Series), 1985-1992 .... C.P.C. (2d)
Carswell's Practice Cases (Third Series), 1992 to date .... C.P.C. (3d)
Charter of Rights Decisions, 1982 to date .... C.R.D.
Construction Law Reports, 1983-1992 .... C.L.R.
Construction Law Reports (Second Series), 1993 to date .... C.L.R. (2d)
Criminal Reports (Canada), 1946-1967 .... C.R.
Criminal Reports (New Series), 1967-1978 .... C.R.N.S.
Criminal Reports (Third Series), 1978-1991 .... C.R. (3d)
Criminal Reports (Fourth Series), 1991 to date .... C.R. (4th)
Dominion Law Reports, 1912-1922 .... D.L.R.
Dominion Law Reports, 1923-1955 .... [] D.L.R.
Dominion Law Reports (Second Series), 1956-1968 .... D.L.R. (2d)
Dominion Law Reports (Third Series), 1969-1984 .... D.L.R. (3d)
Dominion Law Reports (Fourth Series), 1984 to date .... D.L.R.(4th)
Dominion Tax Cases, 1920 to date .... D.T.C.
Eastern Law Reporter, 1906-1914 .... E.L.R.
Estates and Trusts Reports, 1977 to date .... E.T.R.
Exchequer Court Reports, 1875-1922 .... Ex.C.R.
Exchequer Court Reports (Canada), 1923-1971 .... [] Ex.C.R.

Federal Court Reports (Canada), 1971 to date .... [] F.C.
Fox's Patent, Trade Mark, Design and Copyright Cases,
   1940-1970 .... Fox Pat. C.
Insurance Law Reporter, 1934 to date .... [] I.L.R.
Labour Arbitration Cases, 1948-1972 .... L.A.C.
Labour Arbitration Cases (Second Series), 1973-1981 .... L.A.C. (2d)
Labour Arbitration Cases (Third Series), 1982-1989 .... L.A.C. (3d)
Labour Arbitration Cases (Fourth Series), 1989 to date .... L.A.C. (4th)
Land Compensation Reports, 1971 to date .... L.C.R.
Lower Canada Reports, 1851-1867 .... L.C.R.
Manitoba Law Reports, 1884-1890 .... Man. L.R.
Manitoba Reports, 1891-1962 .... Man. R.
Manitoba Reports (Second Series), 1979 to date .... Man. R. (2d)
Maritime Provinces Reports, 1930- 1968 .... M.P.R.
Montreal Law Reports (Queen's Bench), 1884-1891 .... M.L.R. (Q.B.)
Montreal Law Reports (Superior Court), 1885-1891 .... M.L.R. (S.C.)
Motor Vehicle Reports, 1979-1988 .... M.V.R.
Motor Vehicle Reports (Second Series), 1988 to date .... M.V.R. (2d)
Municipal and Planning Law Reports, 1976-1990 .... M.P.L.R.
Municipal and Planning Law Reports (Second Series),
   1991 to date .... M.P.L.R. (2d)
National Reporter, 1973 to date .... N.R.
New Brunswick Reports, 1825-1929 .... N.B.R.
New Brunswick Reports (Second Series), 1969 to date .... N.B.R. (2d)
Newfoundland and Prince Edward Island Reports,
   1971 to date .... Nfld. & P.E.I.R.
Newfoundland Reports, 1817-1949 .... Nfld. R.
Northwest Territories Reports, 1983 to date .... [] N.W.T.R.
Nova Scotia Reports, 1834-1929 .... N.S.R.
Nova Scotia Reports, 1965-1969 .... N.S.R. 1965-1969
Nova Scotia Reports (Second Series), 1970 to date .... N.S.R. (2d)
Ontario Appeal Cases, 1984 to date .... O.A.C.
Ontario Appeal Reports, 1876-1900 .... O.A.R.
Ontario Labour Relations Board Reports, 1944 to date .... [] O.L.R.B. Rep.
Ontario Law Reports, 1901-1930 .... O.L.R.
Ontario Municipal Board Reports, 1973 to date .... O.M.B.R.
Ontario Reports, 1882-1900 .... O.R.
Ontario Reports, 1931-1973 .... [] O.R.
Ontario Reports (Second Series), 1973-1991 .... O.R. (2d)
Ontario Reports (Third Series), 1991 to date .... O.R. (3d)
Ontario Weekly Notes, 1909-1932 .... O.W.N.
Ontario Weekly Notes, 1933-1962 .... [] O.W.N.
Ontario Weekly Reporter, 1902-1916 .... O.W.R.
Practice Reports (Ont.), 1848-1900 .... P.R.

Québec Law Reports, 1875-1891 .... Q.L.R.
Québec Official Reports (Court of Appeal), 1970-1985 .... [] Que. C.A.
Québec Official Reports (Queen's Bench or King's Bench),
    1892-1941 ....Que. Q.B. or Que. K.B.
Québec Official Reports (King's Bench or Queen's Bench),
    1942-1969 .... [] Que. K.B. or [] Que. Q.B.
Québec Official Law Reports (Superior Court), 1892-1941 ....Que. S.C.
Québec Official Law Reports (Superior Court), 1942-1985 ....[] Que. S.C.
Québec Practice Reports, 1898-1944 .... Q.P.R.
Québec Practice Reports, 1945-1982 .... [] Q.P.R.
Real Property Reports, 1977-1989 .... R.P.R.
Real Property Reports (Second Series), 1989 to date......................... R.P.R. (2d)
Recueils de jurisprudence du Québec, 1986 to date............................. [] R.J.Q.
Reports of Family Law, 1971-1978 .... R.F.L.
Reports of Family Law (Second Series), 1978-1986 .........................R.F.L. (2d)
Reports of Family Law (Third Series), 1986 to date...........................R.F.L. (3d)
Saskatchewan Law Reports, 1908-1932 .... Sask. L.R.
Saskatchewan Reports, 1979 to date .... Sask. R.
Supreme Court Reports (Canada), 1876-1922.....................................S.C.R.
Supreme Court Reports (Canada), 1923 to date .... [] S.C.R.
Tax Appeal Board Cases, 1949-1971 .... Tax A.B.C.
Taylor's King's Bench Reports, Queen's Bench, 1823-1827 ....Tay.
Territories Law Reports, 1885-1907 ....Terr.L.R.
Trade and Tariff Reports, 1990 to date... T.T.R.
Upper Canada Chambers Reports, 1846-1852 .... U.C. Chamb.
Upper Canada Chancery Chambers Reports, 1877-1890.................... Chy. Chr.
Upper Canada Chancery Reports (Grant), 1849-1882 ....Gr.
Upper Canada Common Pleas, 1850-1882 .... U.C.C.P.
Upper Canada Error & Appeal Reports by Grant, 1846-1866........ U.C.E. & A.
Upper Canada, Queen's Bench Reports, 1823-1831 .... U.C.Q.B.
Upper Canada, Queen's Bench (or King's Bench) Old Series,
    1831-1844.. U.C.Q.B. (O.S.) or U.C.K.B. (O.S.)
Upper Canada Reports, Queen's Bench, 1844-1881 .... U.C.Q.B.
Weekly Criminal Bulletin, 1976-1987 ....W.C.B.
Weekly Criminal Bulletin, Second Series, 1987 to date...............W.C.B. (2d),
Western Labour Arbitration Cases, 1979 to 1985 .... [] W.L.A.C
Western Law Reporter, 1905-1916...W.L.R.
Western Law Times and Reports, 1889-1896 ....W.L.T.
Western Weekly Digests, 1975-1976..W.W.D.
Western Weekly Reports, 1911-1916 and 1955-1970 ...........................W.W.R.
Western Weekly Reports, 1917-1950 and 1971 to date .... [] W.W.R.
Western Weekly Reports (New Series), 1951-1954 .... W.W.R. (N.S.)
Yukon Reports, 1987-1989 .... Y.R.

Recommended Abbreviations for Major English Report Series

A. REPORT SERIES COMMENCING BEFORE 1865

Cox's Criminal Cases, 1843-1945 .... Cox C.C.
English Reports (Reprint) .... E.R.
Law Journal New Series Common Pleas, 1831-1975 ...........................L.J.C.P.
Law Journal New Series Exchequer, 1831-1975....................................L.J.Ex.
Law Journal New Series House of Lords ....L.J.H.L.
Law Journal New Series Privy Council, 1865-1946 ..............................L.J.P.C.
Law Journal New Series Queen's Bench (or King's Bench),
    1831-1946.. L.J.Q.B. (or L.J.K.B.)
Law Journal Old Series, 1822-1830 .... L.J.O.S.
Law Times, 1859-1947 ....L.T.
Revised Reports (Reprint), 1785-1866 .... R.R.
Weekly Reporter, 1853-1906 .... W.R.

B. REPORT SERIES COMMENCING AFTER 1865

Law Reports First Series, 1865-1875

Law Reports Admiralty and Ecclesiastical Cases ...............................L.R.A. & E.
Law Reports Chancery Appeal Cases .... L.R.Ch. App.
Law Reports Common Pleas ....L.R.C.P.
Law Reports Crown Cases Reserved... L.R.C.C.R[1]
Law Reports Equity ....L.R.Eq.
Law Reports Exchequer ....L.R.Ex.
Law Reports House of Lords (English & Irish Appeals) 1866-1875...... L.R.H.L.[2]
Law Reports Privy Council Appeals ....L.R.P.C.
Law Reports Probate and Divorce .... L.R.P. & D.

---

[1]   Also cited L.R.C.C.
[2]   Also cited L.R.E. & I.

Law Reports Queen's Bench ....L.R.Q.B.
Law Reports Scotch and Divorce, 1866-1875 .... L.R. Sc. & Div.

Law Reports Second Series, 1875-1890

Appeal Cases .... App. Cas.
Chancery Division ....Ch. D.
Common Pleas Division to 1880 .... C.P.D.
Exchequer Division to 1880 .... Ex. D.
Probate, Divorce & Admiralty Division, 1876-1890 ...................................P.D.
Queen's Bench Division ....Q.B.D.

Law Reports Third Series, 1891 to date

Appeal Cases ....A.C.
Chancery Division .... Ch.
Family Division, 1972 to date... Fam.
Industrial Cases Reports, 1975 to date ....I.C.R.
Industrial Court Reports, 1972-1974 ....I.C.R.
Probate, Divorce & Admiralty Division .... P.
Queen's Bench (or King's Bench) ....Q.B. (or K.B.)
Reports of Restrictive Practices Cases, 1957-1972......................L.R. (vol.) R.P.
Weekly Law Reports, 1953 to date...W.L.R.

C. OTHER

All England Law Reports, 1936 to date..All E.R.
All England Law Reports Reprint, 1558-1935 .... [ ] All E.R. Rep.
Criminal Appeal Reports, 1909-1992 ....Cr. App. R.
Justice of the Peace, 1837 to date.. J.P.
Lloyd's List Law Reports, 1919-1950 .... Lloyd's Rep.
Lloyd's List Law Reports, 1951-1967 ....[ ] Lloyd's Rep.
Lloyd's Law Reports, 1968 to date ....[ ] Lloyd's Rep.
The Times Law Reports, 1884-1950 ....T.L.R.
The Times Law Reports, 1951 and 1952....................................... [ ] T.L.R.
Weekly Notes, 1866-1952 .... [ ] W.N.

Status of Reporters

In many instances, more than one citation is included when a reference is made to a case authority. If a parallel citation is given, refer first to the official reporter, next to a semi-official reporter, and last to an unofficial reporter.

A. NATIONAL

Supreme Court of Canada

Official   *Canada Supreme Court Reports* [1975 to date].

Official   *Canada Law Reports, Supreme Court of Canada* [1923-1975].

Official   *Canada Supreme Court Reports* (1876-1922), vols. 1-64.

Federal Court of Canada

Official   *Canada Federal Court Reports* [1971 to date].

Official   *Canada Law Reports (Exchequer Court)* [1923-1971].

Official   *Exchequer Court Reports of Canada* (1875-1922), vols. 1-21.

Unofficial   *Federal Trial Reports* (1986 to date), vols. 1 to date.

Other

Unofficial   *National Reporter* (1974 to date), vols. 1 to date.

Unofficial   *Dominion Law Reports* (4th) (1984 to date), vols. 1 to date.

Unofficial   *Dominion Law Reports* (3d) (1969-1984), vols. 1-150.

Unofficial   *Dominion Law Reports* (2d) (1956-1968), vols. 1-70.

Unofficial   *Dominion Law Reports* [1923-1955].

Unofficial   *Dominion Law Reports* (1912-1922), vols. 1-69.

B. REGIONAL

Unofficial   *Western Weekly Reports* [1971 to date].

Unofficial   *Western Weekly Reports* (1955-1970), vols. 14-75.

Unofficial   *Western Weekly Reports (N.S.)* (1951-1954), vols. 1-13.

Unofficial   *Western Weekly Reports* [1917-1950].

Unofficial   *Western Weekly Reports* (1911-1916), vols. 1-10.

Unofficial   *Atlantic Provinces Reports* (1975 to date), vols. 1 to date.

Unofficial   *Western Appeal Cases* (1992 to date), vols. 1 to date.

C. PROVINCIAL

Semi-official   *Alberta Reports* (1977 to date), vols. 1 to date.
(until 1986)

Unofficial   *Alberta Law Reports* (3d) (1992 to date), vols. 1 to date.

Unofficial   *Alberta Law Reports* (2d) (1976-1992), vols. 1-85.

Semi-official   *Alberta Law Reports* (1908-1932), vols. 1-26.

Unofficial   *British Columbia Law Reports* (2d) (1986 to date),
vols. 1 to date.

Unofficial   *British Columbia Law Reports* (1977-1986), vols. 1-70.

Semi-official   *British Columbia Reports* (1867-1947), vols. 1-63.

Unofficial   *Manitoba Reports* (2d) (1979 to date), vols. 1 to date.

Semi-official   *Manitoba Reports* (1890-1967), vols. 7-67.

Unofficial   *Manitoba Law Reports* (1884-1890), vols. 1-6.

Unofficial   *Manitoba Law Reports* [1875-1883].

Semi-official   *New Brunswick Reports* (2d) (1969 to date), vols. 1 to date.

Unofficial   *New Brunswick Reports* (1825-1929), vols. 1-54.

Semi-official   *Newfoundland & Prince Edward Island Reports* (1970 to date), vols. 1 to date.

Unofficial   *Newfoundland Law Reports* (1817-1946), vols. 1-15.

Semi-official   *Northwest Territories Reports*, [1983 to date].

Semi-official   *Territories Law Reports* (1885-1907), vols. 1-7.

Semi-official   *Nova Scotia Reports* (2d) (1969 to date), vols. 1 to date.

Semi-official   *Nova Scotia Reports* (1965-1969), vols. 1-5.

Unofficial   *Nova Scotia Reports* (1834-1929), vols. 1-60.

Unofficial   *Ontario Appeal Cases* (1984 to date), vols. 1 to date.

Semi-official   *Ontario Reports* (3d) (1991 to date), vols. 1 to date.

Semi-official   *Ontario Reports* (2d) (1974-1991), vols. 1-75.

Semi-official   *Ontario Reports* [1931-1973].

Semi-official   *Ontario Law Reports* (1900-1931), vols. 1-66.

Unofficial   *Ontario Reports* (1882-1900), vols. 1-32.

Unofficial   *Ontario Appeal Reports* (1876-1900), vols. 1-27.

Semi-official   *Ontario Weekly Notes* [1933-1962].

Semi-official   *Ontario Weekly Notes* (1909-1932), vols. 1-41.

Semi-official   *Recueils de jurisprudence du Québec* [1986 to date].

Semi-official   *Recueils de jurisprudence du Québec, Cour d'appel* [1970-1985].

Semi-official   *Recueils de jurisprudence du Québec, Cour du Banc de la Reine/du Roi* [1942-1969].

Semi-official   *Les Rapports judiciares officiels de Québec, Cour du Banc de la Reine/du Roi* (1892-1941), vols. 1-71.

Semi-official   *Les Recueils de jurisprudence du Québec, Cour superiéure* [1967-1985].

Semi-official   *Les Rapports judiciares officiels de Québec, Cour superiéure* [1942-1966].

Semi-official   *Les Rapports judiciares officiels de Québec, Cour superiéure* (1892-1941), vols. 1-79.

Semi-official   *Recueils de jurisprudence du Québec, Cour provinciale, Cour des Session de la paix, Cour du bien-être social* [1975-1985].

Unofficial   *Québec Appeal Cases* (1987 to date), vols. 1 to date.

Unofficial   *Saskatchewan Reports* (1979 to date), vols. 1 to date.

Semi-official   *Saskatchewan Law Reports* (1907-1931), vols. 1-25.

Semi-official   *Yukon Reports* (1987 to 1989), vols. 1-3.

Bibliography

While acknowledging significant sources, this list is not exhaustive. In particular, it omits manuals and catalogues prepared by various publishers.

W.S. Anderson, ed., *Ballentine's Law Dictionary, with Pronunciations*, 3rd ed. (San Francisco: Bancroft-Whitney, 1969).

M.A. Banks, *Banks on Using a Law Library: A Canadian Guide to Legal Research*, 6th ed. (Barrie, Ontario: Thomson Canada (Carswell), 1994).

G. Block, *Effective Legal Writing for Law Students and Lawyers*, 4th ed. (Westbury, N.Y.: Foundation Press, 1992).

The Bluebook: A Uniform System of Citation, 15th ed. (Cambridge, Mass.: The Harvard Law Review Association, 1991).

J.E.C. Brierley et al., *Private Law Dictionary and Bilingual Lexicons*, 2nd ed., rev. and enlarged (Cowansville, Qué.: Québec Research Centre of Private and Comparative Law, 1991).

J. Burke, *Jowitt's Dictionary of English Law*, 2nd ed. (London: Sweet & Maxwell, 1977).

E.M. Campbell et al., *Legal Research Materials and Methods*, 3rd ed. (Sydney: The Law Book Co., 1988).

Canadian Guide to Uniform Legal Citation, 4th ed., McGill Law Journal (Toronto: Carswell, 1998).

J.R. Castel & O.K. Latchman, *The Practical Guide to Canadian Research*, (Toronto: Carswell, 1994).

The CLIC Guide to Computer-Assisted Legal Research, 1988/89 ed. (Ottawa: Canadian Law Information Council, 1988).

P. Clinch, *Using a Law Library: A Students' Guide to Legal Research Skills* (London: Blackstone Press, 1992).

M.L. Cohen & K.C. Olson, *Legal Research in a Nutshell*, 5th ed. (St. Paul: West Publishing, 1992).

M.L. Cohen & R.C. Berring, *Finding the Law: An Abridged Edition of "How to Find the Law, 9th ed."*, 9th ed. (St. Paul: West Publishing, 1989).

How to Find the Law, 9th ed. (St. Paul: West Publishing, 1989).

A Complete List of British and Colonial Law Reports and Legal Periodicals, 3rd ed. compiled by W.H. Maxwell and C.R. Brown (Toronto: Carswell, 1937).

J. Dane & P.A. Thomas, *How to Use a Law Library*, 2nd ed. (London: Sweet & Maxwell, 1987).

R.C. Dick, *Legal Drafting*, 2nd ed. (Toronto: Carswell, 1985).

R. Dickerson, *The Fundamentals of Legal Drafting*, 2nd ed. incorporating "Legislative Drafting" (Boston: Little, Brown & Co., 1986).

D.A. Dukelow & B. Nuse, *The Dictionary of Canadian Law* (Scarborough, Ont.: Thomson Professional Pub. Canada, 1991).

A. Dworsky, *A User's Guide to the Bluebook*, rev. for the 15th ed. of *The Bluebook* (Littleton, Colo.: F.B. Rothman & Co., 1991).

S. Elias, *Legal Research: How to Find and Understand the Law*, 3rd ed. (Berkeley, Calif.: Nolo Press, 1992).

J. Gardner, ed., *Words and Phrases, Legal Maxims* (Toronto: Thomson Canada (Carswell), 1986).

B. Garner, *A Dictionary of Modern Legal Usage* (Oxford: Oxford University Press, 1987).

E. Good, *Citing and Typing the Law: A Guide to Legal Citation & Style*, 3rd ed. (Charlottesville, Va.: LEL Enterprises, 1992).

Guide to International Legal Research. The George Washington Journal of International Law and Economics (Salem, N.H.: Butterworth Legal Publishers, 1990).

J.M. Jacobstein & R.M. Mersky, *Fundamentals of Legal Research*, 5th ed. (Westbury, New York: Foundation Press, 1990).

Legal Research Illustrated, An Abridgment of Fundamentals of Legal Research, 5th ed. (Westbury, New York: Foundation Press, 1990).

J.S. James, ed., *Stroud's Judicial Dictionary of Words and Phrases*, 5th ed. (London: Sweet & Maxwell, 1986).

E.M.A. Kwaw, *The Guide to Legal Analysis, Legal Methodology and Legal Writing* (Toronto: Emond Montgomery Publications, 1992).

Legal Research and Writing (Toronto: Canadian Bar Association - Ontario and Young Lawyer's Division Ontario, 1986).

The Living Law: A Guide to Modern Legal Research (Rochester, N.Y.: The Lawyers Co-operative Publishing Co., 1986).

D.T. MacEllven, *Legal Research Handbook*, 3rd ed. (Toronto: Butterworths Canada Ltd., 1993).

D.T. MacEllven, G. Tanguay & L.K. Rees-Potter, *Guide to Purchasing Law Reports* (Ottawa: Canadian Law Information Council, 1985).

E. Maier, *How to Prepare a Legal Citation* (New York: Barron's Educational Series, 1986).

Manual of Legal Citations, 2 Vols. (London: University of London, Institute of Advanced Legal Studies, 1960).

R. Max, *Law Dictionary*, 2nd ed. rev. and expanded by M.O. Price and Oceana Editorial Staff (Dobbs Ferry, N.Y.: Oceana Publications, 1970).

D. Mellinkoff, *Legal Writing Sense & Nonsense* (New York: Scribner, 1982).

H.N. Mozley, *Mozley & Whiteley's Law Dictionary*, 11th ed. by E.R. Hardy Ivamy (London: Butterworth & Co., 1993).

C. Nemeth, *Legal Research* (Englewood Cliffs, N.J.: Prentice-Hall, 1987).

J.R. Nolan, and J.M. Nolan-Haley, *Black's Law Dictionary*, 6th ed. by West Publishing Co. Editorial Staff (St. Paul: West Publishing, 1990).

The Osgoode Hall Law Journal Citation Guide, rev. and expanded by Board of Editors (Toronto: Osgoode Hall Law School, 1984).

Oxford English Dictionary, 2nd ed., prepared by J.A. Simpson and E.S.S. Weiner (Oxford: Clarendon Press, 1989).

M.O. Price, *A Practical Manual of Standard Legal Citations*, 2nd ed. rev. and expanded (Dobbs Ferry, N.Y.: Oceana Publications, 1970).

M.M. Prince, ed., *Bieber's Dictionary of Legal Abbreviations*, 4th ed. (Buffalo: W.S. Hein & Co., 1993).

Bieber's Dictionary of Legal Citations, 4th ed. (Buffalo: W.S. Hein & Co., 1992).

M. Radin, *Law Dictionary*, 2nd ed., rev. and expanded, by Miles O. Price and Oceana Editorial Staff (Dobbs Ferry, N.Y.: Oceana Publications, 1970).

A.E. Randall, "The Revised Reports" (1912), 28 L.Q. Rev. 276.

K. Redden, and E.L. Veron, *Modern Legal Glossary* (Charlottesville, Va.: Michie, 1980).

P.G. Renstrom, *The American Law Dictionary* (Santa Barbara, Calif.: ABC-CLIO, 1991).

L. Rutherford, and S. Bone eds., *Osborn's Concise Law Dictionary*, 8th ed. (London: Sweet & Maxwell, 1993).

J.W. Samuels, *Legal Citation for Canadian Lawyers* (Toronto: Butterworth & Co. (Canada), 1968).

J.B. Saunders, ed., *Words and Phrases Legally Defined*, 3rd ed. (London: Butterworths, 1988).

M.J.T. Sinclair, *Updating Statutes and Regulations for All Canadian Jurisdictions* (Ottawa: Canadian Law Information Council, 1985).

W.P Statsky, *Legal Research and Writing: Some Starting Points*, 4th ed. (St. Paul: West Publishing, 1993).

W.P. Statsky et al., *West's Legal Desk Reference* (St. Paul: West Publishing, 1991).

Sweet & Maxwell's Guide to Law Reports and Statutes, 4th ed. (London: Sweet & Maxwell, 1962).

C. Tang, *Guide to Legal Citation and Sources of Citation Aid: A Canadian Perspective*, 2nd ed. (Don Mills, Ontario: Richard De Boo Publishers, 1988).

L. Teply, *Legal Research and Citation*, 4th ed. (St. Paul: West Publishing, 1992).

V. Tunkel, *Legal Research: Law-Finding and Problem-Solving* (London: Blackstone Press, 1992).

R.S. Vasan, ed., *The Canadian Law Dictionary* (Don Mills, Ont.: Law and Business Publications, 1980).

J.A. Yogis, *Canadian Law Dictionary*, 4th ed. (Woodbury, N.Y.: Barron's Educational Series, 1998).

Index